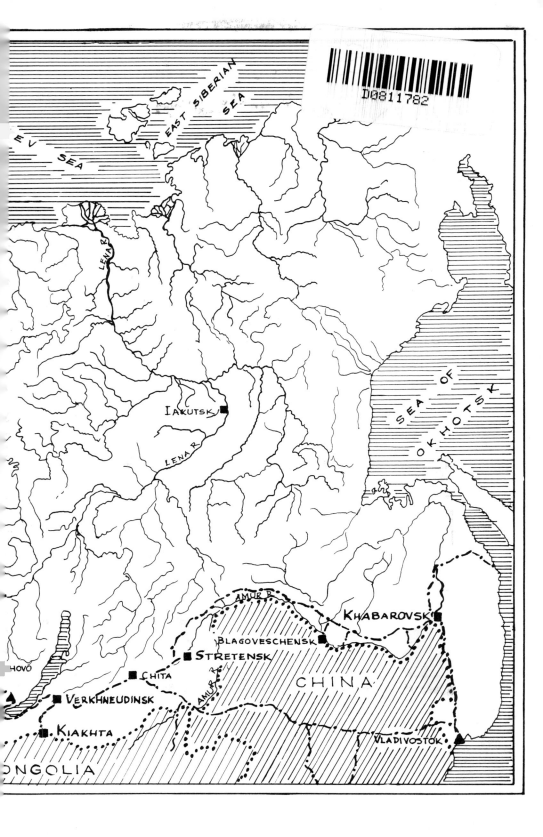

THE STRUGGLE
FOR A DEMOCRACY
IN SIBERIA, 1917–1920

THE STRUGGLE
FOR A DEMOCRACY
IN SIBERIA, 1917–1920

Eyewitness Account of a Contemporary

Paul Dotsenko

Hoover Institution Press

Stanford University, Stanford, California

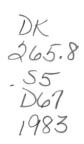
The Hoover Institution on War, Revolution and Peace, founded at Stanford University in 1919 by the late President Herbert Hoover, is an interdisciplinary research center for advanced study on domestic and international affairs in the twentieth century. The views expressed in its publications are entirely those of the authors and do not necessarily reflect the views of the staff, officers, or Board of Overseers of the Hoover Institution.

Hoover Press Publication 277

First printing, 1983
Manufactured in the United States of America
87 86 85 84 83   9 8 7 6 5 4 3 2 1

Library of Congress Cataloging in Publication Data

Dotsenko, Paul, 1894–
   The struggle for a democracy in Siberia, 1917–1920.

   Bibliography: p.
   Includes index.
   1. Siberia (R.S.F.S.R. and Kazakh S.S.R.)—History—
Revolution, 1917–1921.   2. Anti-communist movements—
Siberia (R.S.F.S.R. and Kazakh S.S.R.)   I. Title.
DK265.8.S5D67   1983   957'.08   83-8545
ISBN 0-8179-7771-6

Design by P. Kelley Baker

*In memory of those who gave their lives
in the struggle for a democracy in Siberia*

Contents

Preface

For me—a man who had been deprived of all his rights, who arrived in Yeniseisk province in Siberia in chains, and who within three years became governor of that province—to write a memoir would mean to end up with a film scenario. That was not my intent in writing this book. As a political worker, I wanted above everything, in the memory of all those who perished in Siberia in the name of a democratic ideal, to lift the curtain behind which much of the historical truth is hidden. For in the vast expanses of Siberia, amid the political developments of 1917–1920, the fight for democracy took place on two fronts, as much against the Black reactionary layers of the ruling class as against the Reds. The Reds aspired toward a dictatorship under the mask of the proletariat, the Blacks simply toward a dictatorship.

The somewhat unusual methodology of this book—which is neither a memoir nor an impersonal, fastidious historical work, but a little of both—has allowed me the freedom to express my personal views and at the same time to include excerpts from sources representing various political beliefs, for greater objectivity. A historian has to work within a limited framework, researching events long past from the sidelines, as it were. I, on the other hand, was right there, embroiled in those events from beginning to end. This has given me the advantage of being able to restore lost links to their proper places in the sequence of events.

I shall consider that I have achieved my purpose if this work awakens sufficient interest among historians to encourage them to pursue further research concerning the events in Siberia of which I have written.

I wish to express my sincere gratitude to Nina Shebeko for the difficult and painstaking work of translating this manuscript; to Prof. Richard Pierce, who, having read the initial chapters, found them to be of historical value and gave me the incentive to continue my work; to Anna Bourguina for her friendly criticism of the character of my work and for acquainting me with the interesting material in the collection of Boris Nikolaevski; and to the staff of the Hoover Institution in general and Arline Paul and Marina Utechin in particular for making available to me the rare books and manuscripts in the Institution's collections.

I would like to mention especially Hilja Kukk of the Hoover Library, who courageously undertook to read my manuscript from beginning to end and then proceeded to explore with tireless enthusiasm the possibilities of having it published.

I am indebted to Mark Von Hagen, an instructor in the Department of History at Stanford University who worked as coeditor with me, and to Betty Jean Herring for typing the manuscript.

To Prof. Terence Emmons I am infinitely grateful for his invaluable critical commentary, for all his advice and interest, and for the detailed corrections he made in the manuscript. It is due solely to his cooperation and help that this work has been published.

Introduction

I have lived under all the forms of government Russia has had: autocracy, republic, soviet, republic once again, and, last, right-wing dictatorship. These changes, like the ever-changing pictures in a kaleidoscope, all took place in the vast expanses of Siberia.

My childhood and youth were spent in the Caucasus, against a turbulent political background. At the beginning of this century, the struggle against autocracy intensified, now flaring up, now subsiding, but in the process steadily filling prisons with new fighters for human rights and civil liberties. This wave engulfed the remote districts of Russia, among them North Caucasus.

In Novorossiisk, workers in the railroad industry called a strike in November 1902. The strike was of short duration, but it was followed by another one in January 1903 in which the workers demanded better economic conditions and the right to organize labor unions freely. The government's usual answer was to arrest the leaders and administratively exile[1] the more active among them—some to even more remote areas of the empire and some to the places of their birth.

In early July 1905, the railroad workers again announced a strike, this time a prolonged one. The government sent a railroad battalion to replace the workers, and the trains resumed running on an almost normal schedule. The workers, realizing that the strike could be prolonged and have a disastrous economic effect, decided to force the issue by lying on the tracks and blocking the trains. The commander of the military detachment ordered the tracks cleared, but the workers ignored the order. To break their resistance, the order to fire was given. Several men were killed and many were wounded.

Several days later, a civilian funeral was held for those killed in this unequal confrontation. By the time the funeral procession reached the cemetery, it had grown into a huge political demonstration. A detachment of Cossacks was sent to disperse the crowd. The officer in command ordered the demonstrators to disband peacefully, but his command was ignored. The Cossacks then galloped several blocks down the street from the cemetery, abruptly wheeled about — directly in front of our house — and, at the command "Sabers bared!" charged back to the cemetery. This time the demonstrators dispersed. I was an involuntary witness of these events.

The strike ended and the workers resumed their duties, feelings of discontent continuing to ferment within them. In October a general strike was called, including postal and telegraph services, paralyzing the government. The Novorossiisk Democratic Republic was proclaimed with not a drop of blood spilled. This was actually not surprising because at the time there were no military garrisons stationed in the city. But the governor called for troops from nearby districts, and by the end of December 1905 the brief existence of the republic had ended. The members of the soviet were arrested and tried three times by the military district court, but a verdict was not reached until spring 1910 because it was discovered that the court investigator had used fraudulent depositions.

The wave of freedom was replaced by new repressions. My older brother was arrested in 1908 for political activities and administratively exiled to Siberia for three years. My father was also arrested and spent three months in prison for concealment for not having reported to the police that his son was living in one of our houses. My cousin Nikolai Dotsenko, who had taken part in the revolutionary movement of the years 1905–1907, was sentenced in 1909 to twelve years hard labor for being a member of the Socialist-Revolutionary Party; because he was tubercular, the court shortened the sentence to eight years. His mother, unable to survive the shock, developed a rapid form of consumption and died in 1911, leaving four children, the eldest a girl of seventeen. Together this daughter and I went to the governor-general with the bold request that Nikolai Dotsenko be allowed to attend his mother's funeral. Due perhaps to the unusual nature of our request and our arguments, the request was granted.

Nikolai, shackled and guarded by two soldiers with unsheathed sabers, appeared at the funeral. His friends, in the meantime, had made plans for his escape during the services. When Nikolai was apprised of this opportunity to gain freedom, he declined because he did not wish to compromise his guards. I wonder whether in the entire history of political struggle in Russia anything comparable to this could be found—an occasion when political opponents did not forget that they were first human beings, with respect for human dignity. One official, breaking rules and custom, allowed a convict to attend his mother's funeral and the other man refused an opportunity to escape because of his concern for the fate of those responsible for him. Nikolai returned to prison to complete his eight-year term.

Having grown up in such an atmosphere, it is small wonder that I too should have been caught on a wave of this stormy sea. As soon as I had completed some courses in the College of Commerce, at the age of eighteen, I plunged into political work, at first among the workers in cement factories and afterward among the sailors of our navy.

Generally speaking, the year 1912 was one of mass arrests in all the ports of the Black Sea. For the most part those arrested were sailors of the navy and the merchant marine. The sailors were arrested because they were participants in an organization preparing an uprising of the Black Sea fleet against the government. In the event of a successful insurrection by the naval forces, the sailors of the merchant marine were to declare a strike so that the government would be unable to use the merchant fleet to transfer troops. But others were not overlooked by the gendarme government; in addition to the sailors, the Batum prison held at that time a large group of Georgian Social Democrats and the Bolshevik Ordzhonikidze. In Sevastopol, 152 sailors of the navy were brought before a court martial; 17 were executed and the others were assigned prison terms of various lengths. And approximately four hundred sailors were transferred to other seas.

In early October 1912, the Socialist-Revolutionary Party held a regional conference in the city of Batum. Representatives from the North Caucasus and from the cities of Baku, Tiflis, and Batum were present. At the end of the conference, on November 11, 1912, when we were at the point of returning to our respective places of work, we were all arrested due to some provocation or other.

Only two of the Socialist-Revolutionaries arrested in Batum were sent to Odessa, the gathering point: David Editkin and I. In Odessa court trials were artificially prepared by the Security Department. I was not taken to a prison there, but to the Gendarme Administration, where I was detained for ten days. Colonel P. P. Zavarzin, head of the Gendarme Administration, and the head of the Security Department held lengthy political discussions with me in an attempt to change my convictions and persuade me to join their service. Finally, convinced that their efforts were useless, Colonel Zavarzin remarked: "What do you hope for? Perhaps in 25 years you will gain control, but what awaits you now is penal servitude and then exile to Siberia for life." I replied that essentially there was little difference between our viewpoints, for he had admitted that there would have to be a change in the existing form of government. The difference was only in the time element: he thought the change would take place in 25 years or so and I thought it would occur much sooner. As for the length of my exile, that would be entirely up to me. This ended our talks, and I was thrown into prison with the stipulation that it be solitary confinement—no messages, no packages, no visitors.

It is difficult to determine the total number of arrested sailors of the merchant marine. The arrests continued for more than two years, and the Gendarme Administration sifted through those who had been arrested, releasing some after several months, administratively exiling some, and holding some subject to court summons. By the end of May 1913, 237 people were being held in the Odessa prison in connection with this "sailor affair." One of the last to be arrested in that category was Mikhail Adamovich, leader of the merchant marine union and editor of the journal *Moryak*. He was arrested in Alexandria, Egypt, where the union, which was illegal in Russia, was headquartered. Adamovich and the archives of his union were seized during the night. A month and a half later, also at night, he was transferred under heavy guard to a Russian vessel moored in the shipyard. The head of the Security Division waited for the ship in Constantinople, and the arrested man was transported safely into Russian waters with a convoy of two torpedo boats.

The English Labour Party instigated an inquiry in Parliament to determine why the British government had surrendered Adamovich to Russia. Minister of Foreign Affairs Edward Grey answered that the existing treaty concerning the nonsurrender of political prisoners was in force only in England proper and did not extend to her territories. Thus England helped the Russian gendarmes to create a criminal conspiracy aimed at overthrowing the existing form of government, for the indictment was built on suspicions and suppositions partially supported by the correspondence taken from Adamovich in Alexandria.

After the mass arrests, the gendarme authorities concentrated on 70 of us who were to be actually brought to trial. Our "criminal conspiracy" group consisted mostly of people who had never met until prison and in some cases not until the trial itself. The trial lasted several weeks, and the verdict was announced on November 11, 1914:

three were sentenced to hard labor and fifteen to life exile in Siberia, eleven were acquitted, and the rest were sentenced to prison terms of various durations.

I was pronounced guilty of belonging to the Socialist-Revolutionary Party and sentenced to four years of hard labor; but in consideration of my age (I was not yet 21 when the crime had been committed), the two years I had spent in solitary confinement prior to the trial, and the condition of my health, the sentence was changed to exile for life in Siberia. And in spring 1915 that is where I was sent. Colonel Zavarzin had not forgotten our talks even with the passage of three years, and noted "tendency to escape" on the papers accompanying me. Naturally the prison administration interpreted this as a warning that I was dangerous, so I was handcuffed. For three months, not parting day or night with the chains on my wrists, I traveled the long route from Odessa to Krasnoyarsk, where at the end of May 1915 the handcuffs were at last removed.

My exile was to be spent at the middle flow of the Angara River. There were no roads at all in that region, so we trudged along the rocky riverbanks until we reached a small settlement called Chadobets. There we were told that this would be our permanent abode—without permission to leave, of course—and that from that moment on we must provide our own food, shelter, and clothes. Thus began my new life in Siberia.

At the time of the February Revolution, I was in the same district, in the city of Kansk. My first sensation of joy was quickly overshadowed by the uncertainty of the future. The revolution opened a wide road toward the creation of a government based on democratic principles, but even at that time other events gave cause for alarm.

At the end of March 1917, a company of soldiers came to the meeting place of the committee of the Socialist-Revolutionary Party and announced their wish to sign as party members. They were warmly welcomed by committee members R. Eideman (who was also commander of the military company),[2] Elena Sleshchinskaya, and me. But this spontaneous act on the part of the soldiers did not throw us into rapture: discussing what had happened, we concluded that without political training the force could easily crush us. The political mood of the soldiers in the reserve regiments was unstable; if in May and June I was cheered at meetings, by November I was shouted down by the same soldiers. We were thus obliged to take upon ourselves a yet even larger load of work than the burden we already carried. For example, by the end of 1917 I was a member of the district committee of the Socialist-Revolutionary Party, a member of the District Provision Board, a member of the District Zemstvo Board, and a member of the Executive Committee of the Soldiers', Workers', and Peasants' Deputies. This meant a sixteen- or eighteen-hour working day. There was no time left for creative work or for the political education of the masses. This is how it was and this is how it continued to be until the moment the Bolsheviks seized power.

Once the Bolsheviks had consolidated their power in Siberia, they began to bear down on the opposition. At the end of January 1918, I was arrested as an adversary of Soviet power and as a "reactionary" and declared a hostage. In prison I actually enjoyed a much needed rest, and I even gained some weight. Nevertheless, to await the Bolsheviks' final disposition of me did not enter into my plans. I established contact with people on the other side of the prison wall and planned my escape. In two months, with cooperation from the outside, I had escaped from the Krasnoyarsk prison. Arriving in Tomsk, I contacted representatives of the Siberian government, whose immediate goal was to organize an armed uprising against the Bolsheviks. I was invested with full authority for the military affairs of Yeniseisk province.

Ten days after my escape from prison, masquerading as a demobilized soldier, I returned to Krasnoyarsk and took lodgings on the second floor of a house next door to the headquarters of the Bolsheviks' Red Guard unit. Deputy Minister of War A. N. Grishin-Almazov and Pavel Mikhailov, a member of the West Siberian Commissariat, were also in Krasnoyarsk. We had traveled on the same train but in different carriages. Together we organized a staff of seven, a nucleus for the military organization of the district. From that time on, my daily problem was to organize and gather forces capable of overthrowing Bolshevik power in the region. On June 18 at eleven o'clock in the morning, the first shots were fired. By nightfall we were masters of the situation: the Bolsheviks were fleeing to the north.

After the overthrow of the Bolsheviks in Siberia, I was appointed deputy district commissar. Soon thereafter, because of the fatal illness of Commissar P. Ozernykh, I was performing the duties of district commissar.

In November 1918, I sent a telegram to the minister of internal affairs asking to be relieved of my duties, but the government delayed in appointing a replacement. By this time, it was evident to me that the government was not master of the situation and was not sharing its new methods of governing the country. Not waiting for official orders, I simply transferred the command, in military fashion, to my subordinate and left for the Urals. I submitted my resignation and enlisted as a volunteer for active duty, arriving at army headquarters in December 1918.

In mid-1919, the Siberian army abandoned Ekaterinburg. Three days later I too moved on, having witnessed to my lasting sorrow the sad spectacle of retreating Siberians—a people who had never before known defeat.

> Siberia is a good land
> The winter is savage
> The fly is mean
> The people are convicts.

This is how the Siberians, a people whose roots to their land are deep, characterized themselves and their home: Siberia, in whose social and political life I played an active role for approximately five event-laden years.

This book is my record, as a living witness and an active participant, of political events as they took place at that time in Siberia.

1
Siberia and the February Revolution

Historical and political events in Siberia during the period of the revolution just prior to the Bolshevik seizure of power have been described by both emigre and Soviet historians, but the existing literature devoted to the Siberian liberation movements is rather meager and certainly tendentious: subjective evaluation is the rule for much of the material dealing with this subject. Lately there have been some works published in the Soviet Union that are uncompromisingly pro-Communist Party. The latest "scholarly research" even avoids using materials published by the history departments of the 1930s. The material published abroad is, more often than not, written by people who took no active part in the initial work of organizing the overthrow of the communist regime and therefore highlights only scattered episodes of its final stages. As a result, all the movements are depicted as a struggle between two gigantic powers, the White and the Red—or, more simply, as the Czech uprising in Siberia. The fact that the uprising was organized by democratic elements supported by the people as represented by city and district governments and cooperatives is completely ignored in these accounts. For a better understanding of the events in Siberia, the political situation and economic condition of the inhabitants, the background for these events, must be considered.

The composition of Siberia's population in the early twentieth century differed significantly from that of the rest of Russia. Its existence as a separate and special province was recognized, in fact, as early as the reign of Catherine II. In a decree of October 19, 1764, Siberia was referred to as "the Siberian tsardom," and a year earlier in another decree, "an edict was published to mint a special Siberian coin at the Kolyvano-Voskresensk factories with the coat of arms of the Siberian tsardom."

Government officials discussed the question of a special form of administration for Siberia, but nothing was accomplished by the end of Catherine's reign. Instead, Siberia was divided into West and East Siberia and assigned viceroys (*namestniki*) with unlimited authority.

During the reign of Alexander I, the state, once again recognizing the special nature of Siberia, sought to put an end to arbitrary acts on the part of various governors-general there. Interior Minister O. P. Kozodavlev introduced a bill to limit the authority of local chiefs (*nachalniki*) in Siberia by establishing an organ of supreme authority for the Siberian provinces that would include some officials assigned from the center and some elected by local residents of various estates. The bill would limit the authority of the nachalniki by empowering them only to break tie votes on decisions in their role as chairmen of the province. Moreover, Kozodavlev added, "It seems to me that while limiting the authority of the nachalniki, it would not be unwise to increase the authority of the magistrates and urban administrations."[1]

In March 1819, Mikhail Speransky was appointed governor-general of Siberia. After a comprehensive survey of local conditions, he introduced a bill recommending the creation of a separate higher administration for Siberia. He set as the major goals of his reform: (1) to limit the personal authority of the nachalnik and to bring the actions of that office in line with public opinion (*glasnost*); to restrict arbitrariness and abuses by legal means; to establish regular procedures for decisions so that they would no longer be personal and domestic, but rather official and public; and (2) to increase supervision; to consolidate fragmented and ineffective laws into one code and, in so doing, create an institution to replace both the insufficient purview of the distant central government and the insufficient purview of public opinion.[2]

In a letter to Interior Minister V. P. Kochubei, Speransky writes, "How can I rule without moral authority? I am told 'by laws,' as if laws really exist in Siberia, which has always been governed by arbitrariness, and as if laws can be executed without executors." And in a letter to A. D. Stolypin dated June 13, 1819, he writes, "How do you imagine that I will be able to administer Siberia, which no one has ever been able to do up to now?"[3]

Such an attitude toward Siberia, conditioned by the economic, geographic, and administrative peculiarities of the area, could not help but be reflected in public opinion. The local merchantry had long been distinguished by its independence and liberalism. Siberia was the scene of an eternal battle between bureaucrats and the newly arrived merchants, on the one hand, and bureaucrats and local elements, on the other.

In the mid-eighteenth century, Irkutsk enjoyed the reputation of something of a small republic with a particularly free atmosphere. For example, in 1733 the central government sent a replacement for the bribe-taking Governor-General A. Zholobov. The new man died shortly after his arrival, and Zholobov refused to recognize his replacement. In response, a provisional government was created in Irkutsk, consisting of a Cossack ataman, Bishop Innokenty, and a clerk (*podyachii*), to petition for a new governor.

Because of a change in the policy of the Russian central government, the reform projects of Speransky and Kozodavlev were never realized, but the ground was prepared for a Siberian intelligentsia to begin the struggle for improved Siberian administration. Much as the Decembrists in central Russia had taken the initiative in 1825 to reform the state, so in Siberia in 1860–1865 Cossack officers began to organize circles to discuss improvements in the administration and economic development of Siberia. A Cossack officer, G. Potanin, initiated these discussion circles.[4] Within a short time the movement had spread to other cities in Siberia. The largest group was centered in Tomsk, where local intelligentsia, rather than army officers, predominated. Thus was born a political movement that entered history under the name of *oblastnichestvo* (regionalism).

Some men, like N. Yadrintsev, Potanin, and others, advocated an autonomous Siberia. Their program was modest: (1) opposition to the view held at the center that Siberia was suitable only as an exile colony; (2) a remedy to the problem that St. Petersburg, by not opening a Siberian university, artificially stimulated an exodus of educated young people from Siberia to the capital; (3) opposition to subordination of the Siberian economy to the interests of the ruling class in European Russia.

The oblastniki based their program on the fact that the colonization of Siberia had been a "popular" one, by runaways and people dissatisfied with their lot, who sought refuge and independence. In a proclamation written by Potanin at the beginning of 1865, the Siberian patriots declared, "Siberia, as the land of free men and untapped natural wealth, reflects the aspirations of many generations of Russian peasants, seeking in a distant and unknown land deliverance from serfdom, the land shortage, and oppression. The state has enslaved

Siberia but has not succeeded in breaking the spirit of its freedom-loving people."[5]

The major demands of the oblastniki during this period included: the opening of a Siberian university, the granting of more rights of self-government to the local population, and the improvement of administration in Siberia. These were modest aims; but the gendarme regime manufactured a case against "the Siberian separatists," and in 1865 a court pronounced Potanin, Yadrintsev, and others guilty of plotting the secession of Siberia from the Russian Empire. Instead of reform, Siberia was subjected to a new wave of administrative arbitrariness that included the termination in 1888 and 1889 of what remained of consultative organs at the governor-general level.

During the "days of freedom" in 1905, a Siberian oblast union organized a congress and adopted a resolution on the need to establish regional self-government in the form of a Siberian oblast duma that would decide all administrative, socioeconomic, educational, and other issues of local concern. Despite the reaction of the years 1906–1917 and the halt to reforms promised to Siberia, the continued rapid population growth and the development of Siberia's extracting and manufacturing industries alarmed central authorities. "Siberia is growing at an incredible pace," wrote Prime Minister P. A. Stolypin in a letter of September 26, 1910, to Tsar Nicholas II. He urged on the tsar a series of urgent measures to deal with Siberia. Otherwise, he warned, "an immense and rough democratic country would grow up unconsciously and uncontrollably to one day crush European Russia."[6]

What, during this period, was the ideology of the Siberian intelligentsia? This question can be answered without hesitation: populism (*narodnicheskaya*). Except for a few factories in the Altai region and the gold mines in the north, Siberia was still without industry or an industrial proletariat. The cities were populated by merchants engaged in local trade, by small manufacturers, and by civil servants sent from central Russia who considered their stay in Siberia a temporary one. The overwhelming majority of the population was peasant, so naturally the local intelligentsia focused its attention on the concerns of the rural population. The journal *Notes of the Fatherland*, edited by N. A. Dobrolubov and N. G. Chernyshevsky, had tremendous influence on the education of young Siberian progressives. Chernyshevsky's idea of free agricultural communes was particularly popular.

Outside the cities, approximately 90 percent of the population belonged to the peasant class, but this was a peasant class quite different from its counterpart on the other side of the Urals. This prosperous peasantry never had to contend with land shortage, or with landowners. Only a small percentage of the peasants did not own land, the so-called *samokhod* (self-supporting), who received no help from the resettlement bureau. All the rest were allotted fifteen *desyatin* per male. Even one Soviet historian, M. M. Stishov, speaking of the "deep stratification" in peasant society, was forced to admit that households with ten or twelve horses and cows were not uncommon in Siberian villages. And such peasant households were not placed in the kulak category. In the Siberian scheme of things, they were considered a type of prosperous *serednyatskii* (middle peasant) husbandry.[7] From 1910 to 1917, the land under cultivation in Siberia increased by 80 percent. Economic prosperity and, to a certain extent, the influence of the political exiles created an independent, free-thinking type of peasant. The Siberian peasants did not shirk community work and put forth a great deal of effort to form cooperatives.

The ethnic composition of the population of Siberia was quite varied then. The larger of the Asiatic groups, such as the Buryats, the Yakuts, the Khirgiz, and the Eskimos, lived apart from outside agencies. To a great extent this was also true of the Cossacks, with their separate government, and also of the peasants—of both the old inhabitants and the new settlers.

At the beginning of the twentieth century, railroad and industrial workers began to migrate to Siberia. It was then that the embittered struggle between Marxists and populists exploded there. Beginning in 1901, Social-Democratic Party cells were organized among railroad workers and students in Tomsk. Lenin, who arrived in Krasnoyarsk in 1904, helped organize a cell among the railroad workers while waiting to be assigned a place of exile. So things continued until 1905, after which the Social-Democratic Party enjoyed a considerable growth period.[8] By 1917, in a population of ten million Siberians there were 300,000 laborers, including refugees from territory occupied by the Germans. The workers served primarily the railroads, the gold mines, and local industries. But in Stishov's words, these workers remained "literally dissolved in the general mass of the peasantry and the petty bourgeoisie of the cities."[9]

Siberia thus welcomed with enthusiasm the change in government that occurred in February 1917. The idea of an autonomous Siberia received wide acclaim, not only among the Russian population there, but also among the non-Russians, who began organizing their own autonomous governments. It was as if elemental forces were driving Siberia toward a federalist government.

Siberia for the first time was given the privilege of electing *zemstvo* (district), *uezd* (county), and *volost* (intracounty) boards. The intelligentsia and liberal industrialists dreamed of creating an oblast government and introducing long-range economic development to the region. The workers in Siberia, as in all of Russia, came under a new law concerning labor protection, social insurance, shortening of the workday, and old-age security. There were no large landowners in Siberia, so there was nothing to divide—not that the local peasants needed it, for they had sufficient land.

What was important was the psychological change that took place among the people. The peasant was transformed from a cipher required only to perform an endless number of government-imposed obligations to a man with rights of his own. The idea took hold that to build one's own life was just as much an individual's concern as it was the concern of the government administration. Such were the hopes of the Siberians for a time. Harsh reality cheated them of these hopes, and fate decreed a future that no one at that time could even have surmised. From the first days of the February Revolution, as democratic elements were busy organizing a central power and introducing the beginnings of democracy into city and district institutions, the Communist Party was preparing a new coup d'etat.

In May 1917 a bureau was created for the purpose of organizing a congress of oblastniki. Even the Bolsheviks did not protest this, and they sang dithyrambs to Potanin. The All-Siberian Convention of Oblastniki was held on October 8; present were representatives from city and zemstvo governments, cooperatives, the non-Russian population, and peasant soviets supporting the platform of the recognition of Siberian autonomy. Among the delegates from peasant soviets was a scattering of Bolsheviks. Of all the legal parties, only the Kadets were not represented because they were against granting autonomy to Siberia.

The convention called for a constituent assembly for Siberia on the basis of a general franchise. The special All-Siberian Convention of Oblastniki that followed on December 6 put forth a declaration against the seizure of central power by the Bolsheviks in November and adopted a resolution on elections to the Siberian Constituent Assembly. The few Bolsheviks present at the convention were already in opposition because the convention was against "Soviet power" as an executive government agency and in favor of the authority of a central constituent assembly and organs of local self-government. The Bolshevik Party could not come to terms with this point of view, but, recognizing its own weakness, it refrained at that time from taking any repressive measures against the convention.

2
The Bolshevik
Seizure of Power

The unexpectedness of the revolution caught the liberal and socialist parties totally unprepared; as a result, democracy took a great many false steps and made many political blunders. In late February and early March 1917, Russia was covered by a network of soviets of workers' and soldiers' deputies; there were as yet no peasants' deputies, although no less than 85 percent of the entire population were peasants. To describe in detail the underlying reasons for this, I shall use as an example the province of Yeniseisk, the citadel of bolshevism in Siberia. Several leading Bolsheviks—A. Okulov, M. Frumkin, N. L. Meshchernyakov, B. Shumyatsky, and I. A. Teodorovich—lived there; and Y. M. Sverdlov, I. Stalin, and V. Lenin had spent parts of their exiles there.

After the revolution, the political parties were able to organize soviets of workers' and soldiers' deputies almost immediately simply because the workers and the soldiers were already in the cities. The peasants, on the other hand, who were more in sympathy with the Socialist-Revolutionary Party, were spread over the great expanses of Siberia. In addition to the immense amount of preliminary organizational work needed, time was required to prepare the organization of peasant conventions; and when could the peasants best afford to interrupt their farm work? Because of this, the First Convention of Peasants' Deputies was called only at the end of June 1917—four months after the soviets of workers' and soldiers' deputies had begun to function. By this time the Bolsheviks, having had time to organize, were riding around the countryside advising the peasants not to attend the convention. Further, the representation was most uneven: there was one deputy per 100 workers, two deputies per company of soldiers (120–200 men), and only one deputy per 2,500 peasants. The intelligentsia, as a separate group, had no representation anywhere.

In spite of all the Bolsheviks' efforts, the soviets of soldiers', workers', and peasants' deputies fell under the influence of other groups. On his return from exile, Sverdlov stopped in Krasnoyarsk for several days between March 20 and 30, 1917, and formed a small group, the so-called Pravdisty, thereby laying the foundation for the work of the Bolsheviks, who employed the method of "decay from within" in Krasnoyarsk. They began with the party to which they had once belonged, the Social Democratic (Bolsheviks, Mensheviks, and Internationalists), because they wished to rid themselves of that party's influence. By April 30, 1917, they had succeeded and had set up their own Bolshevik group. The next step was to seize the soviets of soldiers' and workers' deputies. In accomplishing their objective, they relied not on the local people among whom they had no roots, but on soldiers of the reserve regiments sent from central Russia.[1]

In order to paralyze the underground work of the Bolsheviks, the Executive Committee of the Soviet of Peasants' Deputies recommended the formation of a united committee of the soviets of soldiers', workers', and peasants' deputies. Taking into account that representatives of the peasants had just been elected at the District Congress, the Bolsheviks agreed to discuss only the holding of joint sessions of all the soviets; but any such concessions on their part were strictly superficial. At the first joint meeting, two irreconcilable viewpoints came to light: (1) support of the Provisional Government and elections to the Constituent Assembly, and (2) the slogan "Down with the bourgeois government—all power to the soviets" (as legislative bodies).

At the time of the Bolshevik attempt to seize power in Petrograd in July 1917, the Siberian Bolsheviks, sensing their own weakness, made no such attempt. They continued, though, to disrupt the work of the government apparatus, paying special attention to the disbanding of the army and to setting up their own underground cells. Further work was determined by Lenin's instructions to the Sixth Congress of the party in Petrograd on July 26, 1917.

1. The counterrevolution has to all practical purposes taken the government into its own hands.
2. The leaders of the soviets and of the Menshevik and Socialist-Revolutionary parties have irrevocably betrayed the work of the revolution.

3. All hope for a peaceful development is ended: victory can be gained only through the use of arms.

The slogan "All power to the soviets" is no longer the correct one because it fails to take into account the utter betrayal of the Mensheviks and Socialist-Revolutionaries. The Bolshevik Party must combine legal with illegal work.[2]

These instructions illustrate well that the Bolsheviks had decided to make use of all democratic freedoms to overthrow the democratic order.

The official Soviet historian of the civil war in Siberia, V. Safronov, summarized the Bolshevik program at the congress: "In adopting its resolutions, the congress took for granted that the peaceful period of the revolution had come to an end and that all political and organizational work must be directed toward preparation for an armed uprising."[3]

Safronov remarks further, "The problem was to show the masses the class makeup and the role of the Socialist-Revolutionary–Menshevik soviets so that the masses would not place their hopes on the existing soviets, but would refuse to participate in them and to fight for them. Party organizations had to shift the center of gravity to the preparation of an armed insurrection, and for this the soviets as they were presently constituted were useless."[4] This reveals the demagogy of Bolshevik Party propaganda, according to which the soviets of workers', soldiers', and peasants' deputies belonged to the first period of the revolution and did not reflect the wishes of those who had sent them, but, rather, defended the interests of the bourgeoisie. And all this was because the Bolsheviks did not have a majority in these soviets.

For tactical reasons, however, this did not prevent the Krasnoyarsk Bolsheviks from sending out an appeal on August 18, 1917, signed by Alexander Okulov, the Bolshevik chairman of the Soviet of Soldiers' and Workers' Deputies, warning, among other things, of the threat posed by the bourgeoisie to revolutionary organizations, including the soviets. Okulov even called for using the soviets as a rallying point in the struggle for democracy, for land, for peace. This appeal was made because the Executive Committee of the Soldiers' Deputies had heard that two companies and artillery were on the way to Krasnoyarsk from Irkutsk to restore order to the local garrison, namely, to put a stop to arbitrary leaves and to interfere in the matter of sending infantry troops to the German front. On August 20, the commander of the garrison, who had been cooperating with the soviets, was replaced; and the Soviet of Soldiers' Deputies acceded to the demands of the commander of the military district. The acquiescence was short-lived.

On August 28, 1917, the appearance of Gen. L. G. Kornilov on the scene greatly encouraged the Bolsheviks. Lenin characterized the situation thus: "This fresh wind, which brought with it the promise of a good storm, was just enough to blow away all that was decayed in the soviets, and the initiative of the revolutionary masses began to make itself felt as something majestic, powerful, invincible."[5] In preparing for the insurrection, the Bolsheviks took as much advantage as possible of Kornilov's march, which to them was a "fresh wind." Once the district soviet had organized a District Executive Committee of Peasants' Deputies, in early August, the question arose whether to unite with the Committee of Soldiers' and Workers' Deputies. On behalf of the soldiers' and workers' deputies, Okulov continually delayed action on this for fear that hands would be tied by the more conservative elements among the peasant deputies.

Two days after Kornilov's march, a meeting was held in Krasnoyarsk in which the maintenance of order and the prevention of possible counterrevolutionary action were discussed. The meeting was attended by 29 people, representatives of the district governments; the city duma; the political parties—Bolshevik, Menshevik, Socialist-Revolutionary, and the Left Socialist-Revolutionary; the Central Bureau of Labor Unions; the railway workers; the Irkutsk Circuit Bureau; the commander of the garrison; the district commissar of the Provisional Government; and the soviets of soldiers', workers', and peasants' deputies. It was resolved to form a joint committee of nine people, three representatives each from the soviets of soldiers', workers', and peasants' deputies. The Bolshevik Okulov was elected chairman of this committee, and I was elected vice-chairman. Interestingly, during the debates the Bolsheviks I. Belopolsky and V. N. Yakovlev and the Left Socialist-Revolutionaries N. Mazurin and A. N. Lebedeva argued that it was essential to transfer full power to the soviets. Okulov maintained that at that moment the question of seizing full power was not at issue. I have dwelt on this episode somewhat in detail because it illustrates the usual distortion that political events undergo at the hands of some Soviet historians, who think nothing of grossly misrepresenting facts in achieving their major objective of portraying "the triumphant progress of the Bolsheviks."

Safronov writes: "Reflecting the mood of the workers, soldiers, and peasants, the Executive Committee of the Soviets of the Workers' and Soldiers' Deputies united with the Executive Committee of the

District Soviet of Peasants' Deputies and on the first of September proclaimed that it was assuming power over Yeniseisk province."[6] How could there be any talk of the seizure of power when the commissar of the Provisional Government continued to execute his duties in governing the province?

This is also true of the statement that "from the first days of the revolution, Kansk uezd carried out the October program; Kansk uezd refused to organize zemstvo institutions, and immediately conferred on the soviet all zemstvo functions. This decision was made at peasant congresses."[7] All this is far from the truth. It is true, however, that a portion of the purely economic functions of the zemstvo (such as roads and hospitals) were assumed by the soviets because there were no zemstvos at that time in Siberia. But it is not true that the peasant soviet "refused to organize zemstvos." Elections to the zemstvos were held throughout the district. A letter of the Kansk city administration of November 14, 1917 (No. 700), included the announcement that I had been elected to the District Zemstvo: "The delegates of the Kansk District, A. F. Timofeev, Z. M. Rogalevich, and P. S. Dotsenko, have also been elected to the Executive Committee of the Soviet of Peasants' Deputies and, at the same time, are members of the District Zemstvo Administration. As members of the District Committee of the Soviet of Peasants' Deputies, they were against the October overthrow."

The mood of the Kansk Soviet of Soldiers' Deputies changed in mid-July, after the Bolsheviks had agitated for their return home to central Russia to take part in land redistribution. At the same time many of the Socialist-Revolutionaries, members of the Kansk organization, also left for other parts of Russia. This situation was further complicated by a split in the party of the Socialist-Revolutionaries. The Left Socialist-Revolutionaries resigned from the party and joined the International Socialist-Revolutionary Party, taking up the cry: "All power to the soviets!" The splinter groups in Krasnoyarsk were then headed by S. Lazo, Mazurin, and Lebedeva, and in Kansk by R. Eideman.

Kornilov's march made it possible for Eideman, an officer, to assume the dominant role in the Kansk Soviet of Soldiers' Deputies. According to Frumkin, a contemporary Bolshevik observer, "A bitter struggle was always going on with the Socialist-Revolutionaries. The underlying reason for the struggle was the question of the authority of the soviets. We were in constant opposition to the 'coalitionist' government and continued transforming the soviets into the single organ of power."[8] It was in this atmosphere that the November elections to the zemstvo institutions gave the Socialist-Revolutionaries an overwhelming majority of the votes. This clearly shows that the people wanted to organize local democratic agencies of self-government. With the tide of popular opinion against them, the Bolsheviks nevertheless continued to prepare for an armed insurrection.

Once they had seized power in Petrograd in October 1917, the Bolsheviks continued working toward the seizure of power in Siberia. How did the rest of the population react to these events? Safronov describes the mood: "The Socialist-Revolutionaries continued their stubborn resistance. The Socialist-Revolutionary–Menshevik Central Executive Committee of the Soviet of Peasants' Deputies refused to recognize soviet power in central Russia. In Yeniseisk province the Executive Committee of the Soviet of Peasants' Deputies also refused to join with the soviets of soldiers' and workers' deputies. The provincial soviet of peasants' deputies also did not recognize soviet authority."[9] The appeal issued by the Executive Committee of the Peasants' Deputies was not circulated. It had been confiscated in the printing office by the Bolshevik Belopolsky. In it the Provincial Committee of Peasants' Deputies protested against the usurpation of power; and this was no exception to the view held in other regions of Siberia. "In the region of Akmolinsk Oblast, from the moment of the socialist revolution, there was not a single soviet of peasants' deputies that would agree to join the soviets of workers' and soldiers' deputies or that would declare in favor of soviet power."[10] The Bolsheviks, encountering such opposition and knowing full well that the population of Siberia hoped for a constituent assembly, moved slowly toward their goal of seizing power in Siberia. In fact, the process extended to the very end of January 1918.

What was the prevailing mood of Siberia on the eve of the October Revolution, and how strong were the Bolsheviks? In Irkutsk, for example, because of the insignificant size of the working class—6,000 to 7,000—the mood was set by employees of commercial and administrative agencies.[11] Two hundred thousand people voted in the November elections to the Constituent Assembly in this district; the Bolsheviks received only 33,000 votes and failed to get even one of their candidates elected. In March 1918, the Bolsheviks forcibly dispersed the Irkutsk District Congress of Peasants' Deputies. The Bolsheviks claim that in Yeniseisk province, their main center, they dominated the soviets of workers' and soldiers' deputies in the cities of Krasnoyarsk, Kansk, and Achinsk; but outside the cities the Bolsheviks had little influence, and the former agencies remained in power.[12]

For a more comprehensive understanding of the viewpoint of the peasant population, it will help to point out several measures adopted by the Yeniseisk Provincial Congress of Peasants' Deputies: first was the appeal to pay taxes due; second was the decision to require military service of the old inhabitants in the regions of the Angara, Chuna, and Mura rivers; and the third and most "revolutionary" demand was that during wartime, profit from any enterprise must not exceed 15 percent, and that any profit above that would be confiscated by the government; fourth was the stipulation that the strictest measures would be taken against the production of *samagon* (moonshine).

Results of the November elections to the Constituent Assembly in Yeniseisk province were not favorable to the Bolsheviks, even though by that time they were virtually the rulers. Together with the Left Socialist-Revolutionaries, they were able to win only about one-third of the votes and two deputies; all the other deputies were Socialist-Revolutionaries. The villages fell into a state of anarchy. The situation was further complicated by the fact that most members of the newly organized soviets were newcomers to the area with no ties linking them to the interests of the local population. Village and city alike were affected by economic disorganization and lack of goods and currency. Demobilized soldiers, who did not have the required documents for obtaining train passes, were seizing entire railroad cars and not allowing regular passengers to board. And over all this hung a general pall of apathy toward the political events of the time.

The Central Committee of the Bolshevik Party, preparing for an armed insurrection as early as September 1917, directed groups of party workers to Siberia to bolster the strength of the local Bolsheviks. "The Bolsheviks in Siberia were given a two-fold assignment: to support the armed insurrection in the center and, in the event of its success, immediately to supply Petrograd and Moscow with provisions."[13] With this in mind, the Bolsheviks in Siberia adapted themselves like chameleons to their surroundings. They unfurled their slogan "All power to the Soviets!" and proclaimed that power in their hands would guarantee quick election to the all-Russian Constituent Assembly.[14] In the meantime, all their energy was devoted to forming detachments of the Red Guard and the Red Army. Workers were enlisted into the Red Guard; the Red Army was, for the most part, made up of prisoners of war. Simultaneously, reelections were held to the soviets of soldiers' and workers' deputies wherever the Bolsheviks did not yet have a majority. For example, in Irkutsk two reelections were held during November 1917 to the Soviet of Workers' Deputies, "assuring in the long run the victory of the Bolsheviks."[15]

Thus the Bolsheviks prepared themselves for the "peaceful conquest" of Siberia. The large garrisons were disbanded, as they no longer served any useful purpose as a military unit. A small percentage of former soldiers transferred their allegiance to the Bolsheviks. The Bolsheviks were quick to take advantage of the fact that anti-Bolshevik forces were unorganized and lacked central leadership, and each region acted on its own. The "peaceful conquest" was carried out in the following manner: "Entire expeditions from Krasnoyarsk were launched against the Mensheviks and the Socialist-Revolutionaries wherever they held strong positions."[16] These expeditions consisted of party workers, as well as military detachments. As soon as they had succeeded in gaining a sufficient concentration of military strength, they would demand the disarming of all military units that did not recognize Soviet authority. This happened first in the city of Omsk on November 1, 1917. The military schools refused to surrender their arms, and the Bolsheviks accused them of revolution against the Soviet regime. In preparation for the destruction of the cadet corps, the Bolsheviks had a few days earlier successfully disbanded the Third School of Praporshchiks (ensigns) by dispensing to each man 250 rubles and a length of cloth. With the School of Praporshchiks out of the way, they attacked the cadets, numbering about two thousand men. It should be kept in mind that these were wartime military schools. The students were not members of the privileged classes, but were mainly former soldiers, partly of the petty bourgeois of the cities, and children of workers. Because of their insignificant numbers and lack of support from the outside, these schools surrendered after a one-day battle. The large Cossack detachments in the city remained neutral, taking no part in the battle.

In Irkutsk the battles lasted from December 8 to 15. There were heavy losses on both sides, including some of the civilian population. The Bolsheviks, fearing total destruction, were forced to sign a peace treaty in order to gain time. According to the terms of this treaty, authority was to be held by the city government. Two days later, under the command of Left Socialist-Revolutionary Eideman, detachments of Red Guardsmen arrived from Krasnoyarsk, Omsk, Achinsk, Kansk, and the mines of Cheremkhov. Now that he had reinforcements, Boris Shumyatsky, the representative of the Central Committee of the Bolshevik Party, tore up the treaty, on which the ink had not yet dried, and declared that "over the ruins of Irkutsk he would raise the Soviet flag." Under these conditions, the opposing side finally agreed to disband, providing that those who wished might leave the city unhindered.

Concerning the "uprising" of the Cossacks in the city of Krasnoyarsk on January 17, 1918, the Bolshevik observer Frumkin wrote:

In the beginning of January an order was issued by Moscow to disarm the Cossacks. This was a problem that had come up before us time and again. Not wishing to enter into an armed conflict with them, our representatives, Peterson and Lebedeva, proposed to Ataman Sotnikov that the Cossacks surrender their arms. The Cossack leaders asked for twelve hours in which to discuss their proposal among their *sotniyas* [150–200 men]. At midnight the Cossacks abandoned their barracks and crossed over the Yenisei River on their horses to the village of Torgashino, about seven versts from Krasnoyarsk. The city was declared under siege and artillery was directed against Torgashino. The Cossacks marched out of Torgashino and began a descent toward the south, their numbers melting on the way until, at the end of the month, they had all melted away.[17]

Since I had been maintaining contact with a Cossack ataman, I was well informed of the situation. Taking into account the prematureness of the insurrection, the fact that there was no contact with other regions, and the objective of preserving strength and avoiding needless bloodshed, the members of the military command in Krasnoyarsk decided not to accept the Bolshevik challenge but to go south, where they would then call a military meeting. During the night, at 30 degrees below zero, the Cossacks crossed the frozen Yenisei River to reach Torgashino. In the haste of departure, they neglected to take with them topographical maps of the locality, and they discovered later that from Torgashino it was impossible to cross the mountain range on horseback. So they once again made a night crossing—this time to the west shore of the Yenisei River—and moved south. Because the Cossack command had not set any military goals for the time being, the Cossacks who had been called up from the villages through which this detachment passed did not go any farther, but simply returned to their homes and stayed there. In the language of the Bolsheviks, this peaceful retreat of the Cossacks from Krasnoyarsk was called a "rebellion."

This was the conception of "historian" Safronov, who describes these events in a somewhat different light: "The social base of the rebels proved to be very weak. Not only the peasants, but the working Cossacks failed to follow Sotnikov. By taking decisive measures, the Krasnoyarsk, Minusinsk, and other soviets quickly formed detachments of Red Guards and arrested about three hundred people, among whom were the leaders of the Committee of the Right Socialist-

Revolutionaries, for attempting to help the rebels. [I was among those arrested and declared a "hostage."] A contribution of 750,000 rubles was exacted from the bourgeoisie. The Third Western Siberian Conference of Soviets recommended in its resolution concerning authority that wherever peasant soviets are in opposition to Soviet authority, power should be taken by the soviets of workers' and soldiers' deputies."[18]

What was called a rebellion really meant merely that not everyone at once recognized the authority of the usurpers. In their struggle to win over the peasants during that period, the Bolsheviks relied on the soviets of workers' and soldiers' deputies. Those in opposition to Soviet power in the province of Yeniseisk and in Akmolin Oblast can be estimated—without risk of error—at 90 percent of the population of Siberia. Only by using armed force in the cities were the Bolsheviks able to establish hegemony and dictate their conditions to the countryside.

Yet another touch must be added to the "peaceful" transition of power to the soviets. In the beginning of December 1917, a member of the Social-Democratic Party, Anatoly Baikalov, was arrested by the Bolsheviks in Krasnoyarsk because at meetings he had called for resistance to the orders issued by the soviets. Several weeks later he was brought to trial. Presiding over the tribunal, which had been ordered to pronounce a sentence recommended beforehand by the party committee, was a third-year law student. By the time the tribunal opened at eleven o'clock in the morning, a tremendous demonstration, both inside and outside the courtroom, was in progress. The demonstrators demanded that the prisoner be freed. The trial was postponed and Baikalov temporarily released. At one o'clock in the afternoon, the student who had presided over the tribunal was dead. The official version was that he had taken his own life, but according to unofficial sources he was shot by Lydia Subbotina, a member of the Bolshevik Party Committee, because he had violated party discipline. Baikalov was not brought to trial again.[19]

To what extent the "transition to Soviet authority was peaceful" in Siberia can be judged by the events in Omsk, Irkutsk, and Krasnoyarsk described above. The Bolsheviks in Siberia were not numerous, but they had at their disposal large detachments of internationalists who were former prisoners of war.

These internationalist detachments were the most solid and reliable military support of the Siberian soviets. They had seen military action and were skilled in handling all kinds of weapons. They had been living in compact masses in concentration camps. They quickly broke up into detachments according to types of weapons and by nationalities, and chose their own commanding staff. The internationalists disciplined themselves along military lines. They executed unquestioningly the orders of their leaders. Their attitude toward any assignment—be it standing guard duty, tracking someone down, or with gun in hand marching against an enemy of soviet authority—was irreproachable.[20]

During the organization of the Siberian Bolshevik Party, more than 30 sections of internationalists (mostly non-Russians) were also formed. The most active in Krasnoyarsk were the Latvian and Polish sections.

"By the spring of 1918 there were in existence more than a dozen internationalist detachments numbering more than ten thousand men ready to come to the defense of Soviet authority."[21] And again: "It should be noted that for the purpose of putting down 'rebellions and riots,' the Krasnoyarsk [internationalist] detachments constantly shifted back and forth, not only from city to city, but even from one end of Siberia to the other."[22] In other words, the Bolsheviks had under their command a punitive detachment of prisoners of war numbering no less than ten thousand men. These detachments helped to establish Soviet authority in Omsk, Tomsk, Barnaul, Krasnoyarsk, Achinsk, Irkutsk, Nizhneudinsk, Chita, Tiumen, Tobolsk, Berezovka, Daurii, Blagoveshchensk, and Khabarovsk.[23]

The Bolshevik Shumyatsky wrote: "The burials of the victims of the December battles in Irkutsk developed into a powerful demonstration of twenty thousand Russian, Hungarian, German, Chinese, Korean workers and soldiers of army units. It was a moving procession of the mighty workers' international sealed with the blood of fallen comrades."[24] There can be no doubt to whom the Bolsheviks looked for support in their battle to establish Soviet authority in Siberia: it was to foreign bayonets. To mask this fact, all foreigners who enlisted in the Red Guard were automatically granted Russian citizenship.

One slogan used by the Bolsheviks in seizing power was: "Seizure and distribution of the land"; another was "Peace to the huts—war to the palaces"; and the third was "Down with war—long live peace." The slogans had little influence in Siberia. The first did not apply because there were no large landowners and therefore nothing to divide, and in the vast expanses of Siberia there was no shortage of land. Neither, as a rule, were there huts or palaces in Siberia. And as for the third slogan: peace, but what kind of peace? The Siberian people wanted peace, but certainly not a dishonorable one. The Bolsheviks, having seized power in Siberia, were acutely aware of the general mood of the people, especially of former soldiers; they hesitated, therefore, to come out openly with their call for "peace at all costs." A member of the Bolshevik Party Committee of Yeniseisk province said:

> At the beginning of December—the fifth, if I remember correctly—we received an inquiry from the Central Executive Committee concerning the Treaty of Brest-Litovsk and an order to send by return mail that very day a communication expressing our attitude toward the act. After a short discussion at the meeting of the Executive Committee, together with representatives of army units and labor unions, we reached an almost unanimous answer—negative. Only G. S. Weinbaum, then chairman of the Soviet Executive Committee, felt that it was absolutely essential to conclude a peace—no matter what.[25]

Further, at the All-Siberian Congress of Soviets held in February 1918 (attended by 202 people, including 123 Bolsheviks and 53 Left Socialist-Revolutionaries), a resolution was passed against the conclusion of the Treaty of Brest-Litovsk.

The Resolution of the Second All-Siberian Congress of Soviets
on the Question of Concluding Peace with Germany

August 21, 1918

After discussion of the latest news concerning the possibility that the Council of People's Commissars may agree to peace on the terms offered by the four-power coalition in Brest, which earlier had been rejected by the worker-peasants' government of the Russian Soviet Republic, the Second All-Siberian Congress of Soviets of Workers', Soldiers', and Peasants' Deputies resolves:

1. The adherents of the "international revolutionary" policy rule out the possibility of any kind of annexationist treaty.
2. The Council of People's Commissars, by signifying willingness to sign an imperialist, counterrevolutionary peace, would be taking a fatal step, making a fatal error, and dealing a blow to the further development of the Revolution and the International.
3. In the name of the Siberian Soviet Republic, the Second All-Siberian Congress of Soviets declares that it does not consider itself bound by a peace treaty, should there be one, concluded by the Council of People's Commissars with

the German government. Sending fraternal greetings to the struggling revolutionary proletariat of Austria and Germany, the congress expresses its firm decision to fight to the end for an international socialist peace.

4. The Congress proposes that the Siberian Soviets muster all their forces toward the speedy formation of a Red Socialist Army for the struggle against the counterrevolutionary bourgeoisie.

Critical in this resolution is the fact that the congress not only objected to signing the Treaty of Brest-Litovsk, but declared that if it should be signed Siberia would not consider herself bound by it. It should also be noted that the declaration was made in the name of the "Siberian Soviet Republic." At the same time, the Bolsheviks were dispersing the Siberian Oblast Duma on the grounds that the idea of creating an autonomous Siberia was propagated only by a handful of intellectuals who were out of their minds.

Later, the Bolshevik Party Central Committee replaced its representative, Shumyatsky, and issued new directives. As a result, the Siberian Bolsheviks, for the sake of party loyalty, submitted, acknowledged the Treaty of Brest-Litovsk, and forgot all about the "Siberian Republic."

In evaluating this period, Soviet sources vary greatly, but with the passage of time the accounts tend to stray further and further from the truth, whereas praises for the ruling party increase. For example, Safronov writes: "The Bolshevik organizations accomplished significant political work in the villages, and discredited the Kadets, the Mensheviks, and the Socialist-Revolutionaries. The Bolsheviks prepared the peasants for the establishment of Soviet authority and for the defense of its gains. That is why, when the forces of domestic counterrevolution and foreign intervention attempted to destroy the Soviet regime, the peasant movement rose to its highest crest. The workers and the peasants joined in partisan warfare in defense of Soviet authority."[26]

Earlier sources, including Frumkin, state: "At the beginning of November, elections to the Constituent Assembly were held. The Socialist-Revolutionaries began agitating against us, pointing out that the October overthrow was nothing but a seizure of power by usurpers with no regard for the will of the people, since it was only in the Constituent Assembly that that will could have found voice. The peasant vote went mostly to the Socialist-Revolutionaries, especially in the rich Minusinsk uezd (Yeniseisk province) with its kulak population."[27]

Another Bolshevik historian, V. Vegman, writes: "Regrettably the Siberian Bolshevik organizations did not at that time pay due attention to the villages. As a consequence, the sovietization of the Siberian villages was not conducted widely or thoroughly, and the poor peasantry was not sufficiently well organized. As a result of this mistake, when the armed Czechs and White Guardsmen fell upon the soviets, the poor peasants were silent and did not rise to the defense of the soviets."[28]

The soviets were but one target of the Bolshevik assault in Siberia. At the same time, the Bolshevik Party began its campaign to rid Siberia of its oblast duma as well.

Following the Bolshevik attempt to seize power in Petrograd in May 1917 and the subsequent government crisis, Siberia began to feel the absence of central authority and, as a consequence, to experience the beginning of economic collapse. Seeking a way out of this situation, the Tomsk oblastniki took the initiative of calling a meeting of all oblastniki in Siberia. The First Siberian Congress of Oblastniki was held in August 1917. The delegates at this congress represented the peasants', workers', and soldiers' organizations, the zemstvo and city self-government organs, the cooperatives, and the various nationalities inhabiting Siberia. Approximately 65 percent of the participants at the congress leaned toward the socialist parties. And, it is interesting to note, 40 percent of the delegates were either born in Siberia or had lived there for more than twenty years. The congress recognized that Siberia had an inalienable right to an autonomous government and appointed a committee to draft conditions for elections to the Siberian Constituent Assembly; which, together with the central Russian government, would then determine the forms of oblast government. However, the fast-changing political scene in central Russia was not at all conducive to the normal progress of this committee's work.

The seizure of power by the Bolsheviks in Petrograd in October 1917 made it imperative for Siberians to seek another way out and to speed up the process of establishing a regime in Siberia. For this purpose, an extraordinary congress was called from December 4 to 15 in the city of Tomsk. The work of this congress proceeded in an unbelievably difficult political atmosphere: the Bolsheviks had resorted to armed assault in Omsk and in Irkutsk and set the stage for civil war. They did not, however, interfere with the congress, which was able to complete its work and adopt the following resolution: "Acknowledging the fact that in a time of governmental upheaval and civil strife, the only way to restore national power is through an

All-Russian Constituent Assembly elected by means of general, direct, equal, and secret voting, the All-Siberian Extraordinary Congress adopts the position that Siberia should be ruled by a provisional government."[29] On the basis of this resolution, the Siberian Oblast Duma was formed as a legislative body.

The new Oblast Duma met in Tomsk at the end of January 1918, proclaimed itself the supreme authority in Siberia, and chose the Provisional Siberian Government: N. Ia. Derber, E. Zakharov, A. A. Krakovetsky, M. A. Kolobov, C. M. Tiber-Petrov, A. E. Novoselov, I. Serebryannikov, V. I. Maravsky, S. A. Kudryavtsev, P. Vologodsky, V. Krutovsky, G. Patushinsky, I. Mikhailov, M. Shatilov, and N. Zhernakov. The duma announced the following program:

1. To help the all-Russian Constituent Assembly resume its work;
2. To call a meeting of the Siberian Constituent Assembly;
3. To form a volunteer army.

In pursuit of its goals, the Siberian Oblast Duma drew up new regulations for the political and economic problems faced by Siberia:

1. In matters relating to land: to put into practice the law, as applicable to Siberian conditions, adopted by the all-Russian Constituent Assembly;
2. To nationalize mines and ore in Siberia;
3. To establish a national Siberian bank;
4. To reestablish the railroad transportation system;
5. To establish a good trading relationship with allied nations;
6. To introduce, within the limits of the national laws, the eight-hour working day;
7. To offer free education, both general and specialized, at government expense.

The Siberian Bolsheviks had, meanwhile, solidified their position in Omsk and Irkutsk, rid themselves of the Cossacks in Krasnoyarsk, strengthened the Red Guard, and received reinforcements of five hundred sailors from the center.[30] They were now ready to act on the example set for them by the Bolsheviks in the center, who had dispersed the All-Russian Constituent Assembly, by doing the same in Siberia. They did not have long to wait. No sooner had the Siberian Oblast Duma convened in Tomsk and proclaimed itself the sovereign authority in Siberia than it was dispersed. This occurred on February 6 in response to a directive issued by Shumyatsky, representative of the Central Committee of the Bolshevik Party. Sixteen members of the duma were arrested, together with the chairman, I. Yakushev, and two members of the Siberian Provisional Government, Patushinsky and Shatilov. The remaining members of the Siberian Oblast Duma and of the Siberian government then began their illegal existence, resolving to continue their efforts to overthrow the Bolshevik government.

The dispersal of the Siberian duma and the arrest of its members were the turning point in the Siberians' attitude. If, theretofore, any of the oblastniki had hoped that somehow an agreement could be reached with the center, now that hope was buried. It became more and more obvious that the only means of doing battle with the Bolsheviks was through armed conflict.

At a secret meeting, the Oblast Duma authorized a group of men chosen from the Siberian government to organize an armed uprising. These were men with exceptional organizational skills, and all were members of the Socialist-Revolutionary Party. Though they belonged to the same party, they were not responsible to it, however, but directly to the Siberian government, in whose name they carried out their assignments. This should dispel the legend that the Siberian coup was the outcome of the "Czech uprising." This legend was strongly supported, on the one hand, by the so-called White generals, who did not appear in Siberia until after the overthrow, and, on the other, by the Bolsheviks, who wished to justify their shameful retreat.

Siberian democracy, represented by the Siberian Oblast Duma, organized the overthrow of Bolshevik authority, depending solely on its own resources in those early days of February 1918. The Czechs were not yet in Siberia, and the membership of their central organs did not (and would not until May) have any thoughts of an armed uprising. In the preliminary stages of organizing the uprising in Siberia, one of the problems was to determine a social base; another was to ascertain what material resources would be available for the enterprise and to work out our ideas and slogans for the uprising.

The tactics used by the Bolshevik Party to undermine unity among the ranks of their enemy had had time to bear fruit. Disorder among the anti-Bolshevik parties and the intelligentsia was becoming apparent. The Constitutional Democratic (Kadet) Party, after having lost the elections, welcomed the dispersal of the Constitutent Assembly in Petrograd. The Kadets refused to participate in the movement to overthrow the Bolsheviks. What they really wanted was one strong power at the head during a transitional stage that would lead to constitutional monarchy. Trade and industry circles, fearing confiscation and requisition, hastened to contribute money to the Bolshevik

Party. The Socialist Democratic (Menshevik) Party, undermined from within by the Bolsheviks, was weak and therefore remained neutral, hoping to rid the country of bolshevism by peaceful means.

Within the Socialist-Revolutionary Party—now weakened by the revolt of its "left" members—were some who held practically the same viewpoint as the Bolsheviks; the majority, however, was in favor of supporting the Siberian Oblast Duma. The duma, which maintained a rather optimistic outlook for the future, relied on the considerable sympathies of the peasant population, securing material support from city and zemstvo administration and, most important, from the central cooperative organizations. It fell to the lot of those members of the Socialist-Revolutionary Party who joined the West Siberian Commissariat to undertake both the political leadership of the emergent movement and the basic work of forming combat organizations, drawing together not only members of the party, but willing fighters wherever they could be found—among the intelligentsia, workers, peasants, and democratically inclined officers. The political work consisted not only in convincing the population of the reactionary essence of Bolshevik rule, but in promoting these slogans: "Reinstatement of the Constituent Assembly," "Establishment of democratic rule," "Autonomy for Siberia," and, later, "Re-establishment of a second front against Germany."

Siberia was divided into two regions: west and east. The first, centered in Omsk and extending from the Urals to Irkutsk, fell within the sphere of the West Siberian Commissariat, composed of Constituent Assembly members P. Mikhailov, B. Markov, and M. Lindberg and a representative of the zemstvo, V. Sidorov. Military operations in this region were conducted by Grishin-Almazov. The second region extended from Irkutsk to Vladivostok and fell within the sphere of the resident members of the government, headed by Derber, and the minister of war, Col. A. A. Krakovetsky. I too was involved in preparations for the uprising. In late January 1918, while I was in charge of the financial section at the zemstvo meetings, I was arrested by order of the Bolshevik Party Committee and declared a hostage as a guarantee of their members' safety. This was a situation in which I did not have many choices; I could either quietly wait my turn to be shot or attempt an escape. I chose the latter. My former position as vice-chairman of the Executive Committee of the Soviets held out a measure of hope for success. I was able to contact my political colleagues outside prison; aided by the prison personnel, I received no less than three messages a week and was provided with weapons. As it turned out, though, I had no need to resort to the use of arms to escape.

At eleven o'clock on a sunny morning in early March 1918, I was summoned to the office of the prison head, who informed me that he had received an order from the chairman of the Executive Committee, Weinbaum, to free me. The moment I stepped outside the prison gate, my political friends whisked me to a secret rendezvous with a barber, who transformed me from a blond to a brunet. I was provided with documents, money, and a railway ticket and taken to the railway station. At half-past twelve I was happily on my way to Tomsk. At one o'clock the Bolsheviks discovered that the order for my release was a forgery.

In Tomsk I had several meetings with Potanin, one of the founders of the oblastnik movement in Siberia. We discussed possible measures to bring about the release from the Krasnoyarsk prison of members of the Siberian government: Patushinsky and Shatilov, the comptroller, Zhernakov, and the chairman of the duma, I. A. Yakushev. While in Tomsk, I also made contact with the West Siberian Commissariat, and at one of its meetings I reported on the political situation in Yeniseisk province and the possibility of organizing an uprising there. After some debate, it was decided that Mikhailov, Grishin-Almazov, and I should go to Krasnoyarsk to carry out the organizational work.[31] Thus it was that ten days after my flight from prison I found myself again in Krasnoyarsk.

In Krasnoyarsk we set up headquarters for a military organization of seven men. Colonel Gulidov was the chief of the general staff, and I was head of the organization. To avoid problems, when new members were admitted the "principle of ten" was applied: no one in the organization could know more than ten of its members. Those who joined the organization did so for purely idealistic reasons—in the name of the struggle ahead, not for any monetary compensation. Some did, of course, receive compensation, but they were exceptions and the amounts were limited. Whatever funds the organization had were used mostly for procuring arms. In a period of two and a half months, the total expenses of our organization in Krasnoyarsk did not exceed 10,000 rubles. Referring to our work, Soviet historian P. S. Parfenov recounts that a code for secret communications was worked out at an illegal meeting held on May 3 in Novonikolaevsk.[32] Actually, the code was already in my hands in mid-March, in other words, from the moment the work of our organization began.

3

The Overthrow
of the Bolsheviks

In organizing the Siberian uprising, the leaders ran headlong into the Czech question. The Czech corps was made up of prisoners of war, former soldiers of the Austrian Army who had not wished to fight against Russia. The corps, under Russian command in 1917, saw action on the German front. Once the Soviets had begun peace talks with the Germans at Brest-Litovsk, the Czech forces on the western front, in the Ukraine, were ordered by Tomas Masaryk, president of the National Council, to move toward Vladivostok for a quick transfer to the French front.

A treaty approved by Moscow was drawn up between the Soviets and the Czechs in Penza. It was officially announced in a decree of March 26 issued by Commissar Stalin: "The Czechs are departing not as a military unit, but as a group of free citizens, carrying a certain amount of arms for protection against assault by counterrevolutionaries."[1] According to the terms of the treaty, each echelon could have only one armed company; the arms would be limited to 168 rifles and a machine gun, and 300 cartridges for each rifle and 12,000 for each machine gun. All remaining arms were to be surrendered in Penza.

After surrendering their arms, the Czechs continued east more or less unhindered. By the end of April, about one-third of the Czech Army was in Vladivostok. At the beginning of May, however, an abrupt change occurred. Each separate soviet in each city that the remaining Czechs passed after Penza confronted them with new demands concerning the surrender of arms. At the same time, Czech Bolsheviks, with the cooperation of Russian authorities, bombarded them with propaganda aimed at undermining their morale. It was then that the officials of the Siberian government were informed by the Czechs that there might be armed conflict with the Soviets. The representatives of the Siberian government asked that the Czechs clearly define their proposed course of action. The Czechs replied that they did not wish to meddle in Russia's internal affairs, but would take every measure to preserve order on and control over the railroad since it was their lifeline. The leaders of the Siberian military organization made their plans accordingly. But in mid-May 1918, events took an entirely unexpected turn to upset all preliminary plans.

On May 14, 1918, a Czech clash with the Soviets in Chelyabinsk was provoked by hostile action on the part of some Magyars in the Red Army; as a result, one Magyar was killed. The Chelyabinsk soviet arrested several Czechs, who were later freed by force through the efforts of their comrades in echelons at the railroad station. This incident increased the distrust of the Czechs for the Soviets. The Czechs feared that as soon as they surrendered their arms they would be given over to the Germans. The following actions of the Soviets left no doubt as to their intent. A telegram of May 21 sent from the Operations Department of the Commissariat for Foreign Affairs proclaimed: "By orders of Comrade Trotsky, chairman of the People's Commissariat of Military Affairs, all local soviets are urged to persuade the Czech echelons to organize into workers' artels [trade associations formed for the common good] according to specialty and to enter the ranks of the Soviet Red Army. Do all in your power to help organize the Czech communists."

Two days later, a second telegram was sent: "In confirmation of the former order, emergency measures should be taken to detain, disarm, and disband all echelons and companies of the Czechoslovak corps, as a remnant of the old regular army. It is from these that Red Army units and workers' artels should be formed. If help is needed from the Czech commissars, apply to the Committee of Czech Social Democrats in Penza, Samara, Petropavlovsk, and Omsk. Report on the measures taken and the results achieved to the People's Commissar on Military Affairs in Moscow."[2] This telegram was not secret, and it served to put the Czechs on their guard; but they kept to their former principle of neutrality in Russian internal affairs.

On May 25, 1918, the die was cast by a telegram from Trotsky to all local soviets along the line from Penza to Omsk:

All soviets along the railroad line must, under threat of heavy penalty, disarm the Czechs. Any Czech found armed on the railroad line must be shot at once. Each echelon in which even only one armed Czech is found is to be thrown off the train and taken to a prisoner of war camp. The local military commissariats are under obligation to execute this order at once. Any delay is equivalent to treason and the guilty will be severely punished. At this instant reliable forces are being sent to the rear of the Czech echelons to teach the rebels a lesson. Those Czechs who act honorably—surrender their arms and submit to soviet authority—will be treated as brothers and given all possible support. All the railroad workers must be informed that not one railway carriage carrying Czechs is to be allowed to move east. Anyone who resorts to force and renders assistance to the Czechs' eastward movement will be severely punished.[3]

The Siberian soviets in Irkutsk and Omsk implemented Trotsky's order and attempted an armed attack on the Czechs. A member of the Omsk Committee of Bolsheviks wrote:

On May 24 we received a wire informing us that a Czech echelon was approaching. We sent a detachment of 290 Red Guardsmen under the command of Comrade Uspensky to meet this echelon at the Kulomzino Station. On the morning of the twenty-fifth, the Czech echelon drew near. Submitting to Uspensky's demand, the Czechs surrendered 30 rifles. Our comrades noticed that holes had been drilled through many of the railway carriages, evidently for machine guns. When Comrade Uspensky demanded an inspection of the carriages, the Czechs pushed the engineer out of the train, replaced him by one of their own men, and, reversing the engine, returned to Marianovka Station—70 versts from Omsk. Uspensky loaded his detachment into another train that was standing at the station and gave chase. Upon reaching Marianovka Station some of the Red Guardsmen began jumping out of the carriages and opened fire while the majority of their men were still in the carriages. The Czechs answered by cross-fire, not giving the Red Guardsmen a chance to fall into line, and turned them into targets. We lost 70 men, 130 were wounded, and the rest scattered.[4]

After this the Czechs did not have much of a choice; they could either surrender and give themselves up to the mercy of the Soviets or they could make their way using armed force. They chose the latter. But the Bolsheviks were the first to attack the Czech troops, on May 25, 1918.

Because the Bolsheviks had begun military action against the Czechs, the West Siberian Commissariat of the Siberian government decided to take advantage of the situation and ordered its military organizations to stage an uprising. On May 26, 1918, I received the following telegram: "Present your bills of exchange for payment," with instructions for coordinating our action with that of the Czech battalions. The venture was premature: the illegal organizations were not ready for it in all regions. At the May 3 meeting of representatives of the military organizations in Novonikolaevsk, it had been discovered that together they commanded a total of approximately 8,000 soldiers, but the distribution by region was unequal. For example, the organization in Omsk consisted mostly of Cossacks from outlying regions and numbered 3,000, whereas Tomsk had only 500. And Krasnoyarsk, that stronghold of bolshevism, had only 360. The result was that the uprisings did not take place at the same time everywhere. But this did not prevent us from winning a rather swift victory. The Bolsheviks did not suspect the strength of our organization and did not foresee the uprising, so were taken by surprise.

Novonikolaevsk was occupied on May 26 by Russian and Czech troops. On the same day, the Czechs occupied Mariinsk and Kansk. The military organization at Tomsk attempted an unsuccessful uprising on May 28. That night, the Tomsk soviet fled in panic. In Krasnoyarsk, where the soviet had approximately 5,000 soldiers, including Magyar divisions, the military organization with its mere 360 decided to delay action. In Omsk there were many soldiers, but they also waited for the outcome of the battle between the Soviets and the Czechs at Marianovka Station. The picture on June 1 was that the Omsk soviet had two fronts, Marianovka Station in the west and Novonikolaevsk in the east, and the Krasnoyarsk soviet also had two fronts, Kansk in the east (as of May 29) and Mariinsk in the west. The fact that the Tomsk soviet, together with the international divisions, had fled by steamship to Tiumen simplified the operational problems of the insurrectionists. Immediately thereafter the Bolsheviks opened a series of "peace talks," to gain time and prepare themselves for an offensive. The foreigners, namely Americans and French, acted as mediators, knowing absolutely nothing about the overall situation. And to make matters worse, there was no unity among the Czechs. The Vladivostok group of 12,000 Czechs did not come forth, but instead sent a delegation to the west to settle the conflict.

On the initiative of the People's Commissar of Food Supplies, the Omsk soviet conducted peace talks with the Czechs at Marianovka Station. Meanwhile, the Bolsheviks continued extensive arming and sent troops to liberate Novonikolaevsk. A Bolshevik observer reported:

> At the end of the week we had approximately three thousand adequately armed men. We were better equipped than the Czechs: we had 168 machine guns, 4 cannons, and an adequate supply of cartridges. The Czechs had about 30 machine guns. "Our men" drove the Czechs into a marshland near Kainsk and shot them there. In this battle the Magyars distinguished themselves . . . By prolonging the negotiations, the Omsk soviet hoped for the demoralization of the Czech soldiers and sent to them some Czech agitators. The Czechs saw through this subterfuge, shot the agitators, and at one o'clock on June 6 launched an attack in columns. Our machine guns warded off the attack. Hundreds fell in the Czech ranks. Occasionally the Czechs retreated but then attacked again in columns. Nevertheless, in the open field they were beaten back, but not without dealing the enemy considerable losses of five hundred to six hundred men. During the battle the Czechs circumvented the field of action and at half-past nine in the evening appeared at our rear. Our Red Guardsmen were unprepared for such a ruse. The badly fused ranks were broken and panic ensued.[5]

The morning after this battle, the Omsk soviet began a hurried evacuation, and by four o'clock on June 7 it had set out on five steamships toward the north with 279 million rubles taken from the bank. The soviet was forced to flee by ship because the railroad workers, "the mainstay of the Bolsheviks," had dismantled the tracks that led to Tiumen. In the haste of retreat, a division of thirteen hundred men that had been sent to liberate Novonikolaevsk was left behind to its own fate. By evening the military organization had occupied the city without a battle.

"The workmen took over control of the railroad and the prison camp guard and prevented the blowing-up of the bridge (which had been mined at eighteen points) across the Irtysh. The Czechs entered Omsk on June 9, 1918."[6] During the so-called peace talks, the Omsk soviet managed to send 36 million pounds of grain from Siberia to central Russia.

The fall of Soviet rule in the center of bolshevism and the scene of my activities, the province of Yeniseisk, is of interest. Neither in Krasnoyarsk nor in Achinsk were there any Czech troops. There was a small group of perhaps thirty men for the purpose of liaison, who had been disarmed and imprisoned by the Bolsheviks. In Kansk there was a Czech echelon of about five hundred men. The Kansk soviet, acting under instructions of May 28, 1918, from Krasnoyarsk, tried to disarm the Czechs but failed. On May 29 the Czechs, under B. F. Ushakov's command, disarmed the garrison and arrested the members of the soviet. All of them were released from prison within a few days, with the notable exception of P. A. Andreev, who had been in charge of disarming the Czechs.

On June 5, Ushakov reestablished the authority of the former city government. Earlier, the French attaché had sent a telegram (dated June 2) to all the echelons down the line: "Avoid any involvement in the domestic political conflict. The soviets are doing everything possible for evacuation."[7] On May 31 a member of the French mission had sent a telegram from Omsk to the Czechs: "Your actions force the French Mission to wash its hands of this affair. It will be a disgrace if the Czechs are dragged into the Russian bedlam. If the Czechs insist on participating, everything will be finished between them and the French government."[8] Colonel G. Emerson, American representative of the Allied Railroad Commission, telephoned the consul in Irkutsk from Krasnoyarsk requesting that "Gaida and the other Czech commanders be instructed to cease fighting and to stop meddling in politics." As a result, a truce from June 4 to 10 was concluded in Mariinsk. The Soviets, led by Weinbaum, chairman of the Krasnoyarsk soviet, signed the agreement. A Captain Kodlets represented the Czech side and Vice-Consul E. Thomas, the military attaché, and Emerson represented the Americans.

In this breathing spell, the Krasnoyarsk soviet feverishly set about strengthening its army and transporting detachments to the front. A detachment of three thousand men under the command of Aaron Schneider was dispatched to the west, in the direction of Mariinsk. A detachment of eight hundred men under the command of Yakov Dubrovinsky was sent to the east, in the direction of Kansk. Dubrovinsky's detachment stopped at the halfway point on the road to Kansk, at Kliukvennaya Station; Schneider's detachment occupied front-line positions at Mariinsk.

The commander of the Soviet armies and formerly an officer in the Tsarist army characterized the situation at the front in his report to the soviet dated June 7, 1918:

In Kansk the Czech echelons consist of five hundred men. There is no cavalry. There were a few White Guardsmen, but they have been disarmed by the Czechs and sent to outlying districts, where they are organizing prosperous peasants and malcontents . . . On the Mariinsk front the Czech and White Guardsmen units consist of three thousand men. Morale among the Czechs is falling. They are beginning to realize the extent of the desperate situation into which their last venture has thrust them. The Czechs are beginning to understand that it would have been to their advantage to have come to an agreement with the Soviets. At peace talks they are taking a softer line. At the same time agitation is being carried on among their troops. In Mariinsk our troops and those of the enemy are facing each other, separated by a distance of 150 steps. Our positions are, for the most part, secured by natural barriers. Where there are no natural ones, we have constructed artificial ones. So far all is well. There are enough troops to wage not only a defensive war, but also to take the offensive.

Speaking now of technical strength, he noted:

Men may be replaced by machine guns and we have plenty of those. Our artillery is good. Our artillery men have proved themselves to be excellent marksmen at the last battle before Mariinsk. At any rate they are better marksmen than the Czechs. We have at our disposal airplanes and an armored train that can be of immense help. We also have balloons with poisonous gases, which will be employed only in case of extreme necessity. We have engineers to instruct us.[9]

Despite their technical and quantitative superiority, the Soviet armies did not advance; they were trusting time to play into their hands—that each passing day would add to the moral disintegration of their opponents.

The truce ended officially on June 10, but because the Czechs and the Siberian government detachments were waiting for reinforcements (Czech and Russian detachments from Taiga and Tomsk), they did not initiate any military action in Mariinsk. Upon receiving reinforcements and explicit information from me on the situation in Krasnoyarsk, the Russian and Czechoslovak detachments began their offensive, but that was not until June 16. On that very day, the Red Army at Mariinsk was routed. Many were taken prisoner, among them Commissar Schneider. The rest fled in panic. On the Kansk front, all operations were at a standstill because the commander of the Czech forces was completely cut off; the telegraph was in Bolshevik hands. A gold mine worker and member of the Constituent Assembly and his companion, sent by representatives of the Siberian government from Krasnoyarsk for liaison, were recognized by Yakovenko's Red Army detachment and shot. Some of the Bolsheviks who had fled from the Mariinsk front joined members of the Achinsk soviet to hold a conference on June 17, at which it was decided to blow up all the railroad bridges from Bogatol to Achinsk.[10] Thanks to the railroad workers, they were prevented from carrying out this operation.

The Siberian government launched a series of attacks, aimed mostly at military warehouses, against the Krasnoyarsk soviet, which had been weakened by sending its troops to both the east and west front lines. These forays on supply depots unnerved the Soviets, creating a degree of panic. A party committee member reported: "The Whites became insolent and were sending their detachments first to one part of the city and then to another. Skirmishes were not favorable to the Whites. It was quite evident that the Whites did not have a strong organization."[11] Immediately upon receiving news of the defeat at Mariinsk, the Krasnoyarsk soviet began to evacuate to the north. The first contingent to depart was headed by the chairman of the soviet, Weinbaum, on a steamship loaded with valuables appropriated from the National Bank: three hundred pounds of gold, silver, and platinum, in addition to money.

When this news reached the leaders of the Siberian government military organization, the command to stage the uprising was issued. The plan was that the railroad workers would hold a meeting to which they would invite the commander of the Soviet Army to present a report on the situation at the front. So it was that at eleven o'clock on the morning of June 18, a member of the railroad union fired a shot at the commander, who fled, wounded. This same militant union seized an armored train and took control of the railroad station. Arkhipova writes: "The Krasnoyarsk railroad workers, the mainstay of Soviet authority, fired at the commander as he conducted the meeting. There was no solid armed support. The Red Guardsmen threw down their arms and deserted their headquarters. Within a few hours the Krasnoyarsk soviet was boarding ships wrested from the Whites. The frozen city resounded with gun and machine-gun fire in the wake of the departing ships."[12] Thus the Krasnoyarsk soviet, loaded onto five ships and under cover of Magyar machine-gun fire, fled in panic, abandoning to whatever fate might befall them the detachments still at the front.

The 360-man military detachment of the Siberian government in Krasnoyarsk was assigned the following tasks: (1) to arrest prominent Bolshevik leaders; (2) to preserve the National Bank's bonds; (3) to arm the organization; (4) to liberate the prisoners; (5) to seize and defend the means of conveyance, including steamships, trains, tunnels, and bridges; (6) to instigate panic in the rear ranks and to threaten the front, thus diverting a portion of the enemy from the front; (7) to prevent the Bolsheviks from freeing German prisoners held in the camp.

By evening of June 18, some of these assignments were already completed: those Bolshevik leaders who had not been able to escape were arrested; the National Bank was occupied, as were the post office and the telegraph station; the Red Guardsmen still in the city were disarmed and imprisoned; the president of the Siberian Oblast Duma, two officials of the Siberian government, and several Czechs were freed from prison; the military warehouses were seized; the railroad was seized; and most important, the large bridge across the Yenisei was saved. With these operations completed and sentries placed at their posts, the headquarters of the uprising had no more men at its disposal to relieve the sentries or to guard the camps where the prisoners of war were held. By this time the detachments of Red Guardsmen under the command of Dubrovinsky, numbering eight hundred men, were approaching the city. An armored train from the other side of the bridge was sent to meet them; the train was staffed by railroad workers authorized by the Siberian government to guarantee full freedom to all the Red Guardsmen on two conditions: surrender of the command staff and surrender of all arms. In a matter of two hours there was nothing left of Dubrovinsky's detachments, and he was in prison.[13] After the defeat at Mariinsk, segments of Schneider's detachments retreated to Achinsk, where they learned what had happened at Krasnoyarsk. Together with members of the Achinsk soviet, they dispersed in panic.

On June 19 an auxiliary detachment of 250 volunteers was formed, enough for garrison duty only. The next day, detachments of the Siberian government under the command of A. N. Pepelyaev and R. Gaida totaling seven hundred arrived at Krasnoyarsk. All these detachments stayed in Krasnoyarsk for one day. Taking with them the newly formed Yeniseisk Regiment, they moved east in the direction of Irkutsk. There were no Czech echelons in Irkutsk at that time. Because of Bolshevik sabotage, the march of the Siberian government's military organization to Irkutsk was halted. A large Red Guard, including three thousand Magyars—former prisoners of war—was stationed there.

At the time of the uprising, the illegal military organizations of the Siberian government existed only in large centers; there had not been enough time for them to form in districts. But this did not prevent the peasants from ridding themselves of the Bolshevik soviets. The peasants of the Minusinsk region of Yeniseisk province, for example, hearing of the overthrow in the city of Krasnoyarsk, called a meeting at which it was decided to arrest all the members of the soviet; in a few weeks, approximately one hundred were arrested and delivered to Krasnoyarsk. In a month, the authority of the Siberian Provisional Government was established over all of western Siberia.

How can this phenomenon be explained? First, in June 1918, Soviet authority existed only in the region along the railroad. "The countryside lived its own life and was governed by committees formed in Kerensky's time called 'soviets.' The villagers wanted peace and the opportunity to pursue their work. Whoever came from the outside with whatever demands—if contrary to their own—was considered their enemy."[14] Second, the Bolsheviks fell prey to their own lies and propaganda. They seized power with the help of the Red Army, consisting mainly of internationalist units. The Bolsheviks, fully aware that during the Constituent Assembly elections they had received only 10 percent of the votes in all Siberia, nevertheless persisted in maintaining that the working class and peasantry wanted Soviet rule. At the same time, at a meeting of the Krasnoyarsk soviet on June 7, 1918, there was a discussion about the advisability of closing down the railroad factories due to a considerable decline in productivity. At the conclusion of the meeting, the following decision was made: "If the appeal made by the commander-in-chief of the Soviet Army fails to raise productivity, the soviet must then resort to the most difficult of all paths for Soviet authority to take—that of repression against the saboteurs."[15] The Soviet regime had lost its popularity among the workers and peasants. The Bolsheviks nonetheless continued to affirm that they had the full support of the proletariat in general and of the railroad workers, their "main strength," in particular.

Ironically, at a time when Military Commissar Trotsky was conducting negotiations with England's diplomat R. H. Lockhart to send foreign troops to northern Russia with the object of paralyzing the further advance of the Germans, the Siberian soviets sought to frighten the local population with threats of foreign intervention. (The German advance threatened war supplies left by the Allies for use by the Provisional Government against the Germans. The Allies had not begun their intervention against the Bolsheviks in northern Russia at this time.) The population's first view of the intervention was the Bolshevik internationalist detachments made up of prisoners of war. The Bolsheviks became slaves to their own propaganda "about that moral support found among the worker fighters, the consciousness of fighting for one's class interests, for one's principles."[16] The Bolsheviks had no scruples about methods to seize and hold power. All means toward their end were considered good, beginning with instigation, insult, and persecution of their ideological opponents and ending with blatant misrepresentation.

But all this taken together was only an illusion of the permanence of their power. It is in this and only in this that the reason can be discovered why Soviet rule in Siberia (relying mainly on the Red Army, consisting of prisoners of war), after encountering the first serious resistance, fell apart like a house of cards. The Bolsheviks, upon seeing workers (supposedly their main strength) drop their weapons and refuse to fight for the soviets at the first hint of armed confrontation, panicked and fled in haste. That was how it was in Omsk; that was how it was in Tomsk and, finally, once again in Krasnoyarsk, citadel of bolshevism. Misrepresentation and panic were the main factors in the collapse of Soviet rule in Siberia.

4

The Collapse of Opposition Unity

For the representatives of the Siberian government, no great obstacles stood in the way of freeing Siberia from Soviet rule. It was in the process of establishing a democratic regime that serious difficulties were encountered.

Acceptance into the original military organization required:

1. Recognition of the principle of the All-Russian Constituent Assembly;
2. Recognition of the Siberian Oblast Duma as an authoritative local power until the All-Russian Constituent Assembly was called;
3. Nonrecognition of the Treaty of Brest-Litovsk;
4. Recognition of democratic principles in the army, with full authority vested in the commanding staff, allowing for some soldiers' committees in order to maintain discipline.

In order not to weaken the struggle against the Bolsheviks, the existing detachments of the military organization were hastily formed into regiments of the Siberian Army and sent to the front. The democratic nature of this first Siberian Army can be judged by the following incident. On June 7, 1918, E. Harris, the American consul general, paid a visit to the head of the military organization, Grishin-Almazov, at Taiga Station. In the course of their talks, Grishin-Almazov stressed the fact that he and his army were not part of the White Army, but were soldiers of the Provisional Government in Siberia, and that as such they did not have any party prejudices. Their colors, white and green, were the colors of Siberia. The Siberian Army had no epaulets; white and green ribbons were worn instead. Grishin-Almazov did not believe in distinguished service awards of any kind in a civil war.

Such were the first steps in forming the new Siberian Army. Later, the ranks of the rear garrisons began to swell: those who had stood aside for political reasons, taking no part whatsoever in the overthrow, then wished to join.

The West Siberian Commissariat of the Siberian government had to establish a government apparatus, build a regular army, and, at the same time, conduct a war on separate fronts. In creating a state apparatus, the commissariat stumbled on an insoluble problem: lack of personnel qualified for such work. The state apparatus thus came to be bogged down with technicians who, far from sharing the principles of democracy, were often downright hostile to the idea of democratic power. Referring to this situation, Siberian Prime Minister and Socialist-Revolutionary sympathizer P. Vologodsky wrote in his diary: "June 14. It is a comfort to know that the commissars of the Siberian government, almost all of whom are Right Socialist-Revolutionaries, did not pull members of their own party into the ministry, but used business acumen as the sole criterion in filling these posts."[1]

Before the new regime had had time to gain some strength, it was already enmeshed in intrigue and plots. On June 29 the power-hungry minister of finance, I. A. Mikhailov, a former Socialist-Revolutionary, tried to convince Vologodsky that the current members of the Siberian government should take power into their own hands because the "little-known" members of the West Siberian Commissariat had no authority among the Siberian population and none in the eyes of foreigners. "The people of Siberia and the foreigners would be more impressed if authority were in the hands of a government elected by the people, even though this might be done through a far from perfect system of popular representation."[2]

The chairman of the Siberian Oblast Duma readily agreed to this change. Two days later, on July 1, Vologodsky was visited by three representatives of the local Constitutional Democratic Party. "They came with what seemed to me a strange proposal—that the Siberian government not assume power for itself, since the people were already accustomed to being governed by the West Siberian Commissariat and 'they were entirely satisfied by the political and economic measures the commissariat was taking.'"[3] Evidently the Kadet committee thought that the West Siberian Commissariat would be easier to replace by a dictatorship. The Kadet- and monarchist-dominated

Trade-Industry Congress in Omsk resolved to boycott the Oblast Duma. At this congress, one of the Kadets said that "the Oblast Duma cannot under any circumstances be re-established and that the Provisional Government should relinquish all such thoughts." He also declared in favor of introducing a strong one-man government.[4]

On July 13 the Omsk Political Bloc, created by I. A. Mikhailov from among delegates of the Trade-Industry Congress, Kadets, Right Socialist-Revolutionaries, and cooperative organizers, declared "against summoning the Siberian Oblast Duma as the organ vested with supreme power because it stands in the way of strengthening the Siberian Provisional Government, reducing it to the position of an executive organ."[5] Two weeks prior to that, Mikhailov had said that it was absolutely necessary to transfer power to the elected government of this same Oblast Duma; however, as soon as certain members of the government had assumed power, the Oblast Duma became a hindrance to them because they did not wish to be responsible to any authority. "At the same time the military organization headed by Col. V. I. Volkov, not having taken part in battles on the various fronts, took on the character of a secret military organization and continued its work underground in spite of the establishment of the West Siberian Commissariat. Discontent on the part of this organization with the democratic policies of the West Siberian Commissariat and, consequently, with the Siberian government, turned their thoughts toward the idea of a dictatorship."[6]

All this pointed to moral collapse. One military group, having sworn an oath of loyalty to the Siberian government (and having accepted wages from it), immediately began plotting to overthrow this government. Such an attitude among certain circles of the rear-guard could hardly escape notice. A Siberian government official, N. V. Fomin, speaking at a meeting of the Council of Ministers held on July 26, stated: "Among the military there are some who say, 'First, we will take care of the Bolsheviks and then we will begin hanging the Socialist-Revolutionaries.'" At the same meeting, he also said, "The consular corps in Irkutsk does not manifest any special sympathy toward the Siberian government; it objects to the socialist overtones of the Siberian Oblast Duma. The Far East Committee, located in Harbin under the chairmanship of D. L. Khorvat, does not recognize the Siberian government."[7]

Simultaneously, yet another anomaly came to light: members of the Siberian government in Omsk did not wish, under any circumstances, to unite with the other members of the Siberian government, who had been elected at the same time as they by the Oblast Duma but who, after the overthrow, found themselves in the Far East. These representatives formed the Far East Committee in Vladivostok and declared themselves to be not subordinate, but equal to the Omsk government. On August 26 M. P. Golovachev, vice-minister of foreign affairs, reported to Vologodsky on the relation of the Far East Committee to the representatives of the Siberian government. Vologodsky "recommended that extreme caution be exercised" and further advised "that it would be better to approach the government of Khorvat than the Siberian government."[8] Here we have the chairman of the Council of Ministers suggesting that it would be better to come to an agreement with a group that refused to recognize its own Siberian government than to approach the members of that government. Khorvat's government had emerged as yet another self-proclaimed local and autonomous regime, headed by the director of the Manchurian railroads. Vologodsky had evidently decided that his chances would be better with reactionary elements among Khorvat's officials than with members of his own government. Such a policy could not, of course, promise anything but a complete breakdown in the future. "And then there was the view of the Omsk group, the bureaucrats in the Administrative Council and illegal military organizations: 'five ministers and not one more!' Even the arrival in Omsk of I. I. Serebrennikov, a member of the Siberian government, was cause for alarm in local society and in military circles. The Kadets and the trade-industry circles were advocating a dictatorship."[9]

The Omsk clique aimed at expanding the rights of the Administrative Council by giving it legislative functions and by reducing to a minimum the staff of the Siberian government that was responsive to the Oblast Duma. Both aims were successfully accomplished. A decree of the Council of Ministers dated September 7, 1918, stated that while the majority of the staff of the Siberian Provisional Government were away from Omsk, the Administrative Council should itself decide on matters within the province of the Council of Ministers. On September 8, the Council of Ministers, without the minister of justice, ruled that the Administrative Council should have all authority belonging to the Council of Ministers in matters concerning the Oblast Duma and, in particular, the right to interrupt the work of the duma or even to dissolve it. This decision clearly illustrates the attempt on the part of certain members of the Provisional Government to change the structure of power—with, it is true, the reservation "in the absence of the quorum."

Members of the government, elected by the Oblast Duma, still recognized, as late as July, the duma's legislative rights and their own responsibility to the duma. By September, however, without so much as a preliminary consultation with the duma, the Council of Ministers transferred the legislative functions to the Administrative Council, which consisted, with the sole exception of Mikhailov, of hired, not elected employees. How cunningly the preparations were laid for reducing the government's staff to a minimum is apparent from the September 7 entry in Vologodsky's diary noting the friction between the members of the government—between I. Mikhailov and Shatilov, then I. Mikhailov and Patushinsky, between the Administrative Council and the ministers. The weak-willed chairman of the Council of Ministers, Vologodsky himself, was carried by the current. For example, the government picked a delegation to go to the Far East. Vologodsky, in his discussions with government members Patushinsky and Shatilov, as well as with the chairman of the Presidium of the Siberian Oblast Duma, promised not to take with him G. K. Guins, but to replace him with V. N. Novikov. But the Administrative Council "took upon itself" to add Guins as well as others. Vologodsky, contrary to his earlier promise, reconciled himself to the reconstituted delegation.

By this time the relationship between the civilian and military authorities had begun to worsen. Not only the Czechs, but some newly mobilized Russian officers began to set precedents arbitrarily. At a parade of Russian and Czech troops in Krasnoyarsk, for example, the commander of the garrison, immediately after the greeting, offered the floor to P. I. Troitsky, a representative of the Constitutional Democratic Party, which had taken no part in the overthrow of Soviet authority. I was attending this parade as a representative of the Provisional Government, and I reprimanded the commander for his lack of tact in giving precedence to a representative of a political party over a representative of the government. I informed the government what had happened, and within ten days he was removed from his post as commander of the Krasnoyarsk Garrison.

At that time, Grishin-Almazov made an attempt to restore discipline to the military. But in mid-August 1918, he too, wanting to support the policies of the Administrative Council, found himself in opposition to the influence of the Siberian Oblast Duma. "At the meeting of the government, Delegate Fomin reported that a letter from the minister of war, Grishin-Almazov, had been received in Tomsk. In this letter he declares his 'readiness to protect the government by military force should the Siberian Oblast Duma decide to make changes in it.'"[10]

By the beginning of September, Grishin-Almazov had been removed from his post as commander of the Siberian Army. This preceded the rift between the government and the Oblast Duma, and it had a tremendous impact on all the events that followed. I have mentioned that Grishin-Almazov was one of the organizers of the Siberian uprising. After the successful overthrow of Bolshevik authority, he laid the foundation for rebuilding the Siberian Army on democratic principles: no epaulets, no decorations, for he thought that awarding decorations of any kind during a civil war would be absurd. During this first period, the positions of command were filled according to ability and regardless of former rank. But this method of organizing an army was far from pleasing to many of the old generals and reactionary officers; firmly entrenched at their headquarters, they began to pressure Grishin-Almazov. At the same time, the members of the Oblast Duma were split into two factions: those who supported Grishin-Almazov and those who hoped to have him replaced by Krakovetzky, the original choice for the post.

Grishin-Almazov's speech before the Siberian Oblast Duma in mid-August, to the effect that thenceforth and until the cessation of military action the military should have more privileges, did not call forth the sympathy of the majority of duma members. There is reason to believe that Grishin-Almazov himself, hoping to gain special privileges, fell victim to the intrigues of the Administrative Council. The conflict between Grishin-Almazov and the Oblast Duma made it significantly easier for the plotters to replace him with one of their own men. In approximately two weeks, an opportunity presented itself.

The gist of speeches given by representatives of foreign powers at the State Conference in Chelyabinsk on August 23, 1918, was that Russia could be reborn only with the help of the Allies. Grishin-Almazov's answer to this was that other than beautiful speeches, there had been no help from the Allies, and the question was who needed whom more—the Allies Russia or Russia the Allies. The Consular Corps took this as an insult and, accusing Grishin-Almazov of being against the Allies and the Czechs, demanded his removal. Grishin-Almazov admitted his remark about the Allies, but he categorically denied having made any derogatory statements against the Czechs. He was offered the opportunity to resign. He refused to do so and asked Vologodsky to receive him. Instead, the government simply discharged him.

On the recommendation of the vice-minister of foreign affairs, Golovachev, the government appointed P. Ivanov-Rinov as com-

mander-in-chief of the Siberian Army on September 5, 1918. According to the communication received by Consul General Harris from G.
Grey, the American consul in the city of Omsk, Ivanov-Rinov was
appointed at the insistence of English General A. B. Knox.[11] Such was
the network of behind-the-scenes intrigues and provocations. Grishin-
Almazov was not discharged because of dictatorial inclinations, but
was sacrificed to the good neighbor policy toward the Allies. The
Oblast Duma, in spite of a certain amount of opposition toward
Grishin-Almazov, had by no means been anxious to have him replaced
by Ivanov-Rinov, who was known for his reactionary views.

Some memoirs written about this period suggest that Grishin-
Almazov's dismissal was precipitated by the rivalry between him
and Gaida. As proof, they refer to the following telegram: "To the
commander of the eastern front, Colonel Gaida: Immediately inform
on what basis you countermand the laws of the Provisional Siberian
Government, interfering with the internal life of the country?
No. 426/OP. Commander of the Army, Major-General Grishin-
Almazov. Omsk 27 July 18–30." But the telegram has little meaning
without a knowledge of the events that preceded it. On July 25 in
Irkutsk, Colonel Gaida issued an order declaring the region from
Barabinsk to Krasnoyarsk to be under martial law and the region from
Krasnoyarsk to the east to be under siege, with all civil laws abro-
gated. He also ordered that court-martial trials have a majority of
Czechs serving on them and be established along the entire line. These
military courts had widespread jurisdiction over Russian citizens and
violated the decree of the Council of Ministers dated July 15, whereby
a region could be placed under martial law only by the mutual consent
of the ministers of internal and military affairs.

According to Gaida's orders, Yeniseisk province was under seige;
therefore all power was transferred to the military authorities. On
July 26, about eleven o'clock, a captain of the Czech Army appeared
before me and showed me a telegram from Gaida ordering that all
members of the Krasnoyarsk soviet who had been arrested in the
Turukhansk region should be sent to the pre-front lines. I told him that
Colonel Gaida's orders were unlawful, and that none of those arrested
would be sent to him for court-martial without the knowledge of the
minister of internal affairs. That day the first group of Bolsheviks who
had fled from Krasnoyarsk and who had been arrested in the
Turukhansk region arrived. It was the responsibility of the commander of the garrison to transport them directly from the boat to the
prison. The commander was one of the newly mobilized officers who
had not participated in the pre-uprising military organizations and

who had been assigned to this post when the original participants were sent to the front or assigned to other regions. Perhaps it was due to his permissiveness that the prisoners were dealt with arbitrarily, or perhaps this was even done with his concurrence. Some were beaten, and three (Markovsky, Lebedeva, and Pechersky) were dragged outside with lassos and hacked to death with sabers. The convoy had nothing to do with this lynching. In the main, it was done by Cossacks who had accompanied the prisoners and by a Czech reconnaissance member who had been held in the Krasnoyarsk prison.

Knowing that the government would revoke Gaida's order placing Yeniseisk province under siege and that power would revert to civilian authorities, I ordered that the second group of prisoners not be sent to Krasnoyarsk, but that they be detained in Yeniseisk for an indeterminate period. This is referred to in the memoirs of a member of the Committee of Bolsheviks: "A rumor was spread, which later proved to be not without validity, that Krasnoyarsk had demanded that Comrades Weinbaum, V. Yakovlev, and others be transferred to the Aleksandrov Central. Each of us knew only too well what this meant. Because of circumstances not known to us, this was not carried out. We were kept in Yeniseisk for about three weeks, and almost every day were promised that we would be sent out 'tomorrow.'"[12] On the morning of July 27, I informed Minister of Internal Affairs V. Krutovsky what had happened. That day Vologodsky proposed to Grishin-Almazov that he "revoke this order of Gaida's."[13]

These facts clearly illustrate that it was not the rivalry between Grishin-Almazov and Gaida but, rather, the strict observance of the laws enacted by the Provisional Government that was the determining situation here. An attempt was being made to demarcate the spheres of influence of civilian and military authorities. Once Grishin-Almazov had been discharged and Ivanov-Rinov had replaced him, an era of complete irresponsibility on the part of the military authorities began. "Without even waiting for the transfer order from Grishin-Almazov, Ivanov-Rinov assumed his duties. With the appointment of Ivanov-Rinov, the military world began to feel self-sufficient and independent of the government. A colossal political mistake."[14] Thus, in retrospect, wrote one of the members of the Administrative Council, who had played a prominent role in this series of events.

Ivanov-Rinov, not yet officially installed in his post, issued an order on September 8, 1918, restoring epaulets and reinstating former rank in the army, and by so doing destroyed the democratic spirit that Grishin-Almazov had tried to establish. Neither the Administrative Council nor members of the government who were in Omsk at the time protested the unlawful actions of the commander of the army. Further, by order of Ivanov-Rinov "plenary powers were given to military commanders of certain regions, even down to the right to hold courts martial."[15] "As commander of the Steppe Corps, he issued an order on September 6, 1918, that gave all the commanders of punitive detachments the right to shoot on sight, deciding each case separately and according to their own discretion."[16] Ivanov-Rinov accomplished by himself precisely that which Gaida had tried to do a month and a half earlier and which had been opposed by Minister of Internal Affairs Krutovsky, Commander of the Army Grishin-Almazov, and Chairman of the Council of Ministers Vologodsky.

The government had let the reins fall from its hands, and the instances of self-rule that followed led to the dissolution of discipline among the officers stationed at the various bases. According to one member of the government, Serebrennikov, by that time the Council of Ministers already no longer had complete authority; it was instead in the hands of the military. The commanders of punitive detachments did not have to answer for their unlawful actions—on the contrary, in most cases they were rewarded. This policy of course encouraged flagrant atamanship (*atamanshchina*).[17]

Meanwhile, other intrigues hastened the collapse of the Siberian government. In early July 1918, the government introduced a bill to increase the membership of the Oblast Duma by allowing certain conservative elements of the population to send their representatives, approximately three from each district. These merchant and industrial classes were previously not included in the Siberian Oblast Duma because they were against an autonomous government in Siberia. Realizing that they would be in the minority, as in the Trade-Industry Congress and the Kadet Party, the representatives still declined to participate in the work of the duma and began to agitate in their own newspapers, declaring that the Oblast Duma would be Bolshevik in composition. This type of propaganda planted seeds of doubt in the minds of certain members of the government, who began to fear that they would lose their positions in the near future. The chairman of the Presidium of the Siberian Oblast Duma took steps against this propaganda and at the same time "recommended that the government would be moved to the city of Tomsk due to the unhealthy political atmosphere in the city of Omsk, and he also recommended that the government rely on the support of the Oblast Duma. Some members of the government, including Vologodsky, agreed with this viewpoint. But the government as a whole, torn by internal disagreements, suffered from indecision and with trepidation kept glancing back at Omsk."[18]

One group in the government that was striving for control of power actually played into the hands of the reactionary officers, whose inspirational leader was the Constitutional Democratic Party (Kadets). The resolution of this party states:

> The party must help to free the country from the fog of un-realizable goals (the gains of the February Revolution; all power to the Constituent Assembly, and so on), which, under existing conditions, are ruinous fictions, self-deceptions, and deceit. The attitude of the party toward the Provisional Siberian Government depends on the realization of an agreement between that government and the government of Khorvat and on further progress toward statesmanship. It is understood that the support the party gives the government does not predetermine the attitude of the party toward the question of the permanent existence of a separate Siberian government.[19]

The position that the committee of the Kadet Party assumed actually differed very little from the position of the Bolsheviks. Both were against the Constituent Assembly and against the consolidation of achievements of the February Revolution. This, of course, made it all the easier for the Soviets to conduct their propaganda: "It is either we or the dark forces of reaction—there can be no other power." And it had a demoralizing effect on the Siberian Army.

In Omsk at this time, the Administrative Council—relying on the Kadet Party, the trade-industry class, and reactionaries among the military—"decided to stand up for its rights";[20] that is, to become, from a purely administrative organ, a legislative organ and thereby to usurp the rights of the Siberian Oblast Duma.

Against the background of this political situation in Omsk, during a meeting of the Tomsk Oblast Duma in mid-August, Vologodsky received a telegram from Serebrennikov: "If you do not return to Omsk immediately, there is a real threat that a new government will be formed."[21] The reaction of the weak-willed Vologodsky was to urge the duma to conclude its work as quickly as possible and then to return hastily to Omsk, having preserved the fiction of the government.

On September 10, on his way to the Far East, Vologodsky met with Krutovsky and persuaded him to return to Omsk in the capacity of deputy chairman of the Council of Ministers. Two days later Vologodsky saw Novoselov in Irkutsk but did not inform him that the Siberian government in Omsk was discussing the possibility of drawing him into its midst.[22] As soon as Krutovsky, Shatilov, and Novoselov had appeared in Omsk, the local swamp bestirred itself. The Administrative Council feared it would lose its power because it could execute only purely administrative functions when the necessary quorum of elected members of government was present; in the absence of a quorum, the council was empowered to legislate. There was only one way to avoid this: to contrive somehow to exclude the ministers who had arrived for governmental work. And that is exactly what was done by I. Mikhailov, with the help of the reactionary military group.

On August 23, 1918, a decision of the Provisional Government stated that it was forbidden for those in military service to take part in unions, groups, organizations, etc., that have any political goals. Mikhailov, however, not only failed to adopt measures to abolish such organizations, he entered into contact with them. Members of the government Krutovsky, Shatilov, and Novoselov, and Yakushev, chairman of the Oblast Duma, having arrived in Omsk about September 18, were met at the station on the morning of September 21 by three officers who arrested them and drove off with them. The arrested members of the government were offered the opportunity to sign their resignations, under threat of death, and to leave Omsk within 24 hours. Krutovsky and Shatilov signed the document of "withdrawal from the government," but Novoselov refused to sign and was later hacked to death in a field on the outskirts of the city. Some historians have described this forced removal from power as "an unsuccessful attempt at overthrow" headed by those who were so removed.[23] "Krutovsky, Yakushev, and Shatilov were plotting to overthrow the government . . . Novoselov, who was killed in Omsk, was the victim in someone else's game. The one actually to blame for his death is Yakushev, who was the leader of this entire political adventure."[24] It turns out, then, that the desire of several members of the Provisional Government to enter upon their duties was looked upon by the Administrative Council as a "political adventure"—and this regardless of the fact that the chairman of the Council of Ministers Vologodsky had been trying to persuade some of them to return to Omsk and to active work.

Yes, it was an adventure: not, however, for the arrested members of the government, but for the chairman of the Administrative Council, Mikhailov, and for the illegal military organization headed by the commander of the garrison in Omsk, Colonel V. I. Volkov. The execution of Novoselov was entrusted to the staff commander of Volkov's detachment, A. S. Stepanov-Ivanov, and two of Colonel Volkov's adjutants. A report of the incident was sent to the commandant at Omsk, who supposedly ordered Stepanov-Ivanov's arrest and court-martial, but instead sent him on another assignment and supplied him with money and an alias. Officially, the accused had escaped from the military jail; actually, he resumed his activities under the name of Khorbut.

Stepanov-Ivanov recalls:

> After Novoselov's refusal to sign the resignation papers, the military organization decided to kill him. The reason for this decision was the great popularity of Novoselov as a Cossack in Cossack circles. After I reported verbally to the garrison commander, Colonel Volkov—also the head of the illegal military organization—it was decided that I would send an official written report to my immediate superior, the commandant of the city of Omsk, G. Katanaev. The commandant ordered my "arrest" and court-martial. I was given two thousand rubles and my "escape" was arranged. The military organization then commandeered me to Petropavlosk and other places and, later, to Irkutsk.[25]

After such an admission by a man who had carried out an assignment for a group of conspirators, how lacking in seriousness this remark appears: "'They say' that Colonel Volkov, the commander of the Omsk garrison, not having foreseen such a contingency as the arrest, tore his hair when he heard what had happened."[26] From another historian comes the statement: "Colonel Volkov, on being questioned by A. Argunov, said, 'As an officer who has given his word, I swear that I had no accomplices'"; and Ivanov-Rinov wrote: "On investigating the matter, I arrived at the deep conviction that Volkov had no connection with the murder of Novoselov."[27]

To justify themselves in the eyes of foreigners, the conspirators spread a rumor to the effect that Novoselov had been working with the Bolsheviks.[28] On September 22, Mikhailov cabled Vologodsky: "Yakushev, Krutovsky, and Shatilov began to agitate in Omsk against our Far East policy and for this someone had them arrested."[29] He failed to mention that Novoselov had been brutally murdered and that the Administrative Council had ordered the cessation of activity by the Siberian Oblast Duma. Thus the web of intrigue aimed at reinstating dictatorship began to spread.

The Oblast Duma did not submit to the order of the Administrative Council and in its resolution of September 22 stated that the Oblast Duma considers the staff of the Provisional Siberian Government to be the one constituted by the duma in January 1918, with the exception of Minister of Finance I. A. Mikhailov and Vice-Minister of Internal Affairs A. A. Gratsianov, both of whom the duma considers removed from their duties and subject to trial for attempting to overthrow the government. At this point, Mikhailov ordered that the Oblast Duma's activities be forcibly stopped and that several of its members be arrested. These events did not occur unexpectedly; the conflict among certain members of the Provisional Government had been brewing for some time.

Elsewhere, arbitrary actions continued to characterize the military presence. Such insubordination was not exclusive to the commander of Russian detachments, but occurred also among some Czechs. At a meeting with Vologodsky on September 10, I informed him that several days earlier in Krasnoyarsk a stoker had been tried in a Czech court-martial for having posted socialist proclamations. He had been sentenced to be shot; and the sentence had been carried out.[30] Vologodsky vigorously agreed that such acts were inadmissible. To the best of my knowledge, however, he did nothing to prevent them from happening in the future.

At the time of the May 1918 overthrow, all active Bolsheviks in Krasnoyarsk were arrested by my orders, and I was responsible for the prisoners. A decree of the Provisional Government of August 27, 1918, established regional investigative committees, headed by prosecutors of district courts. From then on, the fate of persons arrested depended on the decisions of these committees. The disposition of prisoners therefore took on one or another lawful form, but this was observed for a relatively short time only. The desire for vengeance was stronger than the obligation to uphold the law.

As mentioned earlier, at the moment of the overthrow there were no Czech troops in Krasnoyarsk, with the exception of a small group of several dozen men that had been left there for liaison purposes. In May they were disarmed by the Soviets and thrown into prison. Two men from this group disappeared without a trace; and this the Czechs could not and would not forget. Gaida's attempts at the end of July 1918 to deal harshly with the arrested Bolsheviks were unsuccessful, but the Czechs who had been imprisoned did not let the matter rest there.

On the evening of October 24, a Czech detachment appeared at the prison and presented an order signed by the commander of the company demanding that five prisoners, including Weinbaum, be given over for court-martial. Should the head of the prison refuse to comply, force would be used. The head of the prison telephoned the prosecutor and asked for instructions. The prosecutor's recommendation was to refuse to give up the prisoners and to appeal to the commander of the military region to reinforce the guard around the prison. But the commander said he simply did not have the necessary manpower to withstand the Czech detachment. There was nothing left for the head of the prison to do but prepare a document to the effect that the Czech detachment took the prisoners by force. That very evening Czech Echelon Number 49 held a trial attended by Czech officers and a representative of the Russian military authority. This court pronounced the death sentence for all those who had been taken from the prison. The sentence was carried out that night.

The Czech commander had, supposedly, given the order to take the prisoners according to Gaida's instructions. This is highly problematical because Gaida had transferred into Russian service on October 9 and had been appointed commander of the Ural front, so he had no legal authority to give orders in matters pertaining to the base—or, all the more, in matters within the sphere of the civilian authorities. Further, at this so-called trial a representative of the Russian military authority was present. This indicates a previous agreement between the Czechs, the commander of the military region, and the prosecutor, who simply hid under cover of the statement "coercion on the part of the Czechs." When I investigated what had happened, it took two whole days to obtain an interview with the prosecutor. Neither the commander of the Siberian Army, Ivanov-Rinov, nor the minister of justice ordered an investigation.

Omsk paid but scant attention to the local situation, engaged as it was in a game for higher stakes. The Administrative Council now had its sights set on seizing all Russian power. The web of intrigue continued to grow around the government, aimed for the most part both at depriving the Siberian Oblast Duma of the political role it had enjoyed during its early existence, as the legislative organ of power, and, at the same time, at decreasing to a minimum the number of members elected to the government by the duma. This was the policy that was so consistently and relentlessly pursued by the Administrative Council under Mikhailov's leadership. The removal from power of Krutovsky and Shatilov, the murder of Novoselov, and the dismissal of the Siberian Oblast Duma still left the Administrative Council with two unsolved problems: (1) to remove its "double" (that part of the Siberian government still functioning in the Far East); and (2) to persuade foreign powers to recognize the Siberian government. A delegation was sent to the Far East precisely to achieve these two objectives. Like a distant beacon shone the ardent dream: to become the sovereign all-Russian government.

Vologodsky noted in his diary on September 16, 1918: "The members of our delegation discussed all aspects of the question concerning the necessity for the Siberian government to assume all the functions of an all-Russian government, and it was decided to send a telegram to this effect to our delegation at the Ufa Conference."[31] The Ufa National Conference, following two unsuccessful gatherings in Chelyabinsk, was called to unite all anti-Bolshevik forces into some semblance of government. A few days earlier, Mikhailov had sent a telegram to Serebrennikov in Ufa that ended with the words, "The Administrative Council, at its meeting yesterday, has resolved not to make any concessions at Ufa, even at the risk of a rupture."[32]

The identical thought processes of the members of the Administrative Council in Omsk and those in Vladivostok, both plotting the seizure of all-Russian authority, is an amazing coincidence. The difference in time was approximately four days. That is how much time was needed for the members of the Administrative Council in the Far East delegation to win over Vologodsky to their side.

As mentioned earlier, in the struggle for power, the leaders of the Administrative Council—now, in fact, *the* Siberian government—had to depend more and more on the newly arrived reactionary elements of the trade-industry class and on officers at the bases. The officers, who had performed the Administrative Council's assignments in arresting members of the government, had by virtue of this very act made the Administrative Council its captive. Taking advantage of these favorable circumstances, the officers expanded their influence far beyond the limits of their competence. Regardless of the 1918 resolution of the Kadet Party that radically swept away all slogans on the basis of which the uprising against the Bolsheviks had been so successful, the Omsk government's Far East delegation, headed by Vologodsky, "entered into an agreement with General Khorvat, recommended by the committee of the Kadet Party, which promised to include him on the staff of the Siberian government."[33] A second delegation, sent to the Far East by the Presidium of the Siberian Oblast Duma with the aim of preventing such an agreement, was arrested in the city of Irkutsk by order of Vologodsky.

5

The Rise and Fall of the Directory

Was there a historical need for the creation of the Directory (Direktoriya)? There had been ten separate local governments in Siberia up to the time that the Ufa National Conference was called (September 8–25, 1918), representing the regions from the Volga eastward to the Pacific Ocean. In September 1918 it was essential to the conduct of war against Soviet Russia that political and military actions be coordinated, but how to achieve this most effectively was a matter of widely divergent opinion. The latest version of the Siberian government intended to proclaim itself an all-Russian government and force all the other local governments into submission. The Samara oblast government wanted, by means of cooperation between the democratic elements and the bourgeoisie, to outline national objectives and to set a course toward achieving them by peaceful means. Differences of opinion came to light even earlier—at the Chelyabinsk Conference on July 15, 1918, when a representative of the Omsk government, I. Mikhailov, declared that the Siberian government's representatives were not authorized to accept decisions of any kind and that their part in the conference would be purely informative. The Siberian government took this position because the Administrative Council had not yet had time to consolidate its power and to get rid of the Siberian Oblast Duma. This was achieved during the Ufa Conference, two days before the election of the five-member Directory, which represented territories freed from the Bolsheviks.

The creation of a central authority was crucial for such governments as those of Samara, the Urals, the Ural Cossacks, the Orenburg

Cossacks, and the Bashkirs: it would strengthen their military positions, as it was on their boundaries that the war was being fought. At the Ufa Conference the Siberian government, pressed by the military situation, was forced to accept a temporary agreement. In helping the Ural government, it had formed the Ekaterinburg front, facing the Red Army; but besides the Russian units on this front, there were also Czech troops whom the Siberian government had to consider. The Czechoslovak National Council was also in favor of a central authority and a unified army command because this seemed the only way out for the Czech Army, which, it hoped, would eventually be replaced by Russian units. These were the preconditions for the formation of the Directory.

But some participants of the Ufa Conference thought that "what was apparently a new and successful attempt at agreement in reality clearly exposed the determined decision of the more important bourgeois and reactionary circles to begin a move of breaking with the democracy and then relentlessly crushing it."[1] This is confirmed by General Sakharov, one of the participants of the conference and a delegate of the Siberian government: "At the Ufa Conference they recognized the Directory, but concealed their true intentions."[2] The ink on the signatures under the declaration of Common Interests was not yet dry when the boundary marks for future struggles were drawn.

The group that had "concealed its true intentions," harboring the dream of a dictatorship, soon found certain representatives of foreign powers willing to lend it not only moral, but organizational support. Omsk was host to one of the chief initiators in the business of overthrowing the Directory and establishing the dictatorship: the English General Knox.

> Somewhere around October 15, 1918, traveling to Omsk, General Knox stopped in the city of Krasnoyarsk. The English vice-consul held a dinner at which were present, besides the host, General Knox, the head of the Krasnoyarsk military region and the representative of the Czechoslovak National Council. During the conversation, General Knox said, "It is evident that Siberia is not yet ready for democracy. What is needed is a dictator. The only question is who is the more suitable for this role—General Gaida or Vice-Admiral Kolchak?" On October 25, when he was already in Omsk on a visit to a member of the Directory, General Boldyrev, General Knox drank tea, threatened to gather a band and to disperse us if we do not come to some agreement with the Siberians. "I am becoming a Siberian," he concluded his joke.[3]

Boldyrev took this as a joke; but further political developments were to show that it was far from a joke, but rather, the outline of a previously worked out plan.

Such conversations could not, of course, pass unnoticed by the officers sitting behind the lines in ever swelling numbers. For many of them the word "democracy" was a source of irritation and aroused their hostility. All this led to a result that is described in my report to the minister of internal affairs.

To the Minister of Internal Affairs   October 23, 1918

Political Department

I wish to report to you, Sir Minister, that in the city of Krasnoyarsk, through the sole initiative of the head of the garrison, a banquet was held on the twenty-second of this month in honor of the officers of the English Army. To this banquet were invited representatives of various departments — city and zemstvo executive boards, the chamber of commerce committee, and, as honored guests, the English officers led by Colonel Ward, the English vice-consul, a representative of the Czechoslovak National Council, and other officers of the Czechoslovak Army. The great majority of those present at the banquet were officers of the Russian Army. The selection of guests was not as carefully checked as might be desired, and there were some present who should not have been there at all. As a result, the banquet turned into a drunken debauchery. Even before the toasts were proposed, one or another of the guests would rise from his place and, waving a goblet in the air, try to speak, but instead would be stopped and led out. Toward the end of the banquet, because of excessive drinking, many of the Russians felt quite merry, and when the chairman of the district zemstvo board began to propose a toast to English democracy, his speech was interrupted by shouts of "enough" and "away." The uproar was so great that Colonel Ward commented through his interpreter, "I see that most of those present are wearing officers' epaulets, but doesn't that obligate them to remember discipline? In England we are accustomed to listen to only one orator at a time, not to several."

This reprimand from the Englishman had its effect; order was restored and the toasts were resumed. After several toasts, however, there was a sudden outburst of "Slavsya, slavsya nash russkii tsar," which caused the chairman of the district zemstvo board to protest. Several Russian officers openly showed their annoyance at the protest. Finally, while the interpreter was translating the response of Colonel Ward to the Czechs, at the initiative of a group of Russian officers, the hall resounded to the strains of "Bozhe tsarya khrani." The representatives of the city and zemstvo executive boards registered their protests and left. The representative of the Czechoslovaks, together with the officers of the Czechoslovak Army, also left the hall. In the wake of the departing guests there was another outbreak of noise. Neither the presence of guests, nor the appeals to stop the clamor were of any use. To restore order the head of the garrison was forced repeatedly to shout the command: "Attention!" The official portion of the banquet came to an end soon thereafter. The Englishmen, who had attended the banquet in the role of honored guests, had not proposed a single toast.

Yeniseisk Province Commissar
P. Dotsenko

As a result of my report, on October 30 Supreme Commander-in-Chief General Boldyrev ordered an investigation. This task was entrusted to the commandant of the city of Krasnoyarsk who, on October 30, proposed that I draw up a deposition of what had occurred. I answered by sending him a copy of my report to the minister of internal affairs. I considered it unnecessary to provide additional testimony because on the eve of the banquet I had met with the head of the military region and warned him of the possibility of just such excesses. As might be expected, no one was subjected even to a disciplinary rebuke.

On October 26, 1918, in Omsk, B. N. Moiseenko, head of the Socialist-Revolutionary Party's military organization, was killed by members of Ataman Krasilnikov's detachment. The atmosphere in Omsk thickened by the hour. The Administrative Council kept presenting the Directory with new demands, slowing the formation of a regular government apparatus. General Boldyrev wrote in his memoirs about those days:

In the building where the Directory held its sessions there was an officer, a member of the military organization under the leadership of Captain Golovin, who had been sent there on October 26 to gather the addresses of the members of the Constituent Assembly. Rozanov arrived together with Kolchak for the report. Both were definitely in favor of gradually decreasing the Directory to one person. *October 27.* V. A. Zhardetsky, N. S. Lopukhin, and the representative of the workers of the ataman village again came to see me together with Kolchak. They are ready to go the limit, hinting at the liquidation of the Directory and the preservation of only the supreme

command. *October 29.* Vinogradov [member of the Directory
and liberal Constitutional Democratic Party] reported, in a
state of great agitation, that the military circles and the
"Muses" of Zhardetsky and company are advocating Kolchak
as dictator. *October 30.* General Sakharov, leaving Omsk on
November 2 together with General Knox, commented that
"the central authority has no unity whatsoever and no leadership for the common cause. The local powers everywhere
acted according to their own designs. Political quarrels behind
the lines had a serious detrimental effect on the fighting
army."[4]

The chaotic administration of the War Office and the lack of discipline
among officers behind the lines created conditions in which neither
private citizens nor government representatives had any guarantee of
safety.

In fact, the situation had become intolerable. On November 1,
1918, I sent a telegram to the minister of internal affairs asking to be
released from my duty as provincial governor. Here is an illustration
of the relations between the military and civilian authorities at that
time. On November 8, 1918, the head of the military region, Fedorovich, in violation of the Siberian government's decree of July 15,
declared the city of Krasnoyarsk under siege and ordered anyone in
possession of arms to be shot on sight. No exception was made for the
representatives of the government. To avoid being shot on the street
because of a misunderstanding, I sent my secretary to the head of the
military region to ask for a clarification of the situation. Here is his
report:

Clerk, Special Assignments	November 9
for Commissar of Yeniseisk Province	No. 1204
To Sir Commissar of Yeniseisk Province	
City of Krasnoyarsk	

    I have the honor to report to you, Sir Commissar, that on this
date, on your commission, I presented myself at the administrative office of the commandant of the city of Krasnoyarsk to
receive permission for you to carry and possess a "Browning"
revolver, medium caliber. Upon entering the building of the
commandant's administration, I addressed an officer, captain
second class, requesting that he take me to the commandant's
adjutant. Instead, the officer asked me the purpose of my
errand, and when I explained it to him, mentioning that I had
with me a copy of your written communication No. 1166 ad-

dressed to the commandant of the city, he told me explicitly that during siege conditions permission for the commissar to carry a Browning cannot be given and that the commissar must surrender it to the commandant's administration. When I said that the provisional commissar's position gives him the right to possess arms, and if he asks written permission to do so it is only to avoid the possibility of an undesirable encounter with the army patrol, which may not recognize the provisional commissar on sight, the officer answered that the commissar must still surrender the revolver in his possession, for which he will be given a receipt, but cannot claim the revolver until the siege is lifted. However, he added, if a revolver is indispensable to the commissar he may address his request for permission to possess it to the head of the garrison.

With this in mind, I went to headquarters, where I handed the officer on duty your written communication No. 1178, addressed to the head of the garrison, and asked that it be brought to the attention of the latter's adjutant, since I had previously been told that the head of the garrison happened to be there at the time, or to the head of staff. In answer to my request, the officer handed back to me your communication and told me that the head of staff does not review applications for permission to possess arms and recommended that with your written communication I should apply directly to the commandant's administration. I indicated to the officer that I had already applied to the commandant's administration and had there been advised to apply to the head of the garrison. The officer's comment to this was that the commandant's administration refers matters to headquarters in order to load work on the latter. "This is a matter for the commandant's administration—apply there."

After this conversation I went a second time to the commandant's administration, where the answer I heard on the first visit was repeated.

This has been recorded and duly reported in anticipation, Sir Commissar, of your further orders.

Clerk for Special Assignments

The head of the military region, Fedorovich, then sent his adjutant to me with the request that I surrender my revolver to him. When I refused to do so, Fedorovich issued an order for me to be fined 500 rubles. He had this action published in the newspapers; moreover, he designated my subordinate, the head of the militia, to carry out the order.

I sent the following telegram to the government:

Omsk   November 13, 1918

To the Chairman of the Provisional Government Avksentyev
To the Chairman of the Council of Ministers Vologodsky
To the Minister of Internal Affairs

Contrary to the decree issued by the Council of Ministers on July 15, the city was declared under siege on the authority of the head of the garrison. The head of the garrison has imposed disciplinary measures on my subordinates for actions performed in the line of duty including arrest. Finally, not guaranteeing my personal safety, he refused to give me permission to carry a revolver and demanded that during the siege I surrender my revolver. I refused to comply with this demand. Today I read in the newspaper that by his order of November 12 the head of the garrison has fined me 500 rubles for carrying arms without permission and furthermore he has designated the head of the militia to carry out this order. Perceiving by the actions of the head of the garrison that he has exceeded his authority and, in the interests of upholding the authority of the regime, I ask that you give orders that will protect my subordinates and me from illegal actions and arbitrary commands on the part of the military authorities.

ID [Acting] Provisional Commissar
P. Dotsenko

Considering that I was authorized by the Siberian government to organize an uprising against the Bolsheviks and that I was head of the illegal military organization in Yeniseisk province, Fedorovich's actions would seem absurd at first glance. But they were not absurd; they represented one of the links in the preparation for a seizure of power in Omsk and removal of the Directory. That is how reactionary military circles understood the struggle against bolshevism.

Yes, the Directory was necessary, but not in the form it took. Under the influence of "great power" mentality at the conference, the principle of federalist order was ignored. In the process of creating a regime, a colossal mistake was made: the Directory was given full power without limitations.

The Directory, still without its own administrative apparatus, immediately abolished all the autonomous governments. Once they had lost their formal right to self-rule, the regions began to pay less and less attention to the center, and each one followed its own inclinations. The results would have been vastly different if the Directory had limited itself exclusively to organizing one government over the domains of military, financial, and foreign affairs and had abstained from the "great power" politics, which were alien to all the non-Russian peoples and the Siberians as well.

The Allied representatives were not content to stay out of the Russian intrigues. On October 25 General Knox, during a conversation with General Boldyrev in Omsk, was already threatening to disperse the Directory with force. And his assistant for military affairs, Colonel Ward, was no less modest in his behavior.

The formation of the so-called all-Russian government was completed in November. Admiral Kolchak was appointed minister of war and announced his intention to visit the front, first the Urals and later Ufa. At the same time Colonel Ward, with General Knox's approval, was on his way to the Urals "for the moral support of our Allies' war-weary veterans, taking with him a choir, musicians, and hundreds of select guards." "Purely by chance," of course, the carriage of Minister of War Kolchak was attached to this train. Colonel Ward sent telegrams in his own name "to all the station masters down the line, ordering them, under threat of severe punishment, to clear the corresponding sections of the way and to hold in readiness at each stop a special locomotive for the admiral's train at the moment it reached a station."[5] In the history of Russia, this was the first such ignominious situation: a Russian minister of war traveling in his own territory under the guard of English troops. Besides, it violated all military discipline to give a foreign officer the right to issue orders to Russian station masters.

After several days of lending moral support to the weary veterans in the Urals, Kolchak was to have proceeded to Ufa, but he went no farther than Chelyabinsk. "There are urgent reasons for our immediate return to Omsk,"[6] he told Ward. On November 16 on his way to Omsk, Kolchak found a communication awaiting him at Petropavlovsk Station informing him that the commander-in-chief, General Boldyrev, was en route to the Ufa front and wished to consult with him there.

Colonel Ward recounts:

> The Admiral invited me to his carriage, described the critical situation in Omsk, and told me that he was puzzled by the sudden decision of the commander-in-chief to leave Omsk and to seek a meeting with him on the way. I strongly suspected that the two government groups had come to blows and that one had decided to destroy the other. I also thought that Admiral Kolchak would be forced to define his position in relation to these groups and that perhaps his life and likewise

the life of his British escort would depend on the answer. I therefore ordered my men to load their guns and to be ready for action at any moment if deemed necessary. The patrol on the platform was ordered not to allow anyone (military or civilian alike) to congregate around the train. Two soldiers, assigned to the admiral, were ordered not to let him out of their sight under any circumstances. They were to accompany him at all times and to report to me.[7]

Such an admission coming from this zealous British officer leaves little to be added. One can only wonder if he himself could account for his actions: a person of high authority, the commander-in-chief of the army, calls for a consultation with his subordinate, and an English officer, suspecting that something is wrong, orders his men to load their guns and prepare for action. This is evidently how the representative of Great Britain, in his political naïvete, understood the struggle against the Bolsheviks.

Once it had abolished the Siberian Oblast Duma, the Administrative Council successfully expanded its functions, even to the legislative realm. It became, in fact, the Siberian government—elected by no one—and began to dream about all-Russian authority.

The Directory, upon arriving in Omsk, was confronted with an important new situation. The Siberian government offered, despite the agreement reached at the Ufa Conference, to recognize the Directory if the Directory would name it the All-Russian Council of Ministers. The weak-willed Directory agreed, stating that it had good intentions of using an administrative apparatus already in working order. The members of the Directory completely overlooked the fact that the Omsk apparatus was geared not to govern a country, but to overthrow a government. The Directory thus committed an irrevocable blunder, jeopardizing its very existence. It had already become a laughing-stock, a nuisance that should be done away with at the first opportunity. Further, the Directory chose Omsk as its seat, where the political atmosphere was unhealthy and greatly interfered with the normal functions of the government, instead of Ekaterinburg, as first planned.

Furthermore, Socialist-Revolutionary leader Viktor Chernov was in Ufa neither during the conference or for the selection of the Directory. Once he had arrived and become acquainted with the outcome of the conference, he declared that in his opinion the Socialist-Revolutionary faction of the Constituent Assembly had fully capitulated. The party had won an absolute majority at the elections to the Constituent Assembly, but among the members of the Directory there was only one Socialist-Revolutionary: V. Zenzinov. He did not count

Avksentyev because he was at that time a member of the Soyuz Osvobozhdeniya,[8] and the two memberships violated the principle of proportional representation.

The Socialist-Revolutionary Party's conference in Ekaterinburg in November was attended by members of the party's Central Committee and by some members of the Constituent Assembly, a total of 45 people. A resolution was passed by 22 votes. This was certainly not an absolute majority, as there were 20 negative votes and 3 abstentions. Even though the Directory was criticized for not having adhered to the original program, the party organizations, in the name of the party's Central Committee, were instructed to support the Directory in the face of the advancing reactionary movement.

The Council of Ministers, however, still insisted in its official communication that the Central Committee of the Socialist-Revolutionary Party had issued a proclamation on October 22, 1918, with an open call to arms against the supreme authority and an appeal to the party to form an army of its own, namely, an illegal military force. In fact, these instructions had invited the Socialist-Revolutionaries to join the most legal of volunteer army units, preferably the battalion bearing the name of the Constituent Assembly, a part of Kappel's detachment, or else the so-called Russo-Czech regiments, which operated under regulations and a form of discipline borrowed from the military code of the Czech Legions. In thus distorting the truth, the Omsk circles found a good excuse to accuse Directory members Avksentyev and Zenzinov of disloyalty to the supreme authority and also an excuse for the mass arrests of Socialist-Revolutionaries.

One circumstance remains unclear: who released part of these instructions to the press at a time when even party organizations had not received them at their locations? According to Chernov, this was done by the head of the party's Information Bureau in Omsk; according to Zenzinov, it was the work of the secretary of the party's Central Committee, V. Chaikin, who two weeks later resigned. The second version is more probable because Chaikin was a bitter enemy of the majority Socialist-Revolutionary factions that had participated in the Ufa Conference.

In the midst of these intrigues, an attempt was under way to avert the Directory's overthrow. On November 12, Vologodsky noted in his diary that the minister of communications, L. A. Ustrugov, had reported a telegram sent by Gaida to all echelon commanders telling them to be prepared for decisive action and to concentrate their forces against Omsk. Vologodsky does not explain what prompted this telegram because it was a mystery to him, too. Perhaps I can shed some light on it based on what I learned from Capt. N. Kalashnikov, head of the Information Bureau of the staff of the First Army.

Simultaneously with dispatch of the telegram, the staff of the commander of the Siberian Army in Ekaterinburg commandeered Kalashnikov to Omsk with a proposal to the Directory that the commander-in-chief of the army, General Boldyrev, should order the army units then located in Omsk to be sent to the front to reinforce the troops holding back the advance of the Red Army. In case the army units entrenched in Omsk and preparing an internal overthrow refused to obey this order, detachments of the Siberian Army sent from Krasnoyarsk, as well as some Czechs from the troops distributed along the railway lines, were standing by. It was about this situation that Kalashnikov wished to consult personally with Avksentyev, the chairman of the Directory. Avksentyev did not receive Kalashnikov but suggested that he inform the head of the Chancellory, A. N. Kruglikov, about the purpose of his visit and then come for an answer the following day. The next day, Kalashnikov received an answer from Avksentyev (delivered to him by Kruglikov), who said he did not wish to interfere in military affairs because all that was in the hands of General Boldyrev. Concerning replacement of the guard, Avksentyev answered, "I do not need your Latvians." Kalashnikov was astounded by Avksentyev's reply. In the first place, it was not a question of interfering in military affairs, but of preventing the overthrow of a government. And the Czechs, good enough for Avksentyev when fighting in front-line positions, had suddenly become "Latvians" as internal guards. Avksentyev had taken it upon himself to answer Kalashnikov without having informed the other members of the Directory. This I learned only later, when I met Zenzinov in the United States and asked him why they had declined the offer of the staff of the commander of the Ural front. He answered that he personally had known nothing about it; but it was his opinion that all this could have done little to change the situation in Omsk at that time.

There is an indication of this in General Boldyrev's statement of November 12: "Minister of Communications Ustrugov handed me, in a state of agitation, four telegrams from Gaida. In one of these he summoned the echelon of the Eighth Czech regiment, then on its way to Omsk, to concentrate at that point and to be prepared for action. A company from Krasnoyarsk was also being called."[9] General Boldyrev had not been informed by Avksentyev about the offer from the staff of the Acting Siberian Army, so all this came as a surprise to him. As a result, instead of neutralizing the secret military organizations, he attacked Gaida. The assurances of the head of the garrison and of the

chief of staff of the commander-in-chief—who were also conspirators—that all was quiet in the city and that no attack on the Directory
was expected were evidently enough to satisfy General Boldyrev; with
that he departed from Omsk.

On November 13 a battalion of French troops arrived in Omsk. At a
banquet given in their honor, I. Krasilnikov demanded that the
orchestra play the hymn "God Save the Tsar." Professor N. Ya.
Novomberg refused to stand, and Krasilnikov threatened to shoot him
then and there. The French guests left the hall one by one. Noting this
episode in his diary, Vologodsky commented, "It seems as though the
officers at fault left for the front two days later." It is true that he does
not indicate which front, but the fact is that in two days they were
already taking part in the consultations at Omsk. "On November 15,
E. F. Rogovsky gave a report to the Directory concerning its imminent
overthrow. The news was, on the whole, received quite calmly. *November 16*. The Council of Ministers severely criticized the activity of the
Directory in general and in particular for having issued laws without
having subjected them to preliminary examination by the Council of
Ministers."[10]

On November 17 consultations were held among the military
group, some of the ministers and representatives of the trade-
industrialists, and the Siberian Committee of the Constitutional
Democratic Party, at first in the train occupied by the French Mission
and later in the Military-Industrial Committee building. These consultations conclusively decided the fate of the Directory, and Admiral
Kolchak was proposed as the "supreme ruler." Kolchak returned to
Omsk on the evening of November 17. The liquidation of the Directory
was entrusted to Colonel Volkov, Zhardetsky, and Minister I.
Mikhailov.

On November 18 some members of the Directory were arrested,
and Admiral Kolchak was officially proclaimed supreme ruler. On
November 19, "through secret orders sent to the Cossack troops, Kolchak announced several promotions: Volkov was promoted from colonel to major-general (with seniority) for distinguished service in
combat, Krasilnikov and Katanaev were promoted from majors to
colonels."[11] It did not take General Knox long to find a *banda* (desper-
ados) to disperse the Directory. The participation of a group of officers
in this crime became, in the words of Kolchak, "distinguished service
in combat." It is true that not all were so fortunate. For example, the
commander of the convoy company that actually carried out this
inglorious work was given, instead of a promotion, a watch as a

personal gift from Admiral Kolchak and was then sent on an assignment with a false passport.[12]

An official government announcement stated: "After giving due
consideration to the current situation, the Council of Ministers has
found that the Directory members named above had connections with
members of the Constituent Assembly and, behind the backs of the
All-Russian Government and the army, were preparing a traitorous
agreement with the Bolsheviks." After a discussion of the situation,
the Council of Ministers decided that complete power should be transferred to the Council of Ministers, but that, in view of the difficult
situation in the country at the time, the power should temporarily be
vested in Admiral Kolchak. This decision is somewhat perplexing: if
the council knew for a fact that Zenzinov and Avksentyev "were preparing a traitorous agreement with the Bolsheviks," why did they not
bring them to trial? It is also unclear what prompted the Council of
Ministers to assume all power in such haste and then, in just as much
haste, to transfer it to Admiral Kolchak. With two members of the
Directory arrested, three remained who could have formed a legal
quorum, making it possible for the Directory to decide its own future.
At the same meeting, the Council of Ministers promoted Kolchak from
vice-admiral to admiral—evidently also for "distinguished service in
combat."

Several facts help to understand the role of the English representatives in the overthrow. The Russian ambassador to England at the
time noted in his memoirs: "Although the local English agents in
Siberia report that the Directory is unstable, that talks are being
conducted between the Socialist-Revolutionaries and the military
party—all the same it was decided to recognize the Directory, and on
November 17 a telegram to this effect was prepared to be sent to
Omsk."[13] Probably there had been a disagreement in London between
the Ministry of Foreign Affairs and the Ministry of War, and in order to
prevent recognition of the Directory, the coup d'etat was speedily
accomplished.

This then was the urgent reason for Colonel Ward's and Admiral
Kolchak's return to Omsk. Ward reports: "Neither the Council of
Ministers nor Kolchak himself could make the final decision until they
had full knowledge of Britain's position in this question. The Czech
troops in Omsk were so positioned that it was impossible for them to
approach the meeting place of the Ministers without stumbling onto
the British, and my machine guns commanded all the streets that led
to the building that housed the Russian Headquarters." According to

Colonel Ward, who knew little enough about Russian conditions and nothing of the language, "Members of the Directory were the most outrageous bankrupts that Russia had ever produced, and the people waited impatiently and hopefully for them to be done away with as rapidly as possible."[14] This is how the English "helped" the Russians in their struggle against the Bolsheviks.

The Omsk press, for the most part, indicated, as did some of the government's own announcements, that the overthrow happened unexpectedly as a result of the dissatisfaction of patriotic groups with the traitorous Directory. How "unexpectedly" all this really happened can be judged from the following: General Sakharov asserted that "Colonel D. A. Lebedev rode to all fronts and saw Generals M. K. Dieterichs, M. V. Khanzhyn, Golitsyn, and Gaida and that they all talked about the necessity of replacing the Directory as quickly as possible with one-man rule."[15] General Sakharov left Omsk for Vladivostok in General Knox's train; speaking about the overthrow, he noted that "actually all this was known even before their departure on November 2, 1918."[16]

Some light is also shed on the "unexpectedness" of the overthrow in the memoirs of the ministers, who were present at the historical meeting. Minister of Supplies Serebrennikov said that Major F. Porotikov, apologizing for his mistaken arrest, said, "The Directory has been arrested and will cease to be—there will be Kolchak." While delivering a speech at the meeting of the Council of Ministers, "Kolchak suggested that they hasten in coming to a decision about the question of the dictatorship since the powers concerned were awaiting this decision with great interest. If the council had not agreed to Kolchak's dictatorship, it is quite possible that it would have been destroyed in the same way and by the same forces used against the Directory." Serebrennikov thought that "Kolchak knew about the conspiracy and agreed to assume the dictatorship."[17]

There is a more detailed statement in the diary of Chairman Vologodsky of the Council of Ministers: "On November 18, Avksentyev, Zenzinov, E. Ragovsky, and A. Argunov were arrested by some Cossack officers. Neither the commander of the Military District, General Matkovsky, nor the chief of staff of the commander-in-chief, General S. N. Rozanov, nor the minister of internal affairs, Gratsianov, knew anything about it. We met at the home of General Rozanov to inform each other about the events of the previous night. The manner in which General Rozanov behaved at this meeting convinced me that he knew more than he said he did and that he was concealing something." That very day, Vologodsky called the Council of Ministers, gave a report on what had happened, and proposed that Krasilnikov be arrested. To my astonishment the proposal was met with the sharpest of objections. G. K. Guins argued that Krasilnikov did what should have been done long ago and that his arrest would not meet with popular approval since the Directory had long since fallen into public disfavor. Guins was heartily supported by the other members of the Council of Ministers. I was extremely dejected by this attitude of the Council of Ministers toward my report. I began to think that this whole affair of the officers' overthrow took place with the knowledge and perhaps even under the leadership of certain members of the Council of Ministers.

The Council of Ministers promoted Kolchak to full admiral and elected him supreme ruler by all but one vote: Vologodsky voted against him.[18]

What role Guins played in this overthrow is not quite clear, but later, when he was no longer in a position of authority, he reviewed these events and reached some conclusions that are far from favorable to the Council of Ministers and Kolchak.

> The fateful unexpectedness of the overthrow placed the Council of Ministers before the fact, forced it to make decisions without preparation, to elect a dictator without having adequately evaluated his qualities, to define his rights without having firmly determined the political goals. Those who overthrew the Directory took upon themselves a heavy responsibility and, judging by subsequent events, they evidently had not clearly thought through the program in terms of the future, but had agreed solely on one measure—the replacement of the Directory by Kolchak. The election of a supreme ruler was an act forced on them by party strife and military conspiracy. Dictatorship, supported by popular vote, has been known to history. This was not the case in Omsk. The idea of a dictatorship was introduced by a small segment of the population. It was up to Admiral Kolchak to win general recognition for himself. His name was not known in the broader national circles. Was there any one who had an intimate knowledge of Admiral Kolchak? In the Council of Ministers, no one.[19]

Is this not an admission of political bankruptcy, irresponsibility, and lack of seriousness, which applies in the same degree to the other members of the Council of Ministers? Having elected Kolchak "supreme ruler" they immediately limited his power: he could not issue laws without the knowledge of the Council of Ministers, the chairman of the Council of Ministers, or the minister of the corresponding department. In other words, he was "monarch in the English manner." Actually, what was it exactly that the Directory was guilty of? There had been no judicial proceedings and no indictment, only the unfounded declaration of betrayal.

Several years after the overthrow, Guins described more precisely the guilt of the Directory in his memoirs:

> Can weak-willed, short-sighted people be blamed for not possessing strong characters and foresight? Before Russia the Directory stands guilty of nothing else. All the talk about the negotiations that supposedly took place between Avksentyev and the Bolsheviks, not substantiated at any time or by anyone, his comments about the army distorted and repeated— all this was nothing but the product of malice and provocation on the part of the attackers. The inability to demonstrate its independence of the Social-Revolutionaries, constant consultations with party workers, garrulity, and lack of reality in politics—herein lies the real guilt of the Directory. However, taking a close look at the conditions under which it worked, it has to be admitted that the Directory, from the very first days of its existence, did not have control over events.[20]

Guins looked upon the association of Zenzinov and Avksentyev with the Socialist-Revolutionaries as their most grievous fault, but nowhere does he provide facts indicating that these men in making their decisions were governed not by national Russian interests, but by narrow party concerns. Neither Guins nor the government as a whole has ever presented such facts. Moreover, how could Zenzinov and Avksentyev, who were in the minority, have conducted a narrow party policy when the other three members of the Directory held different political convictions? That Zenzinov and Avksentyev were Socialist-Revolutionaries was no secret among those who attended the convention at Ufa, especially since their candidacy was supported by the Socialist-Revolutionary faction. At that time, the Socialist-Revolutionaries were not yet possessed of a rich imagination and political sagacity and thus did not suspect that at some time in the future Zenzinov and Avksentyev would be accused of having associated with those who had put forth their candidacy. The Directory had been formed as a result of a compromise and could boast of no one among its members with a particularly strong will.

It should be remembered that the candidacy of each member of the Directory was discussed from all angles by a conciliation board, and that it had to be unanimously approved by all who were present at the conference, including Generals Sakharov and Ivanov-Rinov. Ivanov-Rinov, evidently, voted for Zenzinov and Avksentyev in the belief that at some later time it would not be too difficult to remove them from power. Some people are strong in hindsight, and General Boldyrev refers to himself as being in this category.

> The most serious mistake, in my opinion, was to have assigned the forming of a special brigade of artillery and cavalry to my chief of staff, General Rozanov. This brigade was to have served as the personal guard of the Directory, its closest armed force, which should have preceded the Directory in the move to its chosen seat. In those times this was essential. To my deep regret, I realized too late that the agreement reached at Ufa should have immediately been enforced by bayonets and that the closest and most dangerous enemy was not at the front in the form of the Red Army, but right at hand—behind the lines—in that idealistic mixture present in various groupings, especially among the military, that has lost all sense of discipline and has forgotten the need to sacrifice during that immeasurably difficult first organizational period. I based my activity on trust. Reality has proved that other, severe measures were needed.[21]

At this point, the characteristics of the newly arrived "wisemen" who came to replace the Directory should be examined. Vologodsky, chairman of the Council of Ministers, when called upon to tell the so-called Political Bloc (Omsk Defense Bloc) whether the Council of Ministers could be expected to regain a clean bill of health, answered: "I must confess that I have not in the past been distinguished either for my initiative or for my activity. Now, after ten months of tense, difficult, and responsible work, I am worn out and weaker than ever."[22] Guins, the administrative head of the Council of Ministers, wrote about himself: "Suffering from the sin, common to all Omsk political workers, of ill-preparedness for government work on a large scale, I did not possess the gift of foresight or the strength of perseverance."[23] And again:

> With the coming to power of the admiral, new people appeared on the scene. Some, for instance, Colonel Lebedev, seemed to have sprung out of the ground. The appointment of

this young colonel as chief of staff of the supreme commander-in-chief, that is, virtually the commander-in-chief, was a surprise to all. I am afraid the admiral chose him by chance—simply because he happened to arrive wearing the stripes of the Volunteer Army and brought with him to Siberia, as it were, the spirit of L. G. Kornilov and A. I. Denikin. It did not occur to anyone that this appointment could have been the result of the admiral's inability to judge people.[24]

The person who set the political tone of the government was I. A. Mikhailov, a man of limitless ambition. This evil genius began to weave a net of intrigue inside the government from the moment the Bolsheviks were removed from power in Siberia. Two weeks after the soviets in Novonikolaevsk had been liquidated, with the struggle still under way in other regions of Siberia, Mikhailov was already talking to Vologodsky about "the necessity of transferring the power from the West Siberian Commissariat to a more authoritative organ—the government, which was, after all, elected by the Siberian Oblast Duma." His next step was aimed at limiting the number of members in that government. Having become head of the Administrative Council, he concentrated on extending its powers and began working against the Siberian Oblast Duma to the very point of its extinction. Wishing to free himself from public control represented by the Oblast Duma, Mikhailov created a "surrogate public" in the form of the Political Bloc in Omsk. It was Mikhailov who gave instructions to the representatives of the Siberian government in Ufa. And it was he who played an active role in planning the fall of the Directory. After this had been accomplished, he emerged as chief adviser to the supreme ruler. "Politics, in essence, were entirely in the hands of I. Mikhailov, and, to give him his due, he exhibited a great deal of talent during the time of his almost-dictatorial rule. His resourcefulness was fantastic, and a purely political role suited him well, much better, in fact, than the ministry of finances, which requires greater skill in economics, more perseverance, and a more systematic approach to work."[25]

American Consul General Harris, despite his attitude of a well-wisher toward Kolchak's regime, wrote in his report to Washington that Mikhailov was more occupied with intrigues than with bringing the country's economy into order.[26] Admiral Kolchak placed above all else the problem of organizing the army, but he himself did not show evidence of any organizational abilities. During the fourteen months of his rule, there was a succession of ten ministers of war. Each one left before he had had a chance to become well acquainted with the work. It must be admitted that this was a period of chaotic rule for the country. "Affairs were decided not by the Council of Ministers, but by the Council of the Supreme Ruler, where all the decisions were made according to the wishes of Mikhailov and his 'yes-man,' Sukin. The admiral made no decisions—he was completely lacking in character," noted a former minister of war, General A. Budberg.[27]

In these first confused days of the "dictatorship" one very unpleasant feature was already evident. Admiral supreme commander-in-chief swallowed admiral supreme ruler together with his Council of Ministers. It is no wonder that the quarters of the commander-in-chief resembled an anthill. They already had their own ministries. From these quarters Sukin dictated instructions to the Ministry of Foreign Affairs, while Lebedev decided affairs of internal policy. A special department, the so-called "Oskapverkh," enacted the laws. Neither the chairman of the Council of Ministers, nor the administrative head, nor the minister of internal affairs protested.[28]

Guins stated:

The admiral was a politically naïve person. He did not understand the complexities of political organization, the roles of political parties, or games of ambition as factors of government life. The correlation between the various organs of government was an inaccessible and foreign concept to him, and he therefore contributed only confusion and disruption to the work by assigning the same piece of business first to one and then to another. As an example, correspondence with Denikin concerning political matters was carried out simultaneously in three separate departments: the headquarters of the commander-in-chief, the Ministry of Foreign Affairs, and the Administrative Office. Alas! It has to be said that we did not have a supreme ruler.

The admiral, in explaining to us the Tobolsk operation, wondered why it was a failure, and he listened with acquiescence to the report of a general who had removed the hero of Votkinsky detachment (consisting only of factory workers) for having won the battle without permission. It was then I realized that neither did we have a supreme commander-in-chief.[29]

6

Siberia Under Kolchak

The leaders of the overthrow, at the helm of "all-Russian authority," retained the weak-willed P. Vologodsky as chairman of the Council of Ministers and advanced the unbalanced and even less politically literate Admiral Kolchak to the post of "supreme ruler."

Once in power, Kolchak had at his disposal the Russian gold supply, and he did not forget his foreign friends who had lent him aid. On November 21, 1918, he announced the recognition of all prior foreign debts. The Council of Ministers, in a supplementary communication of the same date concerning the overthrow, stated: "A concentration of power, answering the temper of the time, will at last bring to an end the continuous attacks from right and left on Russia's not yet stabilized regime—attacks that deeply shake the government in its inner and outer workings and endanger the political freedom and basic principles of the democratic order; a concentration of power is essential for action against the destructive work of antigovernmental parties, as well as for ending the arbitrary activity of army detachments, causing disorganization in the economic life of the country and disruption of peace and order."[1]

The government's declaration concerning the preservation of the democratic order and political freedoms was intended for the benefit of the world outside Russia. Inside the country, the situation was exactly the opposite.

Following the overthrow came the comedy of bringing to "trial" the very people who had been authorized to carry it out. Kolchak ordered General Volkov, Ataman I. Krasilnikov, and Ataman Katanaev to be tried by court-martial for having arrested two members of the Directory. On November 21, the court ruled that because Volkov, Krasilnikov, and Katanaev were motivated by patriotic feelings and acted to save the motherland when they made these arrests, they should be acquitted. It was characteristic of all that happened in this period that the defendants had not been arrested even for the sake of formality. By its decision the court established a precedent whereby arbitrary acts on the part of the commanders of detachments, if done in the name of the motherland, were not indictable, and in some instances were even rewarded by promotions.

A committee of the Constituent Assembly had declared that it did not recognize Kolchak, who had done away with the Directory, and on November 19 it had sent out an appeal to the people. On the same day in Ekaterinburg, acting on orders from Omsk, a military detachment had raided the building occupied by the Socialist-Revolutionaries and arrested several members of the Constituent Assembly. From that moment, a wave of repression swept over those members of the Social-ist-Revolutionary Party who had taken an active part in organizing the uprising against the Bolsheviks but who did not recognize Kolchak as the "supreme ruler." On November 30, 1918, the following order (No. 56) was issued:

1. All Russian military commanders must in the most decisive man-ner suppress the criminal activity of the above-mentioned persons and should not hesitate to use arms;
2. All Russian military commanders, beginning with the command-ers of garrisons, must arrest those persons and deliver them to the courts-martial for trial, reporting according to command and directly to the head and the commander-in-chief;
3. All commanders and officers abetting the criminal activities of the above-mentioned persons will also be subjected to trial by court-martial. The same holds true for commanders who display weak-ness and passivity in the exercise of their authority.

By this order, Kolchak not only did not limit the arbitrary behavior of commanders of military units—the practice that was of such great concern to the Council of Ministers—but he did just the opposite, extending military authority by charging the army with functions of a purely police nature. As a consequence, the rearguard of the army began to resemble the Soviet Cheka,[2] and a second front was opened, as it were, against the foe within.

At the same time, censorship of the press was introduced. If before the assumption of power by Ivanov-Rinov and Kolchak there had been some attempt toward a demarcation of military and civilian authority, now, from the moment the order above had appeared, there was complete chaos: government legislation had no power, and everything depended on the discretion of the military leaders. The outcome of such a governmental approach became evident all too soon.

On the night of December 21, 1918, the Bolsheviks in Omsk organized an uprising and freed the political prisoners. Among those freed were members of the Constituent Assembly (Socialist-Revolutionaries and Social Democrats). While the Bolsheviks were unable to seize army headquarters, ministers' offices, or other government institutions, some of the Bolshevik workers who had participated in the uprising successfully entrenched themselves in the vicinity of the railroad town Kulomzino, a few kilometers from Omsk.

Evidently General Ivanov-Rinov knew about the impending uprising and timed his arrival in Omsk accordingly. Order Number 160, dated December 22, 1918, stated: "Ivanov-Rinov, who has just arrived from the east, has ordered that the 'provocateurs' be brought before the court-martial." Guins expresses confusion: "On what grounds does he issue such an order? On whose authority? I do not know. But the minister of justice did not register a protest."[3]

After the uprising had been suppressed, the head of the Omsk garrison issued an order stating that all those who had been illegally freed from prison must return; all those who did not return and were later apprehended would be shot on sight.

The members of the Constituent Assembly returned to prison voluntarily, but on the night of December 23 they were forced out of the prison and brutally murdered. Their bodies were left on the shore of the Irtysh River. P. Vologodsky recalls:

> It became known that certain members of the Constituent Assembly who had voluntarily returned to prison were shot after having been tried and that some were shot without the benefit of a trial, after being forcibly taken from prison by military detachments acting under the orders of Officers Bartashevsky and Rubtsov, acting under no orders whatsoever.
>
> On December 25 at a meeting of the Council of Ministers, I. Mikhailov said that the chairman of the Military Regional Court told him personally that the court had been obliged to hold trials for at least twenty persons, who had in fact already been shot. Mikhailov stated that General Ivanov-Rinov and the chief of staff, D. A. Lebedev, had set themselves the goal of shooting all the participants of the uprising.

The Council of Ministers resolved to appeal to the supreme ruler to order an investigation of the executions that had taken place without benefit of trial and of the irregular actions of the courts-martial themselves and also to ask that the staff of the commander-in-chief confine itself to the area of military activities to prevent further interference in government affairs. Kolchak at first attempted to deny these requests and twice answered in the negative, pointing out that in the process of suppressing uprisings laws are apt to be violated.[4]

The minister of justice, who was conducting the investigation, stated in his report to Kolchak that the staff officer for special assignments who was attached to the quarters of the head of the garrison and the chief of staff of the head of the garrison "have not yet been interrogated because of failure to locate them."[5]

The minister of justice commented further on the "obvious violation of the law during these trials since some of those arrested had been tried in the absence of an indictment and in the absence of incriminating evidence. All these facts must be brought to light first of all by interrogating the chairman of the military regional court in Tomsk and also the members of the court—none of whom can be located."[6]

These events produced a very unfavorable impression abroad. A deluge of inquiries poured in from the consuls, and Omsk hastened to pacify them. On January 27, 1919, G. K. Guins sent a telegram (No. 60) to Russian ambassadors abroad in which he stated:

The investigating committee formed under the chairmanship of the senator will determine who is guilty, and those who are found guilty will be dealt with severely—to the full extent of the law. What has happened did not reflect in any way on the government's complete unity with public opinion. In explanation, I may point out that there are some among the officers and Cossacks who tend to deal with bolshevism in their own way. Whatever infringement of the law there has been, however, is insignificant when compared to the Bolshevik terror; but be that as it may, it could still undermine trust in the regime.[7]

At the investigation in Irkutsk, Kolchak said that he did not know why the minister of justice had not released the members of the Constituent Assembly at once since there was no guilt in their actions. The murder of the members of the assembly was, in his opinion, committed for the sole purpose of compromising him personally.

Among those killed was a Constituent Assembly member from Yeniseisk province, N. F. Fomin, with whom I had worked in a cooperative and in organizing the uprising. He had been commandeered by the Siberian government to the armies of Gaida and Pepelyaev and with them had made the march from Novonikolaevsk to Manchuria. The medical report testified how savage the attack on him had been. Seventeen wounds made by several kinds of firearms, bayonets, and sabers were counted on his body. There was also evidence that he had been beaten. So the reactionary officers dealt with one of the most prominent organizers of the uprising against the Bolsheviks. The details of this barbarous murder are described by E. E. Kolosov in his article, "Kak eto bylo."[8] In depicting the scene, Kolosov wrote: "There were two of us [Kolosov and I] searching through all the snowdrifts in front of the officers' club, where the court-martial was held."

In that article, Kolosov mentioned that the Socialist-Revolutionaries then in Omsk had raised the question of renewing terrorism against the government, but he did not give the reason why this was not carried out: after the February Revolution the party switched to a legal position; therefore the use of terror was abandoned. The only member of the Central Committee of the party who was in Tomsk at that time, N. Y. Hendelman, declared that he did not consider himself authorized to change that decision.

Under the pretext of suppressing the Bolshevik uprising, a military group composed of Volkov, Ivanov-Rinov, and others had successfully done away with some unneeded oppositionists and, at the same time, aimed at unseating Kolchak. But that plan was thwarted by Colonel Ward, commanding an English detachment, who placed Kolchak under his protection. Ward recalled:

> The fact that Kolchak proclaimed himself in favor of calling a National Assembly, to be chosen by a general election and to determine the form of rule Russia should have once order was restored, shattered the dreams of the officers of the old order for a quick return to monarchy. Kolchak's declaration against the extreme elements of both right and left practically pushed the monarchists and Bolsheviks into one camp.
>
> In this respect there is no actual difference between the principles of the Bolsheviks and those of the supporters of the old order. The difference is only in whom the power will be entrusted. For the time being, this secondary consideration has been put aside, and they have united to overthrow the man who is their common enemy.[9]

The conspirators were unable to remove Kolchak from power at this time, but they nevertheless achieved their goal. Just as in September they had put a noose around the neck of I. Mikhailov, by killing government member Novoselov, so now, by killing the members of the Constituent Assembly, who should have been freed, they created a deep rift between Kolchak and democratic elements.

Kolchak argued against bringing the guilty to trial, knowing that they were the same people and the same group that had made it possible for him to seize power, because of his own weak position. The headquarters of the commander-in-chief was not, of course, transferred near the front lines. And the investigation came to naught. As when Novoselov had been killed, it proved impossible to locate the guilty. Once again, a farce was enacted as a suspiciously large number of persons holding responsible military posts suddenly disappeared. It seems surprising that they could have left their duties without orders from their superiors. The investigating committee, which was to have determined who was guilty in order to bring those persons to trial, did not determine anything, although it was common knowledge that these orders had come from General Ivanov-Rinov and the chief of staff of the commander-in-chief, D. A. Lebedev.

Supreme Ruler Admiral Kolchak was silent. Also silent was the government as a whole. It was like drifting in a boat without rudder or sails—abandoned and at the mercy of the waves.

Guins recounts: "In the very first month of the admiral's rule, irresponsible military circles saw the opportunity to act on their own initiative, and in no time at all they were completely out of hand. The civilian authorities showed no signs of decisiveness or courage in dealing with the illegal military organizations and those who encouraged them."[10]

There was a time, however, when the author of these lines saw fit to classify the murders of the Constituent Assembly members as an insignificant infringement of the law. It was all very well to seek some measure of consolation for what happened by calling it a relatively lesser evil than Bolshevik terrorism and to find justification in the explanation that some officers tended to deal with bolshevism in their own way; but this cannot obscure the fact that cold-blooded slaughter had been committed and that the victims were those who had been among the first to raise the banners of war against Soviet rule.

The murders did not end with the members of the Constituent Assembly. In the second half of November 1918, I. P. Stepanov, mayor of the city of Kansk, came to my office for advice. He told me that he was not on good terms with the officers of Krasilnikov's detachment. He was on his way to Omsk on city government business and was now undecided whether to return to Kansk. I promised to investigate the political situation in Kansk, and we agreed that he would consult me on his way back. An agent whom I sent to Kansk informed me that the relations between the representatives of the city, the district zemstvo, and the civilian authorities, on the one hand, and the military authorities on the other, were greatly strained because there were no clear lines of demarcation between the two spheres of influence. In spite of this, he did not think there was any reason for Stepanov to feel in danger because this kind of situation had become so widespread that it was now almost the rule, not the exception. On his return from Omsk, Stepanov came to see me and I gave him the information I had, recommending that he return to Kansk.

But the information that I had been given did not quite cover the entire picture: it gave me no idea what savage feelings might be hidden under an officer's uniform. On December 13, 1918, I resigned my post as governor of Yeniseisk province and on the same day left for the west. It was not until later, when I was in Omsk, that I learned Stepanov's fate.

Kolosov, who was a member of the Constituent Assembly from Yeniseisk province, described the events as follows:

On December 27, 1918, there was an uprising of unknown origin in the city of Kansk. Accusations were made against those suspected of having organized the uprising, which bore all the signs of provocation, and among those arrested was the mayor of the city, Stepanov, a member of the Socialist-Revolutionary Party's center faction. A special military investigating commission placed in charge of Stepanov's case came to the conclusion that the mayor . . . had had nothing to do with the uprising. The same commission also determined that in Kansk false documents had figured in the cases of several others who had been arrested with Stepanov (for instance, Aleksandrov). All this was determined by the official military investigating commission. Nonetheless, Stepanov was held in prison, and, moreover, several officers from Krasilnikov's detachment operating in the Kansk district attempted to spirit him away so that they could deal with him on their own.

These attempts were not successful, but when General Rozanov was appointed, he received from Kansk a request for permission to hang Stepanov. The request was granted and Stepanov's fate was sealed. Stepanov was to be hanged at the railroad station, and he was led there through the city streets in broad daylight. The procession passed by his house, and seeing him from the window, his wife and two children ran out and followed him to the station. There, in the presence of a huge crowd and in full view of his wife and children, who were beside themselves from horror and grief, Stepanov was hanged. Just before the noose was thrown over his head, Stepanov called out, "Long live the Constituent Assembly!" But those who were killing him did not care who he was or what were his political beliefs. His body was lifted high on a corbel near a water pump, and there it hung for twenty-nine hours with trains passing under it.

And in Kansk they were saying: "Behold! There is the mayor of the city of Kansk."[11]

Guins explains: "Krasilnikov, one of the participants in the overthrow of November 18, was responsible for the hanging of the mayor of Kansk. It is said that, when informed that complaints about him had reached the supreme ruler, he answered in drunken, stumbling accents, 'I placed him there; I will replace him.'"[12]

The conversation between the chairman of the Council of Ministers, Vologodsky, and the commandant of the city of Omsk, Katanaev, that took place on February 4, 1919, may well serve as the chef d'oeuvre of the undisciplined behavior of the officers behind the lines. Ataman Katanaev and Ataman Krasilnikov had been promoted to the rank of colonel by Kolchak for distinguished service during combat, the arrest of the Directory on November 18. "The commandant of the city, Katanaev, arrested the editor of the newspaper, *Zarya*, and to my inquiry by telephone as to 'by what law and what decree was he guided, making arrests on his own initiative?' Katanaev answered rather irritably that he is guided by no laws and no decrees made by the government, but acts solely according to the impulses of an honest Russian officer who loves his country."[13] He knew that he would not have to answer for what he had done.

A sort of double play was going on: some of the ministers and Kolchak, in order to strengthen their power, wished to make use of certain military groups, and those groups, in turn, wished to make use of the so-called liberal ministers as a stepping-stone to a further concentration of power until a firm dictatorship could be established—without any further pretense at democracy.

When speaking of the army, a distinction should be drawn between the men fighting at the front and the men stationed behind the lines. While at the front, officers and soldiers fighting side by side waged for the most part a selfless battle against the Red Army. The men behind the lines engaged in intrigues and the overthrowing of governments.

Guins' assertion that "the former leaders of anti-Bolshevik officers' organizations in the main cities of Siberia divided Siberia, as it were, among themselves, establishing military districts and placing themselves at the head of these districts," is simply not true.[14]

All the military organizations east of Omsk served as a basis for the organization of the new Siberian Army. In Tomsk, Novonikolaevsk, Barnaul, and Krasnoyarsk, all the newly formed regiments were part of the First Mid-Siberian Corps, under the command of Pepelyaev, and these regiments immediately set out on a march to the east, toward Irkutsk.

The administrative military posts behind the lines fell to those who had not actually participated in the overthrow. The one exception was in Omsk, where Ivanov-Rinov formed the Second Mid-Siberian Corps and unleashed his military activities in West Siberia. (Because of the formation of the Volga front, his operation came to naught.) The Omsk soviet, after its decisive defeat by the Czechs in the battle at Maryanovka Station, retreated and left Omsk without a battle; but Ivanov-Rinov did not even find it necessary to pursue the routed Bolsheviks. This is how he did his part for the liberation of Siberia.

After the removal of Grishin-Almazov as commander of the army and his subsequent replacement by Ivanov-Rinov, the entire First Mid-Siberian Corps was dispatched in October to the Ekaterinburg front. Approximately three weeks after the overthrow, not one of the officers who had participated in the underground military organization remained in Krasnoyarsk. The chief of staff of the organization was transferred to Semipalatinsk, and all the other officers were assigned to active segments of the army. A succession of assignments followed to the responsible post as head of the military region: all were from other regions.

The result was that the more democratic element among the officers of the Siberian Army was serving on the front lines, whereas the posts behind the lines were filled by the more reactionary element. General Sakharov accused the Socialist-Revolutionaries of having penetrated the Siberian Army, but ignored the fact that from the very beginning they had been instrumental in organizing that army.[15] The Siberian Army, which consisted in the first period of its existence of volunteers, had ideals, in the name of which it waged war with the Bolsheviks; and outwardly it seemed that the Omsk overthrow of November 18 did not reflect that spirit. The army at the front was, at the time, preparing for an offensive that proved to be successful and that culminated in the capture of Perm on December 25. This heroic march under incredibly harsh winter conditions cannot, of course, be credited to the supreme ruler or his close aides. The men in Pepelyaev's corps were already soldered together and fought under the aureole of earlier victories in the east.

But to assert, as did Melgunov, that "the Omsk overthrow had no effect on the front"[16] would be to disregard everything that happened later. In the first place, General Boldyrev was commander-in-chief and had control over the Czech troops as well. With the coming of Kolchak, this situation changed. The Czechs not only refused to acknowledge his authority, worse yet, they left the front lines. Kolchak ordered the arrest of the members of the Constituent Assembly "wherever they might be," but that command was not obeyed.

Among the forces of the Samara government was a battalion of the Constituent Assembly, a Russo-Czech regiment, and the Samara cavalry division—all commanded by a member of the Constituent Assembly. To an inquiry from Omsk, "What are these units doing?" General V. O. Kappel answered that since the departure of the Czechs, they had been holding Samara's lines of defense.

The order requiring the troops to wear epaulets stirred dissatisfaction among the soldiers, and although General Kappel submitted to the order, he remarked: "This order will drive away our fighting material." By this he meant volunteers from the local peasantry. Colonel V. Vyrypaev commented: "As easy as it was before to deal with the local peasants, as soon as the epaulets appeared the peasants' attitude toward us changed abruptly."[17]

When Admiral Kolchak arrived in Perm after the First Mid-Siberian Corps had made its victorious march and taken the city, the officers of the corps staff wanted to have him arrested, and it was only because General Pepelyaev was against the arrest that it was not carried out. In a telegram to Washington dated January 13, 1919, American Consul General Harris reported: "Kolchak told me that, according to the communication received from Dutov, many Cossacks are refusing to fight as a result of the Socialist-Revolutionary propaganda."[18]

There is a paradox here: all the misfortunes at the front and behind the lines were, from the moment Admiral Kolchak came into power, attributed to the "propaganda of the Socialist-Revolutionaries." But the admiral himself had benefited from that very propaganda because it was by virtue of "Socialist-Revolutionary propaganda" that he was able to do away with the Directory and become the supreme ruler.

Further, Harris telegraphed his government on January 30: "The Seventh Czech Regiment and the Twenty-seventh Shadrinsky Regiment refused to carry out orders: 10 officers and 250 soldiers were shot; 5 officers and 50 soldiers were brought to Ekaterinburg for trial and then were also shot."[19] Soon thereafter, the Bashkir military units simply went over to the side of the Bolsheviks. At the same time, Omsk had a distrustful and somewhat contemptuous attitude toward the army of the Volga area, referring to it as "the Constituent Assembly supporters" (uchredilovtsy).

The retreating army, holding back the enemy, suffered without warm winter clothing, while Omsk, instead of sending equipment, shells, and cartridges, sent orders to delay action for two weeks. Convinced that written and telegraphed appeals to the general staff were being ignored, General Kappel sent two officers to Omsk, who upon their return announced: "In Omsk they have squandered us away on drink. They don't care about us at all and don't want to have anything to do with us."[20]

It could hardly be expected, with all that was going on among the officers behind the lines—debauchery, lack of discipline or restraint of any kind—that such material could be shaped into decent cadres to serve us as reinforcements at the front. And it was hardly surprising, conditions in Omsk being what they were, that the First Mid-Siberian Corps, which had taken Perm, went without pay for two months. For some officers military duty on the domestic front was like manna from heaven. It saved them from fighting a formidable enemy, the regular Red Army; they enjoyed almost absolute freedom of action; and they held good positions in various military offices.

The military leaders recall the reigning mood. "No one among the officers of the general staff in Samara wanted to head the newly formed detachment, but finally Colonel Kappel offered his services." Further, "there were approximately twenty thousand officers in Kazan, but Kazan's contribution to the front lines was practically nil."[21] "The War Ministry and general staff swelled to monstrous proportions." And the War Ministry "considered itself obligated to protect the interests of seniority in the ranks of the officers' corps, ignoring meritorious action in battle, ability, efficiency, and even acts of heroism."[22]

Lebedev, who together with Kappel and Stepanov had taken part in the liberation of Kazan, once told me that an irremediable and sad aftereffect of the victory was that, along with the liberation of Kazan, there was also the liberation of the Academy of the General Staff, which then automatically took over the management of military affairs in Siberia.

A new attempt at overthrowing Kolchak was in the offing. The offer of the Allies to send a delegation to the conference in the Prinkipo Islands for talks with the Bolsheviks aroused much excitement among the officers behind the lines and at the front alike, because of monarchistic tendencies among them on the one hand and atamanshchina on the other. In some it intensified the tendency to orient toward Japan: to give Sakhalin and Kamchatka, as well as the Chinese-Eastern railroad and fishing concessions, to Japan in return for substantial assistance. The monarchists proposed A. A. Kropotkin, president of the landowners' association, to be monarch.

A coded telegram from Ivanov-Rinov to one of the generals fell into Kolchak's hands, opening a slit in a thitherto closed curtain. Kolchak acquainted Colonel Ward with the contents of the message. Ward recalls:

> We knew about the existence of certain elements, who continued counterrevolutionary work often acting with the knowledge and cooperation of officials in Kolchak's administration. On the first of February, an attempt was made to replace the guard at the residence of the supreme ruler by a false one.
>
> General Knox was at last able to unearth some bits of information. I then commandeered an officer to the Russian headquarters with instructions to inform General Lebedev that we were concerned about the safety of the supreme ruler and that if any kind of evil should be plotted against him, we would hold him [Lebedev] personally responsible.
>
> If any of the officers should plot the assassination of Admiral Kolchak with the aim of proclaiming an absolute monarchy without the sanction of the Russian people, let it be known that anyone who, be it from above or from below, should attempt to deal a blow to the present government and to throw Russia again into anarchy and upheaval will be dealt with as with an enemy.[23]

To what depths the prestige of the government had fallen, when an officer of the English army could allow himself to talk and act as if he were the actual supreme ruler. In any case, his worries that in the event of a change in government Russia would be thrown into a state of "anarchy and upheaval" were unnecessary: in his blindness he failed to see that with his own participation all this had already come true. After all, it was General Knox and Colonel Ward who "gathered the band" for the November 18 overthrow, and it was this band that was still in power.

Relations between military and civilian authorities were further complicated by the spread of atamanshchina. The war against bolshevism was fought on many of Russia's frontiers, but nowhere did atamanshchina reach such enormous proportions as in Siberia. And, of course, to brand it a purely Russian phenomenon evoked by the civil war would be to obscure the true reasons for this particular phenomenon.

The flourishing of atamanshchina in Siberia was preceded by a power struggle among certain members of the Siberian government. Instead of establishing discipline under a common command, they sought support from underground military organizations—support for which they would somehow eventually have to pay. With the cooperation of these military organizations (quite helpful when it came to this kind of inner power play) the Siberian government, as last constituted, came into power. It was also by this means that Admiral Kolchak came into power.

Admiral Kolchak did show some opposition to the Cossack ataman in Chita, but purely on grounds that the latter did not recognize his authority. In general, voluntarily or involuntarily, the supreme ruler made no serious effort to control atamanshchina and thereby contributed to its growth. As a consequence, he himself became a captive and the leaders of these organizations became the masters of the situation.

On December 18, exactly a month after Kolchak had come to power, Vologodsky noted in his diary: "I have been confidentially informed that a group of rightist officers, unhappy with Kolchak's indecisive measures against the leftists, has set as its goal the removal of Kolchak even if it means that force must be used—and heading this group is General Ivanov-Rinov himself."[24] The fact that Kolchak had ordered the arrest of Socialist-Revolutionaries and Social Democrats but did not order them shot was enough for this group to judge him as indecisive.

Regarding the situation in Yeniseisk province, the following information, contained in a telegram from Minister of War Stepanov to General Rozanov, is of interest:

It is very evident that our forces lack even the semblance of normal organization. The operation troops, fewer than 3,500 in all, consist of 32 units under various names, and numbered among them are some officers' companies that have long since been lost at the front and an assortment of detachments—some combined, some separate—and some that are insignificant in size.

It is strange that for the two months that we have been under one higher authority no measures have been taken to correct the purely atamanlike structure of separate detachments that are not held together by any single unifying principle so essential to any army organization.[25]

As a general rule, the detachments had an average of not more than one hundred men each. What they did have was a great deal of authority—as expounded in the instructions issued by the command. The following telegram and command exemplify such directives.

Telegram

From the Staff of the Irkutsk Military Region   March 1919
To Lieutenant General Rozanov
   Krasnoyarsk

The supreme ruler has ordered an immediate and resolute end to the Yeniseisk uprising, not excluding use of the most severe and even cruel measures, not only against the insurrectionists, but against the population that lends them aid. In this respect, follow the example of the Japanese in the Amur oblast, who proclaimed that any village concealing Bolsheviks would be destroyed—a course of action evidently dictated by the urgency to win and the difficult conditions of conducting partisan warfare in a wooded area. In any case severe punishment must be meted out to the villages of Kiyaisk and Koisk. I order: (1) In populated areas reliable inhabitants should be organized to form a guard. (2) In populated areas demand that local authorities themselves arrest or annihilate all agitators and seditionists. (3) The concealment of Bolsheviks, propagandists, and bandits must be met with relentless reprisal unless—in populated areas—the nearest army detachment is duly informed of their [the bandits'] appearance, their departure, and the direction in which they are moving. If such is not the case, a monetary fine should be imposed on the whole village and the elders of the village should be charged with concealment and brought before a court-martial. (4) Conduct surprise raids on points and regions that show signs of unrest. The appearance of an impressive detachment will bring about a change in the mood of the inhabitants. (5) Establish strict discipline and order in your own detachments. Any unlawful activity—looting, raping—will not be tolerated, and anyone caught in an unlawful act should be dealt with then and there. There must be an end to drunkenness. Commanders found in a state of intoxication should be dismissed, tried, and punished. (6) Commanders incapable of holding their detachments to the high standards set should be dismissed and court-martialed for exhibiting slackness in the authority entrusted to them. (7) Local inhabitants should be used for purposes of reconnaissance and liaison. Hostages should be held. If the information thus obtained should prove to be false or is not delivered in time or if there is treachery—the hostages should be executed and the houses that belonged to them should be burned. When making camp for the night and when stopping in villages, detachments should be kept concentrated, occupied buildings should be adapted for defense, guards should be posted covering all directions, in line with the principle of quality and not quantity. Hostages should be taken from neighboring, not occupied villages. All able-bodied men should be held under dependable guard in some large building, and in case of treachery or betrayal shot without mercy.[26]

Commander of the Troops,
Lieutenant General Artemyev

Command   March 27, 1919

To heads of army detachments operating in the region of the uprising.

I command that you use the following strict guidelines:

1. When occupying a settlement that previously has been taken over by bandits, demand that the leaders be handed over to you. If this is not done and you have information that they are present, order that every tenth inhabitant be shot.

2. If the inhabitants of a village should meet the government troops with arms, the village should be burned, the entire adult male population shot, and all property—horses, carts, grain, etc.—confiscated. *Note:* All confiscated goods must be officially registered.

3. If the inhabitants do not by their own volition inform government troops approaching their village of the presence of the enemy in that village and it is ascertained that they had the opportunity to do so, a monetary fine should be imposed on that village, binding the inhabitants by mutual responsibility. No mercy is to be shown in exacting the payment. *Note:* All con-

tributions must be officially registered. The funds are to be submitted to the treasury.

4. When a village has been occupied and an investigation conducted, impose an indemnity on all the inhabitants (binding them by mutual responsibility) who have been found guilty of having given aid, even if indirectly, to the bandits.

5. Notify the inhabitants that if they voluntarily supply the bandits with so much as food, clothing, and so on, to say nothing of military provisions, their villages will be burned and their property confiscated for the use of the treasury. The inhabitants are under obligation to cart away all their property or to destroy it, rather than allow it to fall into the hands of the bandits. For property destroyed in such cases, full compensation will be made either in the form of money or property requisitioned from the bandits.

6. In case of any action directed against government troops on the part of an individual, hostages should be taken from that individual's village and shot. No mercy is to be shown.

7. As a general rule, bear the following in mind: inhabitants who openly or secretly aid the bandits should be regarded as enemies and dealt with accordingly. Their property should be used to compensate for any losses caused by military action to that part of the population which remained loyal to the government.[27]

> Lieutenant General Rozanov
> City of Krasnoyarsk

In a dispute with Kolosov, S. Melgunov stated that Admiral Kolchak did not give such orders. They were, he insisted, creations of the Irkutsk Military Region. He offered as proof the text of the telegram sent to General Artemyev by Minister of War Stepanov:

The supreme ruler has ordered that you be informed: his pressing desire is to end, as quickly as possible, the Yeniseisk uprising, not excluding use of the most severe and even cruel measures, not only against the insurrectionists, but against the population that lends them aid. In this respect follow the example of the Japanese in the Amur oblast, who proclaimed that any village concealing Bolsheviks would be destroyed—a course of action evidently dictated by the urgency to win and the difficult conditions of conducting partisan warfare in a wooded area. In any case severe punishment must be meted out to the villages of Kiyaisk and Koisk.

About the telegram Melgunov states: "It is absolutely clear that the supreme ruler issued a very general directive, which the minister of war took upon himself to make somewhat more concrete and which the local authorities greatly enlarged upon. This is why the supreme ruler issued a counter-directive, forbidding the use of force and cruelty against the civilian population and forbidding also the violation of property rights and the burning of villages as a punishment even though participants of the uprising were harbored in those villages."[28]

Melgunov's statement gives the impression that Kolchak, as soon as he learned about the commands issued by Generals Artemyev and Rozanov, countermanded them. This was not the case. Melgunov has conveniently ignored the time factor, though in other parts of his book the exact dates of these directives are indicated. The directives of Generals Artemyev and Rozanov were issued at the end of March, whereas the order to stop the practice of burning villages was issued by General Dieterichs on October 21. Thus, for seven months all the severe measures were practiced with impunity.

After his arrest in Irkutsk, Admiral Kolchak was brought before an investigative commission. "Admiral Kolchak said that he was aware of the directive issued by General Rozanov and that he did not countermand it in its entirety, but only in part, the part that concerned the shooting of hostages. As for the burning of villages, he said that he knew about isolated instances and that it was quite possible for such things to happen during battles."[29]

If he did not know, he was evidently not informed; but this does not mean that the burning of villages on a wide scale did not take place. General Stepanov's telegram states: " . . . not excluding the most severe, even cruel measures against not only the insurrectionists, but against the population that lends them aid." And he further advises following the "Japanese example as a model for crushing rebellions." The Japanese method consisted of dispensing with trials, shooting on the spot, and burning entire villages. Kolchak's belated order to Rozanov to halt the practice of shooting hostages came when General Rozanov had already had time to shoot a score or two.

In Krasnoyarsk, this practice was forbidden; but that cannot be said of the rest of Yeniseisk province, where, according to General Rozanov's directive, the leaders of the 32 separate detachments in the province wielded a great deal of authority, including the power to destroy entire villages and to shoot on the spot, without benefit of trial—something that Krasilnikov took advantage of on a grand scale. In general, all the *oprichniki* (executioners) used their own discretion in meting out quick justice.

It was not until June 24 that General Rozanov rescinded his orders concerning the shooting of hostages and shooting on the spot, without trial. This was changed to "trial by court-martial," which, under prevailing conditions, actually made very little difference. The shooting would take place in any case, but first there would be the semblance of some formality.

In his desire to prove that Admiral Kolchak was not to blame for what was happening locally, Melgunov, knowingly or unknowingly, has allowed some historical inaccuracies to creep into his book. For example, he writes: "After the shocking events that culminated in the hanging of the mayor of Kansk, Krasilnikov's detachment was sent to the front."[30] This statement could lead the reader to the false conclusion that Krasilnikov had been punished. This is far from true. Stepanov was hanged in early February 1919, and for six months thereafter Krasilnikov continued to do as he pleased in that region. In May, General Artemyev, commander of the Military Region of Irkutsk, sent a telegram to the minister of war in which he stated:

I am submitting one of several reports concerning the activity of Krasilnikov's detachment: "Ataman Krasilnikov idles away his time in debauchery and disorderly behavior, and his officers are similarly occupied; the soldiers take the law into their own hands and conduct searches with the object of looting and raping. The entire population eagerly awaits bolshevism. The situation is critical . . . The reports that come from wherever this detachment has been are all the same. Rozanov is aware of this, but he still expands his detachment with commands of the Fourteenth Division. This is developing into a new kind of atamanshchina."[31]

Further evidence comes from the governor of Yeniseisk province, P. Troitsky, who was appointed to the post after I had resigned. Troitsky, formerly chairman of the regional court, belonged to the right wing of the Kadet Party. In his report to the minister of the interior dated September 26, 1919, he stated:

After the capture of Taseev and Troitsko-Zavodsky by Rozanov's detachment, the people of these regions, having declared themselves loyal, were caught in a critical situation: the military command did not take into account that only the loyal inhabitants remained and continued to shoot and to hang. For example, one of those who was executed in Taseev was the village elder, who happened to be one of the most loyal of all the inhabitants in that village and who had, according to the report of the head of the local administration, performed a number of services for the authorities.

Houses are burned indiscriminately—row after row—leaving many of the loyal inhabitants completely ruined. No consideration at all is shown to the inhabitants. Whatever seems desirable to any of the commanders or even to their soldiers, they simply appropriate: carts, products, clothing, and so on. The ranking officers of Krasilnikov's detachment care not a whit about the measures they use; there is not one elder or member of a district zemstvo who has not been beaten by a whip or by a ramrod.

The loyal inhabitants do sentry and guard duty and at the same time find themselves caught between the two sides: the Reds deprive them of the opportunity to work and the government troops deprive them of their possessions. The least intimation that it might be desirable to establish some degree of lawful procedure—demands presented in some lawful form, some kind of accounting or reckoning for the demands, regular requisitions for carts, and so on—is an offense punishable even by death. Terror in its worst form reigns in this region.

Thus the inhabitants do not see the government troops bringing peace and order, nor do they see any distinction between the Reds and the loyalists. General Rozanov's appeal attracted the attention of some who were wavering, but the first party of 30 volunteers to come over to the government side was shot. The others stayed with the Reds. The burning of villages leaves thousands homeless, and they all go over to the Reds.

All orders to cease burning villages, to forbid requisitioning and the use of force, are meaningless. When the village of Shaplenka was pillaged by Patrikeev's detachment and the matter was brought to the attention of the authorities, the authorities handed the correspondence to Patrikeev himself, who then declared that he would burn down the village for having reported him. Behavior of this kind on the part of the detachments may lead to a peasant uprising and, naturally, it nourishes and supports the Reds.

The activity of Krasilnikov's detachment in the district of Kansk was such that there is no one who can attest to its positive side. The negative side (self-rule, arbitrariness, looting, debauchery, raping, burning of settlements, and senseless killings), however, is all here before us, and it could, of course, have no other effect than to strengthen the ranks of the Reds.[32]

In the face of such reports, coming as they did from officials of the regions affected, the government obviously had a clear picture of the chaotic state of affairs behind the lines, but it chose to overlook them and to undertake no measures to halt the activities of the offenders. On the contrary, they were rewarded.

For some reason Melgunov does not mention the following facts in his book *Tragediia Admirala Kolchaka*. Captain First Class Fedorovich, commander of the military region in Yeniseisk province before Rozanov, was rewarded for his services by promotion to the rank of admiral and placed in command of the Vladivostok fleet. He had distinguished himself by having imposed a fine of 500 rubles on the governor for the right to bear arms and by having been instrumental in provoking the so-called Minusinsk peasant rebellion. General Rozanov, formerly subordinate to the commander of the district, was appointed viceregent of the Far East. Ataman Krasilnikov, before being sent to the front, was promoted from the rank of colonel to that of general—and this in the face of his aforementioned activities.

Who was to blame for all this? First and foremost, the central authorities. The government as a whole, including Kolchak, did not prove itself capable of governing the country. In order to avoid responsibility, general directives were issued that led to and made possible all the subsequent local creativity.

No one, from the top of the ladder on down, bothered to observe the law. Generals Artemyev and Rozanov exercised wide license in breaking the existing military laws and substituting for them their own brand of martial rule. General Rozanov had not even been officially appointed by the government as head of the military region, but had been co-opted by General Artemyev—which Governor Troitsky had occasion to remind him. There was no need to observe formality because everything could be settled quite cozily en famille. No one, beginning with the highest military command in Omsk, reflected seriously about what effect the deplorable behavior of the army detachments would have on the attitude of the population toward the government that allowed it—and, more particularly, what reaction martial rule would have on the soldiers newly mobilized from the very areas where it was practiced.

In its naïvete, the government clung to the assurance that the population was, for some unknown reason, obliged to support it. But as violations of civil rights grew more frequent, so grew opposition to the government. Even those who had at first enthusiastically welcomed the Provisional Siberian Government now joined the opposition.

Workers began to strike. The Consumers' Cooperative, which had contributed a great deal of money and many workers toward organizing the uprising against the Bolsheviks, declared at its August 20–25 convention in Omsk in favor of supporting the government on condition that the government would adhere to the principles of democracy.

In the villages, peasants passed resolutions to the effect that until the All-Russian Constituent Assembly was called, no government or zemstvo taxes would be paid. Some villages added to this their refusal to furnish military recruits. Here is an example of the general feeling: "The Zersko-Kureevsk District Congress of September 8, 1918, has resolved, according to the report of Informer-Instructor D. Sorokin, to welcome the Provisional Siberian Government. On the other hand, we enjoin the Provisional Siberian Government to keep sharp surveillance over its officials so that they do not commit arbitrary acts such as whippings, and, in some cases, shootings—as have been experienced in our oblast at the hands of a passing detachment."[33] But the peasants' entreaties did not deliver them from these evils; on the contrary, they often brought severe reprisals.

Arbitrariness on the part of the local military authorities had begun even before Kolchak came to power. The Siberian government had, at first, tried to control it; but with the appointment of Ivanov-Rinov, the staff officers fastened on their epaulets and loosened their self-discipline.

If I remember correctly, the idea of sending small detachments to the villages to demonstrate the authority of the regime and to exact delinquent taxes from the peasants belongs to Minister of Finance Mikhailov. The military authorities seized upon this idea because officers had no wish to go to the front.

In mid-September 1918, a peasant uprising in the Slavgorod district in the Altai region was suppressed with excessive cruelty, an action completely discrediting the authority of the Siberian government and laying the foundation for the forming of a whole series of partisan detachments in the Altai region.

Because Yeniseisk province played one of the more prominent roles in the history of the partisan movement, it is essential to discuss in detail the relations of its peasants to the regime on the eve of the approaching storms.

In June 1918, the peasants of the Minusinsk district, one of the granaries of Siberia, threw off the Bolshevik yoke without using arms, arrested all the members of the soviet, and delivered them to Krasnoyarsk into my custody. But even by early September, there were indications of a change in the mood of the peasantry due to the unseemly behavior of the military detachments there. On September 10, as I reported to Chairman of the Council of Ministers Vologodsky on the political situation in the province, I drew his attention to this and expressed the fear that the tactless actions of separate military detachments could cause an eruption of peasant indignation, with all the possible consequences. My talks on this subject with the head of the military region, Fedorovich, had brought no results. Vologodsky, Guins, and Novikov had a long talk with Fedorovich, but nothing positive came of it, and the military detachments continued their debauchery. Vologodsky noted in his diary: "The commissar of the province, P. Ozernykh, and his aide, P. Dotsenko, came to me with their reports. Their understanding of the economic situation in the province and the mood of the people produced a good impression. There was a lengthy talk with Naval Officer Fedorovich, head of the local garrison, concerning the dividing line between his duties and those of the commissar of the province. Evidently there is some friction, but everything is being handled in the proper manner."[34]

Vologodsky failed to record in his diary that he recommended that I somehow make an effort to better my relations with Fedorovich. To this I had replied: "How we personally feel toward one another is not the point; the point is that Fedorovich looks the other way as far as the disgraceful conduct of the various small detachments under his command is concerned; moreover, there is no real need to send these detachments to the villages at all. I fear that this activity may cause a spontaneous upheaval among the peasants. In that case, the question, with all its implications, would be: Would the government be able to uphold its authority and to calm the stormy waters?"

Exactly two months later, on November 11, 1918, I received a telegram from the commissar of the Minusinsk district: "In the village of Dubensk, on Saturday, November 9, there was an armed attack on a detachment composed of militiamen, Cossacks, and infantrymen, a total of 40 men. At the same time when the commander of the militiamen was conducting an investigation in the village of Dubensk, about 100 armed peasants from neighboring villages began to encircle the village. During the ensuing conflict 1 Cossack and 1 militiaman were killed, and 12 men disappeared without a trace. The remainder of the detachment returned to the city."[35]

Several things were unclear to me about this telegram: in the first place, what kind of investigation was the commander of the militia conducting? Second, why was he accompanied by a detachment of 40 men? Third, what prompted the peasants of Dubensk to ask for help from the neighboring villages?

One thing was clear—an explosion had occurred. The people's resentment had burst into the open, and something had to be done. I offered to go there, taking advantage of my position as a former member of the Provincial Committee of the Soviet of Peasants' Deputies, to try to smooth over the incident without any further bloodshed. Yeniseisk province had already been declared under martial law by an arbitrary order of the head of the military region.

My proposal was rejected because Fedorovich decided that the "rebels" must be taught a lesson. He did not, however, have a sufficient number of detachments at his disposal to do this. Thus he asked for help first from the Czechs and then from the Italians, and was turned down by both because they refused to take part in a punitive expedition. He had to resort to calling detachments from Irkutsk.

Within a week, the district commissar informed me that to the best of his knowledge the number of insurrectionists had reached over six thousand. I submitted my report to the minister of the interior on November 16 and expressed my own opinion about these events.

> The figure quoted should be taken with a grain of salt because there is no reason to think that the peasantry of Minusinsk district, which has contributed more than five thousand volunteers to help overthrow Soviet rule, should suddenly become impregnated with bolshevik ideas and go over to the Bolshevik side in such great numbers.
>
> There is no doubt that Bolshevik agents are at the head of the movement, but there is equally no doubt in my mind that the underlying reasons for the uprisings should be sought elsewhere than in the bolshevism of the peasants of Minusinsk district.
>
> In general, with the transfer of power in the province to the head of the garrison there has been a noticeable trend to the left and a mood of opposition among the people—even in those layers of society that had with such enthusiasm helped to overthrow Soviet role and to support that of the Siberian Provisional Government.[36]
>
> Acting Commissar of Yeniseisk Province
> Dotsenko

My reservations concerning the number of insurrectionists were mistaken. According to additional information received, the rebellion spread like a brush fire, pulling into its orbit more and more of the populated areas. Within ten days, the peasant army had grown to an incredible figure of ten thousand men.

Excerpts from the report to the staff of the Irkutsk Military Region from the leader of the punitive expedition characterize this "army"— how it was armed and what its goals were.

Approximately ten thousand insurrectionists in all were gathered against the city. Of them only two thousand were armed; their weapons included various kinds of rifles, shotguns, and revolvers of all makes—from ancient good-for-nothing ones to the modern Nagan, Browning, and Colt. The main body advanced on the city armed with axes, knives, pitchforks, or simply sticks specially equipped for the purpose with metal tips.

The detachments that had risen in revolt were calling upon the peasants to help them throw off the Cossack yoke, to hold the Eighth Peasant Congress, which, according to the resolution of the Seventh Congress, would decide whether or not to supply recruits and whether or not to pay taxes. Following these demands came appeals and proclamations, some of which demanded occupying the city of Minusinsk, arresting the government authorities, and establishing a peasant administration.

One of the factors contributing to the wrath against the Cossacks was the unlawful activity of an ataman at Karatuz who had tolerated the law of the fist too often in dealing with the peasants.

According to the report of the chairman of the military administration, resolutions were issued among Cossack circles concerning the unfitness of the ataman and the need to remove him from leadership, and these resolutions were reported by them to higher authorities. Nevertheless, no action was taken.

Unfortunately, the excessive cruelty of the Cossacks in suppressing rebellions and the many instances of unlawful practices—which, in spite of my repeated orders and verbal instructions to the officers, were still allowed—added fuel to the already flaming indignation.

From all the known facts of the investigation and subsequent information, it may be concluded that the present uprising is in the general order of peasant revolts, practically without any political coloring, and there is no reason to suppose that it was instigated by external forces and that it was organized beforehand.

There were no leaders from the intelligentsia in the movement.[37]

The Minusinsk district commissar, in a report personally presented to me, gave a more detailed account of the events leading to the peasant revolt. In early November, the village of Dubensk was visited by a small detachment, ostensibly for the purpose of demonstrating the authority of the regime. Members of the detachment had been drinking heavily, and they sent for the village elder to demand that the village women be brought to them. Receiving a negative answer, the commanding officer gave orders that the village elder be whipped. Such an outrage by the detachment aroused the indignation of the peasants who killed the commander, seven Cossacks, and one militiaman.

The peasants of course expected a reprisal and therefore arranged for help from the neighboring villages. The arrival on November 9 of a detachment of 40 men to conduct an investigation signaled the peasants to rise up armed in self-defense. As a consequence of the irresponsible acts of a handful of drunken men—men in possession of authority—hundreds of lives on each side were sacrificed unnecessarily. And Yeniseisk province was, from that moment on, lost to the government.

The distinguishing feature of this particular movement was its rapid growth. It reached its apogee on November 20, when this mass of poorly armed men advanced on the city of Minusinsk, where they were met with artillery and machine-gun fire. After its defeat, this army within a matter of days melted into oblivion. The workers of nearby copper mines did not support the peasants.

7

The Collapse of Kolchak's Government

At a time when the personal safety of the supreme ruler was wholly dependent on the presence of English troops, there could hardly be talk about normal functions of the government.

How did P. Vologodsky, as chairman of the Council of Ministers, react to his conversation with the head of the garrison, Katanaev, when the latter announced: "I am not guided by any laws or decrees made by the government, but act exclusively on my own impulses as an honest Russian officer"? He entered the episode in his diary and did nothing to curtail Katanaev's practice of self-rule. And Kolchak himself was not overconcerned about upholding the laws.

General A. P. Budberg reports that "most of the decisions made in Omsk were in violation of the constitution—with the approval of I. Mikhailov and Kolchak."[1] And Guins confirms the description: "The Council of the Supreme Ruler turned out decisions like hotcakes made of poor quality flour. Indeed, the decisions that came out of there were astonishing in their ill-advisedness and unexpectedness. On March 31 an order was signed concerning the appointments of Governors-General Rozanov and M. S. Artemyev to the provinces of Yeniseisk and Irkutsk; furthermore, they were guaranteed rights listed in the Siberian government's martial law that had since been revoked."[2]

In early March 1919, it became apparent that there was a disagreement among the ministers. Two groups had formed: eight people from Mikhailov's staff and seven from another demanded changes. Their demands were upheld by the Political Bloc.

Minister of War Stepanov was blamed for having allowed himself to become bogged down in bureaucracy, for having been incapable of organizing the work behind the lines to correspond to the needs of the front, for having been petty and a fault-finder to a degree that created impossible working relations with the civilian authorities, and, moreover, for having demonstrated neither strength of will nor effectiveness of action in the problem of dealing with the arbitrary and unseemly behavior of certain army units and army ranks behind the lines.

The minister of justice was blamed for not having had the courage and firmness needed for dealing with the army commanders and for having overlooked the unlawful actions of army officials.

The minister of supplies was accused of having made commercial deals of a questionable nature.

Also under fire were the railroad officials for their brazen bribe-taking.[3]

Vologodsky suggested that Kolchak replace War Minister Stepanov, who had failed to keep the front lines adequately supplied. Kolchak resolutely turned down the idea of a replacement, asking "How can I demand of Stepanov that he get under control what has become an almost elemental phenomenon, this deterioration to the point of hooliganism among the officers?"[4]

In January 1919 a military council was held in the city of Chelyabinsk to discuss the preparation of an offensive. A. I. Dutov and Gaida proposed that the troops move to join General A. I. Denikin. The chief of the high command, D. A. Lebedev, and Kolchak were both in favor of marching north: Perm to Vyatka to Moscow. (Actually, this was the English plan.)

Lebedev was afraid that joining Denikin would raise the question of supremacy; Kolchak even let slip a phrase to the effect that everything would resolve itself—depending on who reached Moscow first. Is this not an example of dividing the skin of the bear who is still lumbering around in the dense taiga?

Regardless of the sad state of affairs behind the lines and the absence of proper supplies, "orders have come from the quarters of the commander-in-chief to march, even though there are no reserves."[5] Petrov notes: "The commanders of corps were not initiated into the plan of operation." The army occupied Ufa, but could proceed no farther in the absence of reserves. "They began the march in sheepskin coats and valenki [felt boots], and in April they found themselves without greatcoats and boots."[6]

The offensive continued from March 13 to April 29, 1919. At first it was quite successful, but because there were no reinforcements the momentum was lost. This was also the time of year when the roads were bad, which was, of course, a big disadvantage for cavalry action. The units that had been at the front all winter were the ones that gained the victories in the spring. Those that were far behind the lines, from Irtysh to the Pacific Ocean, hardly took any part in that offensive. Consequently, such mutterings were heard in the active army as, "that means we will be left without help until the last one of us is killed."[7]

The retreat began. General Kappel asked for permission to make a break in the front and go behind the enemy lines, but permission was not granted because of the fear that "he will get behind the Bolshevik lines, take Moscow, form a Kappel government there—and won't even let us in."[8]

"In the strictly military sense, the spring operations were not subject to any guidelines; there was no definite, solid plan of action. Atamanshchina had not yet outlived itself, even in the Army." Petrov remarks further, "With conditions behind the lines [on the Ufa front] being in such an unhealthy state, no effective support can be given the retreating front. With each passing day the men in the front lines lose hope of getting help, faith in themselves, and belief in victory."[9]

The Omsk government, on the recommendation of General Knox, replaced Commander of the Army General M. V. Khanzhyn with General Sakharov. At the end of May, the army at the Ufa front continued its retreat. Between it and General Pepelyaev's army, which had advanced far ahead, was a vast stretch of unprotected territory into which large forces of the Red Army poured. General Pepelyaev's proposal to save the situation by quickly bringing in the cavalry met with a cold reception by the high command in spite of the fact that General Sakharov had a huge cavalry division behind the lines. General Lebedev, in the office of the commander-in-chief, rejected this advice and instead ordered the Siberian Army to retreat beyond Perm, when it had an advantage of 300 versts.

On May 26, Gaida sent a telegram to Omsk "demanding the removal of General Lebedev because his actions had created a catastrophic situation along the entire front. The forced retreat of its southern army, with hardly a battle fought, was disorderly, and the Siberian Army suffered a serious drop in morale. In some units, and even within the command staff, there became apparent among the men a reluctance to fight and a desire to return to their homes in Siberia."[10]

Gaida's telegram was, in fact, to a certain extent, born of necessity and intended to serve as a lightning rod because General Pepelyaev's order to retreat had caused great indignation among the Siberians. "It was proposed that General Pepelyaev send one or two divisions to Omsk to disperse the quarters of the commander-in-chief and to take power into his own hands."[11]

No matter how complicated the situation was at the front, Omsk continued its carefree existence. Minister Serebrennikov observed: "A civil service brand of military optimism reigned in Omsk amid the negligence and inaction of the local military authorities. The trade-industrial circles were interested mainly in contracts and not in supporting Kolchak."[12] "The Kolchak administration was not popular [not only among the trade-industrial circles but] among the masses of the city's population."[13] And who set out for Ekaterinburg to talk over with General Gaida the subject of his telegram? None other than General Knox. General M. K. Dieterichs, moreover, called for the army to fight under a new slogan: For the Christian faith.

Despite this situation, General Lebedev continued in his post as head of the quarters of the commander-in-chief, but on June 20, 1919, General Gaida's resignation was accepted. Vologodsky left for a rest, but even then he was not to have any peace. On July 31 he received a letter from Minister of Internal Affairs V. Gattenberg, informing him that "our army is in the final stages of total collapse. We are abandoning our positions; we have lost Perm, Ekaterinburg, Zlatoust. Political intrigues continue. The government has no contact with the people."[14]

At a meeting of the Council of Ministers in early February, it had been reported that a kind of laxity among the Cossacks may be observed of late—an unwillingness to go to the front and a tendency to cling to their own villages. This, however, did not stop Kolchak from issuing an order on July 28 to the effect that "all demands of Ivanov-Rinov should be given priority: funds, equipment, and provisions for the organization of a Cossack corps."[15]

Kolchak knew about Ivanov-Rinov's connection with the illegal military organization aiming at his removal. Kolchak also recognized Ivanov-Rinov's role in that organization. By giving the order to release unrestricted sums of money for the organization of a Cossack corps, he probably wished to buy himself off and gain time in order to free himself from dependence on the illegal military organization. Kolchak also ordered the formation of a detachment of marines to serve as his personal guard.

General Ivanov-Rinov characterized the overall situation at the time for a representative of the Czech newspaper *Narodnye listi*: "The rural population does not support Admiral Kolchak, hundreds of Russian officers are hiding in staffs that are of no use to anyone, the supreme ruler must step down in favor of a colleague in whom the people have trust, all the ministers should be placed on trial; it is essential to free society from the rudeness and demoralization of various counterintelligence organizations and the new regiments—formed for the sole purpose of providing soft positions for the officers—both of which should be abolished, etc. . . ."[16]

Regardless of the serious situation at the front, Commander of the Western Army General Sakharov was occupied by other matters: he was more interested in political intrigues. "I dispatched to the city of Omsk a certain person bearing a special report, which would bring to the attention of the supreme ruler the opinion of the Army [not specifying which army, since the Siberians were against the Treaty of Brest-Litovsk] that it would be to our great advantage to enter into direct negotiations with German circles, and in this way we could obtain real cooperation and help in our holy war."[17]

In August an attempt was made to save the situation by switching to an offensive position, but coordination was lacking, and the venture was unsuccessful. On August 19 General Dieterichs' chief of staff removed Ivanov-Rinov from command of the corps for not having executed an operational command calling for the corps to break through the Red lines from the rear. "Ivanov-Rinov's corps, having won a victory in the Kurgan region, stopped to rest instead of pursuing the fleeing Soviet Army behind its lines. On August 24 Kolchak countermanded Dieterichs' order, stating as his motivation: 'Ivanov-Rinov is quite capable of performing light assignments; it is only the heavy assignments that he is incapable of performing.'"[18] He did not, of course, mention who it was who gave Ivanov-Rinov the heavy assignments.

The authoritative testimony of the former minister of war, General Budberg, offers a comprehensive look at the political and military situation of the period: "What was surprising was how reactionary most of the members of the Council of Ministers were, how hostile they were to all social organizations and how fearful of their criticism. Counterintelligence engages in the fabrication of all kinds of 'plots' so as to receive additional large funds for uncontrolled spending."[19]

Further, "uprisings behind the lines are to a great extent caused not by bolshevism, but because the local authorities behave in such a manner as to incite the hatred of the people. The unbalanced element among the officers has done a great deal to alienate the people."[20]

On the condition of the army, Budberg writes: "The number of companies that appears in the military records exceeds approximately by double the actual number."[21] And again, "The winter and spring were lost for the purpose of creating a real, durable army and a sensible, healthy government structure." Budberg also remarks: "Organizations that were small, but strong in spirit and firmly bound together by the principles of the struggle, were drowned in the sea of subsequent formations. The army swelled to eight hundred thousand companies with but seventy or eighty thousand bayonets spread among them!"[22]

The high command was singularly lacking in brilliance. This, too, contributed to the collapse of the army. "The plundering of the civilian population by soldiers became matter of course. Gradually being extinguished are the last remnants of self-sacrifice and heroism in the service of an ideal, with which the Siberian White movement began and without which victory is impossible."[23]

As uncertainty about the future increased, so, in the same measure, did the talk about removing Kolchak. As early as May 28, Vologodsky had been informed that officers in the Cossack troops were planning to remove Kolchak forcibly from his post as supreme ruler. On August 27 an officer presented himself at Vologodsky's office and announced, "I bring you a message from a secret organization, whose goal is to launch a more persistent and energetic type of warfare against the Bolsheviks than has been the case under the Kolchak administration. If we are to have any success in this, our organization realizes that certain ministers must be replaced by a stronger willed, more resolute, more energetic individual. To accomplish these changes as painlessly as possible, our organization, honoring your patriotism and political integrity, offers you the opportunity to resign your post within three days."[24]

V. Pepelyaev adds: "The Political Bloc informed Kolchak that one of the main reasons for the serious situation observed at the front and behind the lines is the lack of firm and systematic execution of the principles of rights and order as set forth in the programs and declarations of the government, and that deviations from these principles are fast reducing them to complete negation."[25]

In mid-February 1919, at a meeting of the Council of Ministers, the question of reorganizing the government had been raised. The talks continued into mid-August with little or no results. Several ministers were replaced, but a general reorganization did not materialize.

In August several substantial changes were made: on August 10 General Dieterichs replaced General Lebedev as chief of staff; on August 13 Vologodsky asked Sukin and Mikhailov to hand in their resignations because of the public indignation that they had brought upon themselves. This they did without any outward signs of protest.[26] Those who had been relieved of their posts evidently considered the situation hopeless in any case and felt that it was time to quit Omsk.

In September Kolchak received the representatives of the Economic Council; he had created this body but had lately begun to look upon it as a "sovdep" (soviet of deputies), subject to dismissal. The following statement appears in the notes of this semipublic institution: "The activity of the government is not subject to any definite program; it is haphazard and often depends on secret irresponsible influences. Lately the direction that some of the departments have taken is in character contrary to the principles of lawfulness and of people's rights . . . Military authorities interfere in the sphere of civilian rule, disregarding the law and the elementary rights of people. The resort to corporal punishment is so widespread that the people are beginning to question which is better, to be ruled by the existing authority or by the Bolsheviks."[27]

The delegates proposed the creation of a government council, which would have the rights (1) to examine the budget; (2) to exercise control over the activities of the departments; (3) to interrogate department heads, and so on. In other words, the aspiration to create a more responsible government did exist. Kolchak, however, was not open to suggestions. He was wallowing in hopelessness.

According to Guins, Kolchak commented: "The ideal, of course, would be to carry out the principles of legality, but how is this to be done when there are no honest people? Noninterference from the military authorities, a strong council—all well and good, but actually there is no way to subject all the atamans to a central authority, and to change ministers is useless because there are no suitable replacements."[28]

The picture is clear: everything was falling apart at the seams, but nothing could be done about it. The dash of daring and the willpower needed were simply not there. Admiral Kolchak defined his views on governing more explicitly in his talk with Guins during the journey to Tobolsk.

As commander-in-chief, I have set myself a military goal: to crush the Red Army. I do not concern myself with reforms. The answer is not in the laws, but in people. We are building with poor quality material. Everything is in a state of decay. I am amazed at how much corruption there is everywhere. How can anything be accomplished under conditions such as these, surrounded as we are by thievery, cowardice, and stupidity? And the ministers—even those in whose integrity I believe— do not satisfy me as officials.

A civil war must of necessity be merciless. I order the commanders to shoot all captured communists. Now we can depend only on our bayonets. I am the commander-in-chief and therefore responsible for everything. That is how it should be according to martial law. There is nothing I can do now to change this order of things. It is my firm belief that in an interim war, martial law is the only system of power that *can* be effective.[29]

Against the background of collapse at the center, the army's unraveling proceeded apace. The Minusinsk and Slavgorod uprisings had been but the distant rumblings of an approaching storm. Drunk with power, the Omsk intriguers paid no heed to these danger signals. In view of the serious deviations of the regime from democratic principles in governing the country, the public and economic organizations in the rest of the country assumed a watch-and-wait attitude. At the cooperatives' conventions a resolution had already been passed to support the government, but only up to a certain point. At rural gatherings voices were being raised against paying taxes and against contributing military recruits until such time as the Constituent Assembly would be convened. Behind the lines there were indications of a rift between the army and the civilian population. The Allies were interested in holding back the German advance, but not in holding back the Bolshevik movement.

The idea of re-establishing a second front now, after the signing of the armistice with Germany, was out of the question. The Allies set about putting Russia's internal affairs into order. It was with their active cooperation that Admiral Kolchak, taking advantage of the monarchist leanings of some of the officers, had come to power, and the Council of Ministers had proclaimed him the supreme ruler and the supreme commander-in-chief. Admiral Kolchak decided to build an all-Russian regime with the manpower and natural resources of Siberia, a country entirely unfamiliar to him. Furthermore, his experiences as a naval officer could be of little service to him in organizing land forces. In order to fill this gap, he appointed Colonel Lebedev as chief of staff of the commander-in-chief. "Colonel D. A. Lebedev, sent by Gen. M. V. Alekseev to Siberia, appeared in Omsk and played a prominent role in the November overthrow. And then, incomprehensibly enough, since he had had no command experience, *he* soon became chief of staff of the supreme commander-in-chief. This kind of leadership could, of course, have no other than a detrimental effect on the operations of the army."[30]

In January 1919 England's representative, General Knox, informed Admiral Kolchak that neither England nor Canada had any intention of sending troops to the Urals. At the same time, the French battalion at the front refused to follow the orders of General P. T. Janin. With the establishment of one-man rule in the person of Admiral Kolchak, the Czech units saw no reason for their further presence at the front. The proposal of the Allies in February 1919 to send a delegation to the Prinkipo Islands for negotiations with the Bolsheviks split the officers into even more factions and strengthened pro-Japanese leanings.

The echelons sent as reinforcements to the front were, for the most part, depleted by almost 90 percent by the time they reached Chelyabinsk. The newly recruited soldiers, once they had been armed and outfitted, had a way of disappearing en route to their assigned destinations. At a critical moment on the western front, the Forty-sixth Regiment in Tomsk refused to go to the front, as did the Twelfth and Thirteenth Regiments at Taiga Station. On August 3, 1919, there was an uprising within the Krasnoyarsk garrison, and on August 25 there was an explosion in the building that housed Kolchak's guard.

General Dieterichs assumed the post of commander of quarters of the commander-in-chief and appealed to the army to carry on the struggle in the name of the Christian faith. Similar slogans disclosed the complete absence of any political instinct—how was it possible otherwise to ignore the fact that a large percentage of the population of Siberia was composed of non-Russians, practicing a variety of religions? In the regions nearest the action the population was mixed: Russians, Bashkirs, Tatars, Kazakhs, Chuvashi, Votyaks, and others. In Samara and Simbirsk provinces, the matter of land was of great significance. In some regions occupied by the Western Army, zealous officers were determinedly restoring former privileges to the landowners. This bit of political shortsightedness played, of course, right into the hands of the Soviets.

In January 1919 there were disorders in the ranks of the Fourth Soviet Army, commanded by Frunze. The Bolsheviks, however, taking advantage of the mistakes of their enemy, quickly recovered by spreading propaganda, drawing attention mainly to the fact that Omsk was under control of the generals. The result was that in the first three months of 1919, the Red Army grew by 139,600 men. This was a big step forward, considering that until then there had only been 80,000 men in the Ufa-Ekaterinburg regions.

As for the size of the Siberian Army, there are no accurate data available. General Sakharov mentions an army of five hundred thousand in his book, but the onetime minister of war, General Budberg, challenges this figure: according to information he obtained from the records of the Procurement Office, there were always twice as many mouths as there were actual bayonets. But even if the estimate were a modest two hundred thousand, the question remains how many were at the front and how many occupied positions behind the lines. The operative summary shows that the army conducting the attack at the front was not very large. For instance, General Pepelyaev's army, which took Perm, was only eleven thousand strong. This army, threadbare in December's freezing weather, lacking in medical supplies, but high in morale, somehow managed to move forward. But in the spring and summer, never having received adequate reinforcements or equipment or arms, the Western Army lost its spirit.

General Sakharov, in his report to Dieterichs, said, "It was as if it were done intentionally; not even one wagonload of warm clothing was sent to us, no reinforcements, no officers, and even bread and other provender were delivered irregularly, although the storehouses held huge amounts of supplies. It is really too bad, but the army, beginning with the soldier and ending with the commander, does not have faith in the ability of the present government to remedy the situation. The army has no confidence in the government. Under present conditions the hope of victory is fading."[31]

In a typical response, General Sakharov naturally laid the blame for all this on the Socialist-Revolutionaries, who had demoralized the country. It is not clear how he reached this conclusion. Evidently he lumped everything together into one heap: horses, men, whatever. What did the Socialist-Revolutionaries have to do with the failure of the Procurement Office to send arms, bread, and clothing to the front? At the head of the Procurement Office and headquarters stood not the Socialist-Revolutionaries, but the generals, kindred to him in spirit, but exhibiting a deplorable incapacity for leadership in a civil war.

The reasons for the defeat of the Western Army were pointed out in a report presented to Kolchak by General Gaida as early as May 1919.

> One of the reasons for the collapse of the Western Army was the policy and propaganda of the staff, impregnated by an anti-democratic spirit and kindling discord among the various nationalities. The army's advance was suddenly transformed

into a hasty and rather disorderly retreat. This put a stop to the advance of the Siberian Army. And all the strategic advantages of initial success in battle came to nothing.

Within the Western Army some very serious defects were discovered. First of all, it became apparent that the supply system was not capable of the tasks involved with an advance. Furthermore, the retreat was accompanied by the demoralization of the troops. Some units, after killing the command staff, surrendered to the enemy.[32]

In Omsk military circles and among Kolchak's associates, no one disputed, in essence, the analysis of failure contained in the report; but it was waved aside because of the concluding remarks, which were considered tendentious: "The coincidence of our failures at the front, internal turmoil, and public dissatisfaction points to the presence of a common denominator that is the cause of all this. It might be well to seek it in the methods used in governing the country."[33]

No one in Omsk could swallow this bitter pill, and a search began for some excuse to ignore the report. The report had been presented to Kolchak by General Gaida; first it had been approved by the entire staff of the First Army, including General Pepelyaev. But the author turned out to be a Socialist-Revolutionary, Capt. N. Kalashnikov, head of the Information Bureau of the Siberian Army staff! Here was reason enough to discount the report as undeserving of any particular attention.

Not having received a positive response, General Gaida sent a telegram addressed to Vologodsky, chairman of the Council of Ministers, demanding that General Lebedev be removed from office. The staff of the supreme commander-in-chief saw sedition in this, and Admiral Kolchak appointed a special commission of three generals to conduct an investigation. The commission concluded that General Gaida was an able and popular military leader. On the other hand, the strategic and administrative work produced by the quarters of the commander-in-chief was found to be not satisfactory. The orders issued were often absurd and did not correspond to the situation at the front. The form of General Gaida's protest was found to be unacceptable, however, because it did not conform to military discipline: Gaida had sent the telegram to Vologodsky, and not to Admiral Kolchak. The minister of war, General Budberg, was also of the opinion that General Gaida was right in blaming General Lebedev and the staff for issuing orders that were inept and harmful to the situation at the front. Soon thereafter, Lebedev was removed from his post as chief of staff, and Gaida retired.

Regardless of Generals Budberg and Dieterichs' oft-repeated proposal to begin arming the fortifications behind the lines, Admiral Kolchak remained opposed to this measure. Consequently, when the critical moment came, the retreating army found itself without a base to hold on to. The government began a hasty and disorganized evacuation of the city of Omsk.

In the face of this flight from Omsk, a secret military Cossack organization decided to engage in some independent revolutionary activity by staging a "routine" overthrow. In Ishim this unlawful group called a conference of all leaders of its members who happened to be on hand. The measures that should be taken to halt Kolchak's retreating army were discussed at this conference. The plan was to gain a stronghold in the region of the Siberian Cossack troops, untouched as yet by Bolshevik propaganda. It was decided that the only way to achieve success was through an overthrow. The post of dictator was first offered to General Ivanov-Rinov, who declined. Next it was offered to General Volkov, who also declined, giving as the reason his complete depression. It was then offered to a prominent member of the military organization and commander of the Petropavlovsk Regiment, who accepted. A plan was formed for the overthrow and arrest of the commander-in-chief of the army, General Sakharov. But the candidate for the dictatorship delayed and withdrew from participation in the overthrow.

The battles that took place in mid-October 1919, to gain crossings over the Tobol and Ishim rivers, were actually the last fought against the Red Army. After that, the retreating army rapidly collapsed. General Puchkov observed that "the highest military command has temporarily let the leadership slip from its hands."[34]

The defense of Omsk was General Sakharov's responsibility, but he made no moves in that direction, and on November 14 he left the city without a battle. The Omsk garrison, its military education not yet completed, was taken by surprise. The Red Army captured 40,000 soldiers, 10,000 officers, 40 cannons, 897 machine guns, 3,000 wagons, 19 million cartridges, and almost unbelievable amounts of other military supplies and provisions. Moreover, 50,000 head of cattle remained in the region. The Procurement Office that had failed to send adequate supplies to the front now left everything to the Red Army.

What defies understanding is that an army with ten thousand officers in the Omsk garrison should need additional military education in order to defend the city. This kind of reasoning was typical of the officers behind the lines. When in spring 1918 we had organized detachments for the struggle against the Bolsheviks, all we asked of the participants was that they be able to handle arms and that they desire to fight for the creation of a democratic form of government. No special military training was required.

On November 18, 1919, there was an attempted uprising in Vladi- vostok of the Siberian oblast government, with General Gaida partici- pating. This uprising was quelled by General Rozanov's troops, with the cooperation of the Japanese. On December 6 the chief of division seized Novonikolaevsk and demanded that Kolchak convoke the Sibe- rian Constituent Assembly. General S. N. Voitsekhovsky, with the help of a Polish division, put down this uprising. The chief of division and 32 officers faced a firing squad.

On December 7 General Pepelyaev sent Kolchak a telegram:

> I implore you for the last time to order the immediate convoca- tion of the Siberian Constituent Assembly so that the people can take into their own hands the organization of Siberia and choose a Siberian government. We act solely in the name of the defense of our native land from the Bolsheviks and await your agree- ment within 24 hours from today. We have for a long time honestly and openly tried to convince you of the need to take this measure, and you have agreed to it in principle. But time does not wait. We tell you now that we are ready for anything. We will be judged by God and the people.[35]
>
>   Commander of the First Army
>   Lieutenant General Pepelyaev

In answer, Admiral Kolchak summoned General Sakharov who announced that there were enough troops at his disposal to bring order to the army and proposed to Kolchak that the First Army be disbanded. Kolchak agreed. Following this decision, on December 9, General Pepelyaev and his brother, the chairman of the Council of Ministers, arrived in an armored car at Taiga Station for a meeting with Kolchak. They demanded (1) that General Sakharov's orders for the disbanding of Pepelyaev's army be remanded and that Sakharov himself, as a reactionary who had traitorously abandoned Omsk to the Bolsheviks, be removed from his post as commander-in-chief; (2) that the all-Siberian Constituent Assembly should be convened without delay and that to it should be transferred supreme authority; (3) that Kolchak leave Siberia.

Kolchak answered affirmatively only to the first demand; he promised an answer to the others after consulting with the full staff of the Council of Ministers in Irkutsk.

Having received no satisfaction from Kolchak, the brothers Pepelyaev decided to take matters into their own hands and to arrest General Sakharov. After all, they reasoned, "all Siberia is indignant at the crying shame of the surrender of Omsk and the nightmarish evacuation, and at all the horrors that are being perpetrated at the railroad station. To calm down the masses we have decided to arrest the one who is responsible for all this: General Sakharov."[36]

This action of the chairman of the Council of Ministers and the commander of the First Army could be viewed in no other light than as an open challenge to Kolchak, leaving him no other recourse but to take official steps to have Sakharov removed from his post. General Kappel was appointed commander-in-chief of the army. After a telephone conversation with Sakharov, Kappel told the staff officers that "the commander-in-chief, somewhere between Omsk and Novonikolaevsk, would not give the plans for the next few days, nor even a chart of the disposition of the troops. I sincerely wonder how we, led and governed by such characters as these, have been able to last as long as we have."[37]

The staff of the First Siberian Army, now in Tomsk, refused to retreat any farther. In view of this, General Pepelyaev disbanded the troops, allowing the men to go home. The remainder of the Western Army simply rolled on eastward, at times stopping the advancing Red Army. The retreat was complicated in that the army had to pass through territory of partisan activity and through places where the Siberian Army was staging uprisings.

The commander of the Third Army, General Lebedev, onetime right hand of Kolchak, left Ataman Dutov's detachment to its fate and fled a hundred miles from the front. General Volkov, commander of the corps and head of the illegal military Cossack organization, committed suicide. General Ivanov-Rinov abandoned his staff and convoy and disappeared together with the treasurer, thenceforth making his way alone. The candidate for the dictatorship and his entire regiment joined the Bolsheviks near the city of Kansk. Kappel suffered severe frostbite and died of complications soon thereafter. The commander of the artillery corps brought the locks from two hundred French cannons, taken previously from Krasnoyarsk, to the Red Army near Nizhneudinsk, announcing that he was tired of being under orders to those who surrounded Admiral Kolchak.

Thus it was that an army that had been strong in spirit and had marched forth victoriously lost faith in the cause for which the war was being fought, lost heart and rapidly disintegrated. Budberg reflects: "At the top of the military command were ambition, conceit, and ignorance of large operations. The law was forgotten; everyone acted according to his own judgment, behaving arbitrarily. 'It was not the conquest of the Red Army—it was the decomposition of our own military command.'"[38]

8

The Political Center

The farther east the army moved, the thinner its ranks grew. As a result, the entire political situation began to change with kaleidoscopic rapidity.

From the moment Omsk had been abandoned, Admiral Kolchak's government virtually ceased to function. The administrative apparatus, its headquarters now in Irkutsk, was being reorganized, and Admiral Kolchak himself was somewhere between Krasnoyarsk and Irkutsk on a slow-moving train.

When the all-Russian front collapsed, the Siberians conceived of the idea of saving their land from the Bolsheviks by creating an autonomous regime with a democratic form of government.

In mid-October 1919, at an illegal congress of zemstvos and town councils in Irkutsk, a resolution was passed demanding the replacement of Admiral Kolchak's regime. In November the Political Center was created, to be responsible for organizing a new Siberian government. The Political Center was made up of (1) the Zemstvo Political Bureau; (2) the Central Committee of the Union of Working Peasants; (3) the Regional Committee of the Socialist-Revolutionary Party; and (4) the Bureau of Siberian Organizations of the Russian Social Democratic Party.

By this time, the Siberian territory not yet seized by the Bolsheviks was notably diminished. The Political Center could hope for influence only in the provinces of Tomsk and Yeniseisk and in the oblasts of Yakutsk, Trans-Baikal, and the Maritime.

The program of the Political Center called for (1) convocation of the Siberian Constituent Assembly; (2) organization of a buffer state with a democratic form of government; (3) peace with Soviet Russia; 4) opposition to the Japanese intervention; and 5) renouncement of political blocs with reactionary elements.

Following the unsuccessful attempt on the part of the brothers Pepelyaev to convince Admiral Kolchak that he should convoke the Siberian Constituent Assembly and transfer power to it, a series of events decided the fate of Admiral Kolchak and his government.

Admiral Kolchak, sadly lacking in political experience, made decisions based on the opinions of those surrounding him at the moment. At this particular moment, those closest to him were two generals and and a colonel who blindly trusted in the support of Ataman Semenov and of Japan. Any change in the government was therefore deemed unnecessary. If at some previous time Kolchak had, in a personal interview with General Pepelyaev, agreed to convoke the Siberian Constituent Assembly, he now delayed this decision.

The period of negotiating a peaceful evolution of authority had come to an end, and an era of armed conflict had begun. On December 19 the Yeniseisk Regiment claimed power for the Krasnoyarsk zemstvos and proposed that Admiral Kolchak step down as supreme ruler. On December 21 and 22 there was an uprising in Nizhneudinsk and at the Cherekhomsk mines, after which power in these regions was transferred to the Political Center.

In Irkutsk, where there were still remnants of Kolchak's government, the situation was tense. Some members of the government realized that the government power had come to an end, and they began negotiations with social organizations, hoping to find some solution to the situation. But it was too late for that. Kolchak's government had only one road left to follow, and that was the road that led to full capitulation. Although Minister S. N. Tretyakov declared that military authority must submit to civil authority, the military authorities thought otherwise and did not recognize the government. The acting chairman of the Council of Ministers granted political parties permission to meet and discuss the political situation, but the head of the garrison, Gen. E. Sychev, promptly dispersed the meeting.

On December 23, by order of Admiral Kolchak, Ataman Semenov was appointed commander-in-chief of Eastern Siberia. At this time, Ataman Semenov removed the commander of the Irkutsk Military Region, General Artemyev, and appointed in his place one of his own generals, who was sent in command of a detachment from Chita to fortify the garrison. With Semenov's men came an echelon of the

Japanese army. At this time the Allies had under their command in Irkutsk a large Czech army and were maintaining neutrality. Because the Japanese felt outnumbered, they were forced to follow suit.

On December 23, 31 members of the Political Center were arrested by local counterintelligence in Irkutsk and declared hostages. Among those arrested were B. Markov and P. Mikhailov, leaders in the preparatory work of spring 1918 for the uprising against the Bolsheviks.

December 24 marked the beginning of the uprising against the government. The time for talks had ended; now it was the machine guns that would be heard. The uprising, under the command of Capt. N. Kalashnikov, former head of the Information Division of the Urals Army, began in the city of Irkutsk. Irkutsk became a battleground. The civilian population sought shelter wherever it could be found, mostly in basements. Paper money became worthless, essential products vanished from the markets, and fuel was scarce. At this time I was living with my wife and child on the shores of the Angara River not far from the pontoon bridge leading to Glazgovo Station. Every second day I walked to the neighboring village for a bottle of milk for our daughter, and my wife washed diapers in the Angara's icy waters while bullets whistled overhead.

Semenov's detachments were forced to retreat after an unsuccessful attack on Glazgovo Station. Semenov promised to send reinforcements to the Irkutsk garrison, but General Skipitrov was able to spare only two hundred soldiers; he himself returned to Chita.

The battle for the city of Irkutsk continued, with alternating successes, up to January 2, 1920. Continuous fighting during one entire week wore out the men of the garrison, both physically and spiritually. The ataman of the Irkutsk Cossack troops refused to carry on the struggle; two infantry companies killed their officers and went over to the side of the insurrectionists. The Fifty-fourth Regiment also declared its recognition of the authority of the Political Center. In view of this desperate situation, the staff of the military region held a conference at which it was decided that the government should ask the Allied command for aid in evacuation. The acting chairman of the Council of Ministers, A. Cherven-Vodaly, and Gen. P. T. Vagin established contact with General Janin, who pointed out to them that because the railroad station was under control of the Political Center, they should address themselves directly to the center. To the great displeasure of the commander of the military region, General Artemyev, and the head of the garrison, Cherven-Vodaly and Vagin entered into negotiations with the Political Center. As a result, a truce was declared. General Sychev took advantage of the cessation of hostilities to prepare for evacuation, but he encountered opposition from the chief of the Fourteenth Division and the chiefs of the Cadet Corps, who opposed evacuation. This left the garrison with only a battalion of Semenov's men.[1]

The government representatives proposed (1) passage to the east for Admiral Kolchak, his army, and his administration; (2) passage for the gold supply; and (3) continuation of the struggle against the Bolsheviks to be carried on by the Political Center.

The Political Center presented twelve conditions, which included:

1. the immediate resignation of Admiral Kolchak;
2. the resignation of the Council of Ministers;
3. the relinquishing by Ataman Semenov of all the posts assigned to him by Admiral Kolchak;
4. the surrender to the new government of all political workers responsible for the civil war;
5. the bringing to trial of all culpable persons.

During the exchange of views, the delegates of the Political Center agreed to give passage only to Kolchak and to his ministers, on condition that the 31 hostages should be freed. The other points proposed were declared inadmissible. The representatives of the government, in turn, agreed to the resignations of Kolchak and the Council of Ministers but categorically declared against the last three conditions listed above.

The Political Center delegation then made the announcement:

> The government's answer to the twelve items comprising our conditions for the truce strikes us as completely devoid of sincerity. It appears that the government is trying to gain time in order to re-establish its power and mobilize it in the Trans-Baikal region in order to continue the civil war, which has caused enough suffering to our country. According to the terms offered us, the newly established regime would be, from the very beginning, threatened by a regime located in the Trans-Baikal region. Furthermore, not having enough forces for the democratic reorganization which the new regime wishes to undertake, the evacuation of units of the Siberian Army, especially from the front, would leave our gates wide open to soviet troops. And, in any case, the formation of an independent power in the Trans-Baikal region would lead to the capitulation of the new government to bolshevism. It is for these reasons that the delegates of the Political Center cannot consider the government's answer as at all satisfactory.[2]

On January 3, 1920, at a meeting of the representatives of the Political Center, Cherven-Vodaly gave orders to the head of the garrison (through General Vagin) to free all representatives of the Political Center who were then under arrest. A meeting was scheduled for January 4 for further talks. The representatives of the government arrived very late to this meeting, then asked for additional information concerning the application of 3–5 (above). It became apparent later that all these diplomatic talks were aimed by the army staff at lulling to sleep the Political Center so as to gain time for the evacuation from Irkutsk. By the end of the day, the arrested representatives of the Political Center had been taken from prison, and all the valuables had been removed from the government bank as well. On the night of January 3, fifteen boxes of gold disappeared from Kolchak's train. The next day Kolchak resigned and transferred his authority to General Denikin in Nizhneudinsk. On January 5 the Political Center assumed power and announced the restoration of civil liberties.

An initial attempt by the Political Center to gain support of the armies of Pepelyaev and Kappel was unsuccessful. The Siberians refused to retreat beyond their own regions and began to disperse toward their homes. General Pepelyaev fell ill with typhoid fever, and General Kappel died. The command of the retreating army units fell to General Voitsekhovsky—behind whose back General Sakharov really played the lead.

Political Center leaders realized its days were numbered unless some agreement could be reached with the retreating army. The departure of the army to the Trans-Baikal region left the way wide open for the Soviet Army to take the city of Irkutsk. Lacking the support of its army, the Political Center's position was weak from the first day it came to power. The Political Center invested the zemstvos and towns with local authority, then took steps to establish a truce on the soviet front on the condition that autonomy would be guaranteed to the oblasts not occupied by Soviet Russia. The Communists in Irkutsk began a campaign against the Socialist-Revolutionaries and the Mensheviks, hoping to isolate them from the people. It is true that some of the Communists were in favor of supporting the Political Center, but the majority demanded soviets—even taking it upon themselves to create a local soviet of workers' deputies. Moreover, they urged the partisan detachments not to submit to the authority of the commander of the Irkutsk garrison.

The hostages taken from Irkutsk by General Sychev were all brutally murdered—beaten to death by mallets—and their bodies lowered from a barge into Lake Baikal. This aroused universal indignation, especially within the garrison. The Political Center had earlier agreed to free passage for Kolchak; it now demanded that he be delivered into custody. On the same day the commander of the Czech forces informed General Janin that the Czech command would no longer be able to protect Kolchak.

What was the motive for killing the hostages? Was it part of the general policy of those surrounding Admiral Kolchak—to destroy all political opponents, whoever they might be? Or was this the private initiative of the enigmatic General Sychev? Without the knowledge of the Council of Ministers, Sychev ordered the front to be cleared and began to evacuate the city of Irkutsk. And it was he who took the hostages of the Political Center from prison and had them killed. General Sychev had the complete trust of Ataman Semenov but at the same time was a soviet secret agent.[3] The question arises, then: in which capacity was he acting at any given time? It is difficult to determine where the role of the reactionary general ended and the role of the Bolshevik intelligence agent began. Perhaps sometime in the future the truth will be revealed.

We know from General Sakharov that "preparations were being made for the complete annihilation of the Socialist-Revolutionaries."[4] Sakharov also expressed "regret that the Whites were incapable of handling the Socialist-Revolutionaries as well as were the Reds."[5] General Voitsekhovsky, pursuing this policy, senselessly inflicted severe punishment on all garrisons lying in the path of his march east that had dared to demand the resignation of Admiral Kolchak and the convocation of the Siberian Constituent Assembly. After a short stay in the newly occupied territories, Voitsekhovsky moved farther east, liquidating democratic elements as he went and, by so doing, clearing the way for the Bolsheviks.

There is reason to suspect that the killing of the hostages on Lake Baikal had another, more specific motive: the hostages were killed three days after Cherven-Vodaly had ordered that they be released from prison. General Sychev, therefore, had committed an act of direct insubordination to the government. What prompted him to do this? Was it not because neither Ataman Semenov nor his closest associates cherished the prospect of seeing Admiral Kolchak established in the Trans-Baikal region? The presence of Kolchak and his army there would automatically mean the loss of supremacy and independence for Ataman Semenov and his staff. It was also in direct opposition to Japanese policy. By liquidating the hostages these parties hoped to rid themselves of Admiral Kolchak because they were certain that in this case the Political Center would not let him pass through. History had once again repeated itself: in December 1918 Ivanov-Rinov, in order to discredit Kolchak, had also arbitrarily decided the fate of the members of the Constituent Assembly who were to have been released from the Omsk prison.

By this time, Kolchak's relations with the Allies were somewhat strained: Kolchak, no longer in constant contact with the Council of Ministers, acted at his own discretion, and some of the communications he sent were of a challenging nature (at best, they lacked the form customary in diplomatic exchanges). Then, too, the Allies realized that Kolchak, as supreme ruler, was finished, and they were seeking grounds to break off with him.

Even in early December, General Janin had declined Kolchak's request for an appointment. On December 16, 1919, at a meeting of the Entente in London, it was decided to discontinue aid to the anti-Bolshevik governments of Russia, leaving it to America and Japan to pursue in Siberia whatever policy best served their respective interests. In declining to resolve the Siberian question, the Entente was of course throwing a bone of contention to America and Japan, knowing full well that the interests of the two countries were diametrically opposed. Under these conditions, the killing of the hostages on Lake Baikal served to untie the hands of the Allies.

On January 14, 1919, all the Allied missions left Irkutsk, and the next day the Czechs delivered Kolchak into the custody of the Political Center. On January 16, the Allies signed a treaty with Soviet Russia renewing trade relations. This signified that the Soviets had been de facto recognized. Admiral Kolchak—but not the supply of gold that had been with him—was in the hands of the Political Center.

At the same time, the instability of the Political Center was aggravated by insubordination of the partisan detachments of O. Zverev and N. Kalandarashvili to the commander of the garrison, N. Kalashnikov. On January 15, the Political Center ordered Kalashnikov to disarm one of Kalandarashvili's regiments. It was easy to give such an order, but quite another matter to execute it. And Kalashnikov was, at that time, faced with another problem: the defense of Irkutsk from the approaching army of General Voitsekhovsky, who had already liquidated the insurrectionists in Nizhneudinsk and in Cheremkhov during his march. Kalashnikov did not have an adequate army to do battle on two fronts. He therefore proposed on January 17 that the Political Center relinquish its power. Leaders of the Political Center had to acknowledge the hopelessness of its situation, and on January 21 power was transferred to the Revolutionary Committee, consisting of Bolsheviks and Left Socialist-Revolutionaries. Thus ended the last attempt of the democratic elements in Siberia to preserve political independence for the region.

During the almost two-year struggle against communist dictatorship and later against Kolchakovshchina, the ranks of the Siberian democrats were significantly depleted. Many of the important leaders had perished, and those who remained alive no longer had the strength to continue the fight on two fronts.

The tragedy of the Political Center was that it could not establish a more normal relationship with the retreating army. General Sakharov and some of the generals with him had one plan: to take the army and the gold supply to the Trans-Baikal region and establish themselves firmly there. "The Bolsheviks," they reasoned, "can have western and central Siberia; they will teach the rebellious population there a lesson." It would seem that the views of the reactionaries, both right and left, were identical—so victory was theirs.

It was noted earlier that the state apparatus and its general leadership had, by mid-December, virtually vanished into thin air. Each member of the government acted autonomously while waiting to grasp the earliest opportunity to move farther east. The majority of ministers from the former staff had already resigned. Some of the newly appointed ministers were not yet au courant with the situation and did not, in any case, share the same political views as their predecessors.

On January 2, 1919, the acting chairman of the Council of Ministers, A. Cherven-Vodaly, said to General Janin: "I have already mentioned that those of us who came from General Denikin looked upon the policy conducted by Admiral Kolchak's ministers as destructive. We soon realized that it would be difficult for the chairman of the Council of Ministers, Pepelyaev, to accomplish anything because, as minister of internal affairs, he had already incurred the hatred of the community and of the people. The circles close to the admiral were preparing to launch an even more reactionary policy."[6]

There was no unity of thought among those who surrounded Admiral Kolchak. He himself reflected this, as he fluctuated from one extreme to another while blindly holding onto the trust he had placed in the Allies. When Kolchak was handed over to the Political Center, he said: "This means that the Allies did, in truth, betray me. How despicable! And I had, it seems, served them so conscientiously."[7] He was so utterly lacking in political awareness that he also failed to perceive that some of the generals in the Trans-Baikal region to whom he had transferred his authority had no desire to see him there.

When the Political Center shifted its power to the Revolutionary Committee, an investigatory commission was formed to interrogate Admiral Kolchak. On this commission were represented the Bolsheviks, the Social Democrats, and the Socialist-Revolutionaries. One of the Socialist-Revolutionaries, it might be noted, had earlier been an active member of the Omsk political bloc that had supported Kolchak. (This commission should not be confused with the Cheka, which made arrests, pronounced judgments, and carried out verdicts. The investigating commission was confined to interrogation only.)

The questioning continued, with interruptions, from January 21 to February 5, 1920. On February 3, General Voitsekhovsky and his army reached the city of Irkutsk and presented the following demands to the Revolutionary Committee: (1) the army should be allowed to pass through the city of Irkutsk; (2) Admiral Kolchak should be handed over to his army; (3) some of the gold supply should also be given to the army. Prior to this, the Revolutionary Committee had received orders from Moscow that Admiral Kolchak should be sent there. The committee, fearing that General Voitsekhovsky would take Irkutsk by force and free Kolchak, decided to act: on the night of February 6, 1920, Kolchak and the chairman of the Council of Ministers were shot on orders of the committee. It would seem that some force had pursued Admiral Kolchak, relentlessly pushing him ever closer to his grave.

In accordance with a proposal of the brothers Pepelyaev of December 9, 1919, and a later proposal of the Political Center concerning the transfer of power, Admiral Kolchak should have been guaranteed safe departure from Siberia. "General Janin had offered that he, Janin, would guarantee safe passage for the carriage in which Kolchak and his officers were traveling, but Admiral Kolchak refused, insisting on the passage of the entire train, including the convoy."[8] Several days after this offer, Admiral Kolchak released the members of his convoy from their duties and told them that whoever so desired could depart. The entire convoy of five hundred men took advantage of this offer and went over to the side of the insurrectionists.

While the Political Center was being formed in mid-November 1919, its leaders had counted on the support of Pepelyaev's army and the organization of a democratic Siberian buffer state. With all hope of victory lost, the dispirited soldiers of the Siberian Army simply dispersed toward their respective homes. The remnants of General Kappel's corps, not wishing to linger in central Siberia, moved east. The way was now cleared for the unhindered advance of the Red Army.

All these events naturally had a very adverse influence on the general political situation. The Political Center, having assumed power on January 5, 1920, sent a delegation to negotiate with the representatives of the Soviet Fifth Army. The delegation did not arrive in Tomsk until January 18. During the talks, the representatives of the Political Center stressed that the movement of the Red Army toward the east from Irkutsk would inevitably lead to a clash with Japan. Further, if the Soviet Army was prepared for a war with Japan there would be no purpose in forming a buffer state; otherwise, an independent buffer state would be essential.

At that time the general military situation was not favorable for the Soviets, as there were indications of an imminent conflict with Poland. At the end of December 1919, the eastern front of the Red Army was disbanding, and the troops were being transferred to the center. The Fifth Army alone was left to operate in Siberia. An epidemic of typhoid fever raged. And, most important, the relations of this army with the Siberian partisans left much to be desired. The head of the partisan army in south Yeniseisk province was arrested, and one of his regiments was forcibly disarmed. Matters were no better in the Altai region, where, in order to "pacify" the partisans, reserve units of the Red Army had to encircle them.

Considering this situation, Fifth Army Commissar I. Smirnov and War Commissar Trotsky recommended that the Council of People's Commissars come to an agreement with the Political Center. A treaty was signed calling for the creation of a democratic buffer state under the direction of the Political Center. The boundaries would begin west of the city of Irkutsk, from Zima Station, and follow the rivers Oka and Angara.

The chief purpose of creating the buffer state was, of course, to neutralize Japanese intervention. The Bolsheviks in Irkutsk protested on the grounds that this would actually be an anti-Soviet buffer and insisted that the Council of People's Commissars should review the question. Pursuing its usual opportunistic tactics, the council broke its agreement with the Political Center.

According to the new variation that resulted, the buffer would be created exclusively for tactical reasons as a temporary artificial republic. A communist was entrusted with the organization of a government for this Far East Republic. The boundaries were curtailed: they would now begin at the Selenga River and the city of Verkhneudinsk. What the Bolsheviks really created was a fiction of an independent state; the Socialist-Revolutionaries therefore refused to take part in the government of the Far East Republic. The principle of centralism served as the foundation for this government, without even a hint of parliamentary order.

Later, the Bolsheviks in Chita took a stand against the communist, whom they considered a supporter of the independent government, and maintained a friendly neutrality with Soviet Russia. In the end, he, Smirnov, and Trotsky were relegated to the ranks of those who supported the foreign bourgeoisie.

9

Foreign Intervention

The anti-Bolshevik movement in Siberia should not be linked to foreign intervention, despite the coincidence in time. As early as the end of 1917, France and England were discussing the organization of an expeditionary corps of Japanese in the Far East, sounding out the attitude of the United States to this plan. The plan was no secret from the Russian ambassador to Paris who in early 1918 warned the American ambassador that if Japanese forces should land on Russian territory, the Siberian government would protest.

Those members of the Siberian government in contact with foreign representatives always stressed that in the struggle against the Bolsheviks, Siberia needed help only in obtaining arms and ammunition. The presence of foreign armies in Siberia would be admissible only under one condition: the opening of a second front against Germany. The leaders of Europe, however, had something quite different in mind. Their chief goal was, of course, to defeat Germany; but it would not be such a bad thing, they reasoned, if at the same time Russia were to be pulled out of the ranks of the great powers.

England wished to see Russia divided into several separate independent states, with none of them large enough to be a threat to the world. The Entente wanted victory over Germany—but not victory over the Bolsheviks. The Allies realized that the liberation movement in Russia, begun independently of them, could be used to serve their own ends. It is upon this canvas that all subsequent events developed along all the borders of Russia.

The arrival first of the Japanese and later of English troops in Vladivostok served to strengthen the Bolshevik position, and the Bolsheviks lost no time in unfurling the slogan Fight Foreign Intervention. Because few Russians doubted that Japan was eager to annex the Far East Territory, this had its effect. Instead of being internationalists, the Bolsheviks had suddenly become patriots fighting for the preservation of Russian territory. In order to paralyze Japan's activities, the United States also sent a military detachment.

American troops arrived in Vladivostok on August 16, 1918. In the State Department's instructions to General Graves, it was proposed to

> ask all associated in this course of action to unite in assuring the people of Russia in the most public and solemn manner that none of the governments uniting in action either in Siberia or in northern Russia contemplates any interference of any kind with the political sovereignty of Russia, any intervention in her internal affairs, or any impairment of her territorial integrity either now or hereafter, but that each of the associated powers has the single object of affording such aid as shall be acceptable to the Russian people in their endeavor to regain control of their own affairs, their own territory, and their own destiny.[1]

These were the intentions of the State Department at the start. But, under pressure from the Allies, the department deviated greatly from these intentions, often disregarding completely the spirit of the declaration. General Graves wrote about the State Department instructions: "After having carefully read the document and feeling that I understood the policy, I went to bed, but I could not sleep; I kept wondering what other nations were doing and why I was not given some information about what was going on in Siberia."[2]

Indeed, U.S. representatives stationed in Siberia at that time did not have a clear picture of the complicated situation. They were technicians without the necessary background to understand foreign politics, the more so during revolutionary times. A member of the Inter-Allied Railroad Commission wanted to settle the conflict between the Bolsheviks and the Czechs, not perceiving that the Bolsheviks simply used him to bring about a truce that would give them the opportunity to pull up their troops to Mariinsk. The views of Consul General E. Harris, the diplomatic representative in Siberia, were no different from those of the English and French representatives. They all shared a total ignorance of the political situation in Siberia, which was not surprising because the overall situation shifted constantly: what was true in Vladivostok was not true in Irkutsk, and what was true in Irkutsk was not true in Omsk.

Harris was under the impression that 80 percent of the population in Siberia had monarchistic tendencies. He arrived at this conclusion while on a train trip—not even having passed through the center of the country. And he never did understand why the people did not support Kolchak's rule.

All the foreign representatives ignored the fact that the Siberian uprising against the Bolsheviks was achieved without Allied participation, and that it was chiefly accomplished through the active cooperation of the Socialist-Revolutionary Party. The formation of the Siberian Army bore the same imprint. Furthermore, the members of the Socialist-Revolutionary Party were very active in cooperatives of the zemstvo and town autonomies.

In fact, a singular lack of enthusiasm concerning the change in Siberia's form of government was displayed by some representatives of the Allies. Shortly after the overthrow of the Bolsheviks in Krasnoyarsk, the English vice-consul paid me a visit. He had not come to congratulate me, as I at first supposed, but to present a rather odd request. He asked for the release of a member of the Committee of the Bolshevik Party, who had been arrested by my orders—and who was his accountant.

During this time of economic chaos, speculation reached an incredible pitch in the cities of Siberia; the rest of the population was supplied with products exclusively by the cooperatives. Harris saw fit to warn Washington about this concentration of trade in the cooperatives because their prices were lower than those of private merchants. It seemed to him that the interests of private business in the cities were of greater importance than those of the entire village population, comprising about 90 percent of the total population of Russia.

The policy of England, France, and Japan was directed toward supporting the independence of separate Russian detachments and thus preventing the formation of a strong central power. The American State Department representative also followed this policy to a certain extent. Instead of supporting the security of the existent regime, he thought in terms of a future military dictatorship. As early as late July 1918, for example, when the struggle with the Bolsheviks was still at its peak, Harris declared himself in favor of establishing a military dictatorship in Siberia even before the war should end. He believed that only a strong cabinet composed of members of the

Constitutional Democratic Party, Kadets (which had not taken part in the initial struggle against the Bolsheviks), could possibly have any success. Later, when the Directory was established, Harris recommended that it not be recognized. He was under the delusion that the Constituent Assembly was supported solely by the Socialist-Revolutionaries and by the Bolsheviks! And this in spite of the fact that already in January 1918 the Bolsheviks had forcibly dispersed the Constituent Assembly.

In the same vein, Harris considered the coup d'etat in Omsk (when the Directory was pushed aside and replaced by Supreme Commander Kolchak) to be part of the normal course of events. In his report to Washington, he interpreted the events of November 18 to mean that Kolchak was the successor to all lawful Russian governments in existence to the end of October 1917. But his prognosis was short-lived. On November 21, three days after the overthrow, Harris received a communication from the consul in Omsk stating that the Czechs and the Siberian armies may not recognize Kolchak as head of the government. Harris decided to travel to the Urals to acquaint himself with the disposition of the Siberian Army. In mid-December 1918, he reported to his government from Ekaterinburg that the present government in Omsk may not be all we want, but it is the best that has yet appeared and it is attempting to steer a middle course between the Socialist-Revolutionaries and the reactionaries.

It is difficult to imagine what facts Harris used to reach his conclusion. Among the five members of the Directory, only two were Socialist-Revolutionaries, and they were not engaged in any party activity; the members of the Directory, moreover, had not had time to make any laws because they were absorbed in organizing a government apparatus. By the same token, Kolchak did not, in a month's time, produce anything positive with which to recommend himself. His activity at the time was limited to issuing orders of a general character and to ordering the arrest of members of the Constituent Assembly. The foreign affairs consultant under Kolchak told the American consul that "Ataman Kalmykov is a brigand and a plunderer, and Admiral Kolchak does not have the power to stop the activities of Ivanov-Rinov, in particular, and the Cossack atamans, in general."[3]

An official in the American consulate wrote to Harris in March 1919 from the Altai region that the people were pro-Bolshevik not because they were against Kolchak, but because of the repressive measures taken by the military, including the annihilation of entire villages. In August 1919 Consul A. Thomson reported from Omsk that few of those around Kolchak trusted his statements and promises.

General Graves observed: "The acts of these Cossacks and other Kolchak leaders under the protection of foreign troops were the greatest asset to bolshevism that could have been devised by man. The atrocities were of such a nature that they are sure to be remembered by the Russian people and recounted by them for as long as fifty years after they were committed."[4] None of this prevented Consul General Harris from writing to the State Department in early September 1919 that all the pessimistic conclusions of the U.S. ambassador to Japan and Graves should not be taken seriously.

In view of the conflicting opinions among the several American representatives in Siberia, the State Department suggested that Harris call a conference to discuss the general situation in Siberia. Following is a précis of the conference, which took place in mid-September 1919 in Vladivostok:

Pursuant instructions from State Department, Consul General Harris has been in conference with Admiral Rodgers, General Graves, Mr. Smith of the [Inter-Allied] Railroad Commission, and Consul Caldwell of Vladivostok.

We are in accord and of opinion as follows: That the liberal movement as headed by Kolchak is increasing in strength. Indications are that Kolchak is inclined to approach the center parties to make concessions to them and unite with them in a comparatively liberal form of government. His influence would be extended were he to promise a constitutional assembly to the people but sees at present as a chief necessity only the subduing of Bolsheviks and although well disposed to civil institutions regards a pledge to them as of less immediate importance. Kolchak seems sincerely committed to the good of Russia through policies of liberal character with possible personal preference for constitutional monarch rather than for republic, but not at all in favor of old type of government. Kolchak probably represents the most acceptable type of man Russia has available but we do not believe him a great national leader.

The really reactionary associates immediately about Kolchak are not of serious importance although it is perhaps not advisable for him to seek an immediate break with them. He has recently disavowed the actions of some of the more important reactionary leaders who claim his countenance.

In eastern Siberia the zemstvos are not so favorably disposed toward the Kolchak government, for the Cossacks under Semenov and Kalmykov are reactionary and violent, and the people are not sure that Kolchak himself is sufficiently liberal.

Zemstvos in eastern Siberia say Kolchak has reduced their authority.

The betterment of the whole people is essentially dependent on economic prosperity induced through operation of railroads and elimination of Bolsheviks who seek to rule for their own profit by terror, violence, and destruction; and through the prevention of arbitrary acts of violence by reactionary Cossacks in the name of order. The Siberian situation would be improved (1) if after enunciation of satisfactory liberal policies, some form of encouragement, yet not reaching formal recognition, as de facto government, could be given by Allied powers to the liberal movement now headed by Kolchak. We are now actually dealing with Kolchak on railway business and must continue to do so. (2) Some form of financial and material support is necessary. A loan is preferable to a gift, although there is some chance of losing it. If arms and supplies are given, it should be done openly and by agreement of the powers. Japan's secret gift of arms to Semenov and Kalmykov promoted reactionary discord and tended to drive peasantry into control of opposite party of violence when they only asked to be free from oppression. (3) Agreement on part of Allies to refrain from assisting or supporting any of the Cossack factions now embarrassing Kolchak. (4) Adoption of every means short of force to weaken strength and influence of reactionary Cossack leaders. The Cossack people, generally of Siberia, are essentially the same as the rest of peasantry and desire stable government and personal security. (5) Development of industrial and civic prosperity by prompt and efficient operation of railroad. (6) Stabilization of currency.

Japanese military authorities have been fomenting trouble in various directions as set forth in recent weeks by General Graves to War Department, and the conduct of the Japanese troops in Siberia has not been in accord with policies of the United States. But within past few days, Japanese command has expressed its intention to conform more to American policy and to fight bolshevism by creation of economic prosperity, and to use physical force against any Russian party only when such party interferes with railroad or attacks Japanese troops or cantonments.

The Inter-Allied Railway Commission has been acting harmoniously, and the best promise of success in pacifying Siberia is through smooth working of railway, protected by Allied forces against lawless attacks of any minority party of violence. Not only has there been divergence of views between the Japanese military party and the present Japanese government, but it seems probable that both the English and French military representatives in Siberia personally hold very reactionary views as to Russian politics and are not in harmony with the representatives of their own governments on the Inter-Allied committee. Consequently the governments of England and France have no clear-cut views as to the situation here. Indications are that the representatives of France and England, especially France, on the inter-Allied committee wish to delay action by the military committee until their home governments are well informed, and both powers have granted authority to the civil representatives on the railway committee to require their members of the military committee to conform to the general policy as expressed by the Inter-Allied Railway Committee.

The matter is one to be settled in its broad lines of policy by agreement between the Allied powers party to railway agreement.

Apparently if the powers will unify the expression of views by their respective representatives, the Inter-Allied Railway Commission will be able to arrive at harmonious decisions promotive of law, order, good feeling, and prosperity in Siberia.[5]

This resolution was typical—not in the points of agreement, but in the points omitted. Nothing was said of the actual situation in Siberia: the Political Bloc that had earlier supported Kolchak's government had become critical and was demanding reforms; the Second Army, under the command of General Sakharov, had suffered defeat and was retreating; Geneal Pepelyaev's First Army, never having known defeat, was now ordered to retreat and was rolling back rapidly, its spirit broken; and the partisan movement was mushrooming behind the lines. In short, what was lacking was any indication whatsoever of the presence of the very factors that characterize a stable power.

Generally speaking, the United States had no definite policy toward Russia at that time, except not to allow Japan to gain a stronghold in Siberian territory. Representatives of the United States were not armed with explicit instructions; left to themselves thus, they simply could not figure out what was happening around them.

The representative of the American Red Cross believed that all that was needed to change the character of the Soviet regime was to recognize it and provide economic aid. He was still prattling about the strength of Soviet authority up to the week before its collapse in Siberia.

The precise role of the prisoners of war in Siberia was unclear to the Allies. Trotsky offered to send a commission to investigate this matter, appointing one of his own men as translator and liaison with the local soviets. This commission, consisting of a British officer and an American officer, traveled throughout Siberia and found conditions normal: German and Austrian prisoners of war were held in camps patrolled by the Red Guard. The commission did not even suspect that all the local soviets had been instructed to confine the prisoners of war to camps during the commission's sojourn. One exception was Irkutsk, where the diplomatic corps was located and where it was difficult to conceal three thousand armed prisoners of war. It was explained to the commission that all these former prisoners of war were now Russian subjects. Among such Russian subjects in Tomsk was Bela Kun, who later played a prominent role in Hungary; another, in Omsk, was Tito, the future leader of Yugoslavia.

While one representative of the United States and his assistant were conducting negotiations in Moscow concerning the recognition of the Soviet regime, and while Consul General Harris in Siberia was insisting upon recognition and economic aid to Kolchak's government (even when Kolchak had no ground to stand on), then the U.S. War Department chose to send a military observer to Siberia—when there was no longer anything left to observe except the army's chaotic retreat.

The activities of the Allies were completely uncoordinated. Some of them made promises knowing that they would not be kept. Flaunting their affiliation (to which they had little claim) with the participants of the uprising, they provided the Bolsheviks with an excuse to resort to more terrorist acts, thereby causing the deaths of countless innocent citizens. And in the face of all this, not one of the Allies declared that the Bolshevik government, a government of arbitrary rule and terror, should not be recognized.

It is almost inconceivable that at the moment when all Siberia was ablaze with the partisan movement some foreign diplomats should still cling to the belief that the Inter-Allied Railway Commission, which was not even in agreement with itself, would be able to bring order and economic prosperity to Siberia.

It was even less reasonable to talk about Kolchak's liberal tendencies, for he was surrounded by reactionary elements from whom he was apparently in no hurry to disassociate himself. And the reactionary groups themselves did not present a united front, some holding their course for England, others for Germany, and still others for Japan. Kolchak's government, in the interest of foreign relations, strove to uphold the illusion of liberalism.

Many of the ministers, including P. Vologodsky, I. Mikhailov, Starinkevich, and I. Serebrennikov, were not monarchists, but because of the many governmental upheavals of the time they had virtually become captives of the monarchist-inclined military groups. Kolchak, a man of no firm political convictions, flung himself from one extreme to the other. At times he seemed to embrace the program of the constitutional monarchists and at other times, especially during critical moments, he was ready to welcome Socialist-Revolutionaries into his government.

In May 1919 the Allies sent an inquiry to Admiral Kolchak about "whether he intended to convene the Constituent Assembly; whether he intended to hold free elections to the *zemstvo* and city governments; and whether he intended to refrain from establishing the old order and the former class structure."[6] With the help of a member of the French Mission, I. Sukin formulated the reply, which consisted of some vague references to the democratic policy of the government; Kolchak, without having first consulted his Council of Ministers, sent it to the Allies. But to his generals, Kolchak said, "First of all, I answered that I certainly, most certainly, intend to call the Constitutional Assembly, or, rather the Zemstvo Assembly, but not until all of Russia is freed of the Bolsheviks and order is restored. Until then there can be no talk of speech-making. Second, I answered that the Constituent Assembly elected during Kerensky's regime I do not recognize as such and will not allow to convene. If it should take it upon itself to convene, I will disperse it; and those who do not submit to my orders, I will hang. Last, in selecting the future Constitutent Assembly, I will admit only a sound political element composed of hard-working and knowledgeable people, not idle talkers. That is the kind of democrat I am."[7] This is one of the more accurate characterizations of Kolchak's self-made liberalism.

The Entente made proclamations concerning the inviolability of Russian territory and political sovereignty, at the same time sending Generals Knox and Janin to Siberia—General Knox to set up an administrative apparatus and General Janin in the role of commander-in-chief—four months after the Bolsheviks had been driven out of Siberia!

Yes, the foreign missions in Siberia, either by active support or passive, did assist the reaction that occurred. And all, in the same degree, ignored the presence of the democratic layers of society in Siberia. In its declaration of June 1919, the Central Committee of the Socialist-Revolutionary Party stressed that "the road to victory over

Bolshevist anarchy without Allied military help would be a longer road, but it would be the only one that would vouchsafe, at the end of civil strife, the results that could lead to the social and political resurrection of Russia. Russia is no longer the arena of the war against the Central Powers. Russia is engaged only in civil war. And it is not the reaction, but democracy—and only democracy—that can win the final victory in this war."[8]

10

The SR Party and Civil War in Siberia

Siberia has of old been the place of political exile in Russia. In the beginning of the nineteenth century, the Decembrists, and in the last three decades of the century the Populists and the Poles, filled the cities of Siberia. Their presence had a great impact on the worldview of the local intelligentsia and students. From the moment of its formation, therefore, the Socialist-Revolutionary Party had—already there and waiting—a breeding ground from which to draw its activists. In 1905 party committees were already in existence in each of Siberia's large cities, and in mid-1906 a convention of party organizations chose the Siberian Oblast Committee. The first issues of the party's central organ, *Revolutionary Russia*, were printed in Siberia.

Each passing year up to 1917 brought a new wave of exiles, and naturally the ranks of the party workers in Siberia grew ever larger. As early as 1907, with members of the Socialist-Revolutionary Party participating, a peasant union had been organized in one of the grain centers, the Minusinsk district of Yeniseisk province. Many exiled Socialist-Revolutionaries worked in cooperatives and city governments, which newcomers regarded as schools for the education of the masses. To this work, after the February Revolution of 1917, was added the task of creating zemstvos and unions. By the end of 1917, an impressive network of consumers' and producers' cooperatives conducting their own industrial enterprises reached throughout Siberia. Credit cooperatives, which subsidized the purchase of agricultural machines, were just as widely developed. Butter-producing artels (dairy cooperatives) sent huge quantities of their product to the European market, where it could compete with Danish butter. The consumers' cooperative competed easily in the domestic market. Because of the large turnover, trading expenses did not exceed 10–12 percent; and the district unions, which bought wholesale and supported a staff of instructors, did not spend more than 3–4 percent. This friendly cooperation between the exiles and the local population made it possible to build a powerful economic system directed at raising the cultural level and well-being of the region.

Despite all this creative work in Siberia, most of which the members of the Socialist-Revolutionary Party undertook, they were not spared all manner of accusations. In 1917, for example, the Bolsheviks branded the Socialist-Revolutionaries "socialist traitors" and began to "bury" them. Later they could not explain away the fact that the same socialist traitors received an overwhelming majority of votes to the Constituent Assembly, whereas the ruling Bolshevik Party in some regions (for instance, Irkutsk province) failed to put through even a single candidate.

The Siberian Socialist-Revolutionaries played a special role in building the party organization. Siberian economic conditions differed substantially from the general Russian picture: there was no land shortage, nor was there an industrial proletariat. Consequently, the Siberian program and tactics differed somewhat from the general party line.

The oblastniki, with their program of a federalist state structure, and the settlement of the land question on the basis of the *obshchina* (commune property rights) and democratic peasant self-government, were close to the Socialist-Revolutionary program. It is therefore not surprising that at the Congress of Siberian Oblastniki in 1905, Socialist-Revolutionaries already played an active part in the deliberations. The autonomy of the Socialist-Revolutionaries in Siberia also served to bring them closer to the oblastniki. One example will illustrate the degree of autonomy asserted by the Socialist-Revolutionary oblast committee. At the end of January 1918, the oblast committee resolved to begin preparations for an armed uprising against the Bolsheviks, and in February 1918, after the Siberian Oblast Duma had dispersed, the Siberian government elected by the same duma entrusted the West Siberian Commissariat (the majority of whose members had previously been members of the oblast committee) to begin the struggle against the Soviets. The Central Committee of the party, however, sanctioned these actions only in May 1918—when the question of an uprising in Siberia had long been determined.

At the end of June 1918, the same West Siberian Commissariat, on its own initiative, decided to denationalize all private enterprises located on territory occupied by the Siberian government, thereby, in fact, foreshadowing the direction of economic policy of the Siberian government: recognition of private property.

From the right came the accusation that the Socialist-Revolutionaries were organically incapable of fighting the Bolsheviks, and that the masses would never follow them. But suddenly, after all those "burials" it became apparent that the Socialist-Revolutionaries were not only alive but were successfully organizing an uprising against the Bolsheviks, and that with their active participation Siberia would, in a short time, be free from Soviet rule. Then, under the impact of a reactionary wave from European Russia, the Socialist-Revolutionaries were once again being "buried." This time it was said that they were incapable of constructive work, helpless when it came to practical matters, and completely devoid of any business sense; in addition, they were accused of treason to the Motherland. All these accusations amounted to a psychological preparation for a reactionary swing back.

A new regime came to Siberia, the dictatorship of Admiral Kolchak. The Socialist-Revolutionaries were once again "buried," this time not only politically, but physically as well. The example set by the Soviet Cheka was contagious. In a wave of arrests, party members were exterminated without trial or judgment—shot down, cut down by bayonets, stabbed by swords and sabers. And what came of all this? What did the government gain? One of the ministers in the Kolchak administration answers: "The government found itself in almost complete isolation: not one party, not one social organization stood behind it. Enemies, on the other hand, surrounded it, and malcontents were to be found everywhere. Reports came in of cruelties inflicted on the socialist intelligentsia in the cities."[1]

Who was to blame? None other, of course, than the party of Socialist-Revolutionaries. "Among the enemies of the Omsk government, the most powerful was the Socialist-Revolutionary Party. It doomed the Siberian government; it destroyed the Directory."[2] There is not much logic in this statement, but that does not seem to have been important so long as someone could be named as the source of all the evil that had befallen the government. Thus an insignificant, good-for-nothing, inactive party that could not possibly exercise any influence over the masses suddenly found itself listed among the most powerful enemies of the government.

Evidently the Socialist-Revolutionary Party was to blame for its very (albeit illegal) existence. It was also guilty of never having included the idea of a dictatorship in its program and of not running after the chariots of the victors. None of this was new. In Moscow in 1922, at the trial of members of the Central Committee of the Socialist-Revolutionary Party, the commissar of public education declared that the Socialist-Revolutionaries are guilty because they question the preponderant influence of the Bolsheviks over the working classes.

All the persecution directed against the Socialist-Revolutionary Party by Kolchak's government and by numerous atamans achieved but little. It is true that the party was significantly weakened, but it was certainly not vanquished. In the first place, the people of Siberia were accustomed to thinking of the socialist intelligentsia as practical workers, striving to elevate the economic and cultural levels of Siberian life, and not as traitors to the motherland; in the second place, this intelligentsia had taken root and become an integral part of the community, whereas in Omsk at the time the majority of those in authority were outsiders.

The so-called Chernov memorandum of October 22, 1918, received little approval among members of the party, and it caused rifts in certain circles. Some considered it untimely, serving only to pour water into the mill of reaction. This pessimistic memorandum underestimated all the present possibilities of overcoming the Omsk reactionary groups. Chernov and some members of the Central Committee of the party were dissatisfied with the fact that the party, having received over 80 percent of the votes in the election of 1917, had only one representative, V. Zenzinov, in the Directory; they saw this as complete capitulation by the party. The majority of party members who had taken part in the Ufa Conference did not consider representation in the Directory so essential because within several months there would be a meeting of the Constituent Assembly, to which the Directory was wholly accountable. Once re-elections to the Constituent Assembly were held, a permanent government was to be chosen.

Of the present members of the party's Central Committee, only three agreed to sign approval of the composition of the Directory; five others withheld their signatures. Chernov and his supporters approached the question from a purely formal point of view, whereas the great majority of the Socialist-Revolutionaries looked upon it from a strictly practical standpoint, thinking of the absence at that moment of suitable candidates among the present party membership to fill government positions. That is why they agreed to the Directory's composition as it stood. In directing criticism toward the Directory, the Central Committee of the party had in mind not so much the Directory itself as the members of the Socialist-Revolutionary Party who had signed the Ufa Agreement.

Once many of the Socialist-Revolutionaries had been arrested by order of Admiral Kolchak, many of the remaining members assumed an illegal position. A small group of Socialist-Revolutionaries began negotiations with the Bolsheviks on their own initiative. This group announced that their feeling about the necessity for an agreement with the Bolsheviks and the Soviet regime was shared by the presidium of party members at the Constituent Assembly and by other party workers. As a result of their negotiations, an agreement was reached, in the name of their group, to cease any activity against Soviet rule and to lend their support in the fight against Kolchak's government. The representatives of the Soviet regime, in turn, guaranteed to all members of the Socialist-Revolutionary Party belonging to the platform of these three men the same inviolability as granted to individuals who crossed over to the Bolshevik side and to army detachments who went over to the side of the Soviet Army. In accordance with this agreement, detachments of the Siberian and Czechoslovak armies were called upon to cease fighting. This appeal also bore their signatures and the signatures of two other members of the party's Central Committee.

In response, the Ural Oblast Committee of the Socialist-Revolutionary Party immediately declared:

> These negotiations are, on the part of those who conducted them, an act of political breach of faith, provocation, and treason toward the Socialist-Revolutionary Party. The statement made by the Socialist-Revolutionaries that they were authorized by party members at the Constituent Assembly to enter into negotiations with representatives of Soviet authority—the force that had dispersed the Constituent Assembly and is still engaged in a fierce struggle against it— besides being traitorous, humiliating, and insulting to the very idea of rule by the people and its representative organ is an act of unprecedented political imposture because no one ever authorized the members of the Constituent Assembly to negotiate, or, all the more so, to conclude an agreement of any kind with the Soviet regime.[3]

Kolchak's government was well aware of all this: I. Sukin, adviser on foreign affairs, sent a telegram on March 12, 1919 (under Nos. 180/185), to the Russian ambassadors in which he stated: "Those who signed acted only in their own names and on behalf of a group of their supporters, not having any authority either from the assembly or from the party."[4]

The group's appeal to the armed forces to cease fighting had little effect: the detachments of the Committee of the Constituent Assembly, commanded by a Socialist-Revolutionary, formed part of General Kappel's army, and they remained in the ranks and continued fighting. The Siberian Army remained firm. As to the detachments of Bashkirs — some five hundred men — who went over to the side of the Bolsheviks, it is more likely that the reason for this may be found not in the call to cease fighting, but in Admiral Kolchak's nationalist policy. The Czechoslovak detachments had left their front-line positions before the appeal was ever issued. Four Ural Cossack regiments laid down their arms, but the circumstances leading to this were also specific: the Cossacks were exhausted. Because of the poor coordination of the Procurement Office, they suffered from lack of clothing and supplies, and their wounded and sick did not have the necessary medical help. To undertake a grueling march over unpopulated wilderness was simply beyond their means. Moreover, the Ural Cossacks did not need the propaganda of this group of Socialist-Revolutionaries; they had Bolsheviks of their own. As early as the beginning of 1917, a Cossack officer refused to pay allegiance to Ataman Dutov, went to the city of Uralsk, and organized a Cossack detachment of two thousand men that became part of M. V. Frunze's Soviet Army.[5]

Given all these facts, it is hardly possible to consider the Socialist-Revolutionaries responsible for creating a gap in Kolchak's front. On the contrary, the only reason Kolchak's government was not overthrown as soon as it had seized power was the fear of weakening the front.

The notorious Bolshevik amnesty of the Socialist-Revolutionaries, qualified to begin with, was not a general amnesty at all. It was merely a guarantee of individual inviolability granted to all those who crossed to the Soviet side and to those members of the Socialist-Revolutionary Party who supported the platform. The Bolsheviks further required that a declaration of future political loyalty to Soviet power be signed. All those who refused remained in prison.

In Moscow there was talk about legalization and amnesty, even to the extent that a newspaper was allowed to be printed in Petrograd. But then there were second thoughts, and in ten days the newspaper was closed down. At the same time, arrests of Socialist-Revolutionary workers continued. In Moscow, 43 Socialist-Revolutionaries were brought in from Saratov and confined in Butyrsky Prison. And from the city of Ufa, those who had been granted inviolability were being brought in—not as political prisoners, it should be noted, but as prisoners of war.

Members of the Socialist-Revolutionary Party conference held in Moscow in February 1919 reacted to this situation by adopting a resolution "sharply condemning the negotiations of the Ufa delegation members of the Constituent Assembly because they were responsible for the interpretation that this was an act of the party's complete political capitulation to the despotic power of the Bolsheviks."[6]

Refering to this resolution, one of the initiators of negotiations with the Soviets wrote: "We had every reason to suppose that our eastern liquidation effort would meet with a correspondingly serious and responsible attitude. Experience, however, has convinced us that the opposite is true. We have met with a stubborn determination to bring to naught our liquidation of the front and to nullify our agreement with the Bolsheviks, even though it would have meant a common struggle against the dreaded restoration."[7]

As it turned out, the group did commit treason against the party. Because of the distorted interpretation attached to the negotiations and the consequent loss of contact with the Central Committee, the negotiations themselves had an adverse effect on the attitude of the periphery to the center. They also had a devastating effect on the attitude of the peasants toward the party—which they considered to have capitulated. All this was further complicated by the fact that the leading organ of the party, in its then illegal status, did not hold regular meetings of its full staff, and decisions were made haphazardly by a small number of members of the Central Committee who happened to be present. Under these conditions, the center could hardly provide firm leadership. Meetings called on the spur of the moment and attended by a chance gathering of members of the committee were not conducive to working out even a single tactical approach to the problem; and, of course, the situation as a whole took its toll for the future.

In February 1919 a resolution called for a temporary cease-fire against the Bolsheviks, not meant to be interpreted as acceptance of the Bolshevik dictatorship, but as a means of preserving strength, and in March and April of that year a wave of serious uprisings swept through the Soviet Army. Socialist-Revolutionaries participated in these uprisings, but by this time all coordination had been lost, and the periphery acted on its own initiative. The struggle was especially intense in Simbirsk, Samara, and Saratov provinces and in Astrakhan. Frunze was forced to withdraw some large units from the front to put down the rebellions. He sent a special detachment of twelve hundred men, complete with martial law staff, to the city of Sizran alone. As for Siberia, the people there had always lived their own lives, apart from outside influences. The Soviet Army had hardly had time to return to West Siberia when armed conflict against the Bolsheviks broke out, with the participation of the Socialist-Revolutionaries. This conflict continued into 1920, 1921, and 1922, reaching its peak in 1921 in the region of Tumen-Chelyabinsk. The head of the Siberian Cheka informed Moscow in 1922: "The White-bandit bands of Turushkin, Plotnikov, Kaigorodov, and others, attracted by the Socialist-Revolutionaries, have all been annihilated. The Siberian Peasant Union, beginning with its Central Committee and ending with its local branches, has been liquidated, and the greater number of its participants has been shot."[8]

Kolchak's government arrested two Directory members and accused them of having dealings with the Bolsheviks or, in other words, of treason to the government. But the accused men were not brought to trial; they were exiled by the government. Kolchak and his entourage knew well that the charge was false, absolutely without foundation, and that although it could be used for propaganda, it would not stand up in a court of law. The facts reveal the following: in mid-October 1918, a member of the Central Committee of the Socialist Revolutionary Party, A. I. Altovsky, came to Omsk and, together with party member B. Sokolovsky, composed a memorandum to the commander-in-chief of the army, General Boldyrev. They had previously acquainted two members of the Central Committee, who were in Omsk at the time, with the contents. This memorandum had no aim other than to bring to a speedier conclusion victory over the Soviet Army. It outlined a plan of systematic and widespread disintegrating and reconnoitering work to be carried out behind the lines of the Bolshevik forces. The plan was to use the still existent military apparatus of the Socialist-Revolutionary organization in the Volga region to cut off from Soviet Russia not only the provinces of Saratov and Samara and part of the Penza province, but Astrakhan as well. To execute this plan, it was proposed to organize four or five small detachments behind Bolshevik lines. This work was to be directed by a special staff of three under the commander-in-chief, receiving from him strategic assignments and reporting to him the financial and overall state of affairs. The memorandum was delivered to General Boldyrev on October 16, 1918. General Boldyrev, in full sympathy with the plan, suggested that to execute it the authors of the memorandum should contact the head of the reconnaissance division and his aide.[9]

By the end of October the plan was in final form. The Directory, however, to the end of its days, failed to confirm it; the Directory was busy bartering with Omsk about the organization of the ministries. With the coming of power of Admiral Kolchak on November 18, 1918, all of these plans were swept away, which is one reason why the civil war in Siberia became such a drawn-out affair and, in the end, was lost. The question that should be asked here is, "Who helped the Bolsheviks?"

Yet another sin chalked up against the Socialist-Revolutionaries is that they did not support Admiral Kolchak—who, in one of his first acts, ordered the arrest of Socialist-Revolutionaries. But history knows of few cases where political prisoners extolled the virtues of a government that had incarcerated them.[10] A member of the Central Committee, having delivered over the entire government supply of gold taken by the National Army in Kazan—680 million gold rubles—was arrested in Omsk and held there at length under sentence of death. It would seem naïve to expect that a party persecuted by the government should suddenly accept that government and support it; yet such simple-minded sentiment did exist.

The Socialist-Revolutionary Party, advocating as it did the sovereignty of the people and the equal rights of the entire population to participate in the government of the country, was duty-bound to struggle against any dictatorship whatsoever, whether it came from the right or the left. Members of the party, fighting actively on two fronts, held steadfastly to the ideal in the name of which they were willing to go to their deaths. And they died, on the fields of battle, in prisons, in prison camps; yet the idea of the sovereignty of the people has remained alive to this day.

One of the greatest disadvantages of the Socialist-Revolutionary Party at the time was its widespread popularity, and that is what ultimately caused its downfall. This was a party with several thousand members and sympathizers even before the revolution that reached the number five hundred thousand members by mid-1917 and received millions of votes in the Constituent Assembly, but found itself dissolved in the general mass. This was a party destined to have a very short period of time for inner organizational work and for the political education of new members. As a result, the central organs lacked a unified course of action, as membership was chosen on the basis of proportional representation of various factions. There was more than one ground for conflicting opinion—just as there was more than one ground for the solution of tactical problems. All this had a paralyzing effect on action. The pessimism and fatalism prevalent among the intelligentsia in Russia at the time were not unknown among the members of the party, and they served as a brake, interfering with the party's initiative in the struggle. This was apparent in the attempts at organizing a defense of the Constituent Assembly in January 1918, and it was just as apparent when the Directory was in need of defense in November 1918.

At a trial of Socialist-Revolutionaries held in Moscow in 1922, Commissar A. V. Lunacharsky depicted the Communist Party as a rider on the back of a peasant. To this, defendant A. I. Altovsky replied, "It is one thing to ride on the back of a peasant who has temporarily escaped the yoke and quite another to transform people in bondage into free citizens, governing themselves in a free state."[11]

Buffeted simultaneously by blows from the reactionary waves rolling in from right and left, the ship of democracy was crushed. But rising to the surface and floating on the crests of the waves were hundreds of thousands of splinters—and on each was written, "The struggle for the liberation of man is not ended."

11
Conclusion

Following the usurpation of power by the Bolsheviks, we who advocated sovereignty of the people, knowing full well that the Bolsheviks' intent was to make the entire population politically and economically dependent on their good graces, could not refuse to fight for our goal. Likewise, from the moment of the conclusion of the Treaty of Brest-Litovsk, we could not refuse to fight for the independence of Russia.

As the Bolsheviks unfurled their slogan "Long live the civil war," a dilemma faced us: Should we submit in silence, or should we accept the challenge—become slaves, or make a bid for freedom? A small number of us chose freedom, which meant entering into armed conflict with the oppressors. Risking our lives, walking daily on the edge of a precipice, we spent months in painstaking preparation for an armed uprising. Our strength was not in our numbers, but in our ideals. We unfurled our own slogan, calling for a federal organization of the multinational Russian territory with autonomous rule for its different components; for a government system that would allow each national group, within the confines of the whole, the right and opportunity to shape its own destiny according to the traditions of its past.

We won the battles, but we were far from having won the final victory. We laid the foundation for the building of a new government structure, but we did not complete the structure itself. The biblical story about the Tower of Babel was repeated. Having vanquished the Bolsheviks, we acquired new enemies in the persons of those who had earlier voluntarily remained slaves of the dictatorship. Now they were afraid that the regeneration of Russia might take place without their participation, and they began to demand the right not to a proportionate but to a dominating role in the general planning of the government. Because of the civil liberties that had been granted, the reactionary element, rising to the surface, wanted to turn back the wheels of history. Under cover of statesmanship and the preservation of the unity of the country, they sought to restore the old form of government. The situation was complicated by the officers behind the lines, who belonged to this group.

The democratic element, not wishing to endanger the situation at the front, agreed to a compromise: the creation of a coalition government in the Directory, coalition as a temporary measure during the transition from the Bolshevik soviets and the autocratic-bureaucratic state to the creation of autonomous local democratic organs. This was just a compromise measure, and the men elected to the Directory were not notable for strength of character or decisiveness. The Directory members did not take into account the fact that its existence depended upon the support of broad layers of the population, and, yielding to the urgings of the rightists, they liquidated the local oblast governments and the Siberian Oblast Duma. Thus the Directory killed its own life-roots, was left in isolation, and, even before it had had time to put through any laws, had already become the laughingstock of the reactionary elements.

At the very moment when there was hope for a quick victory over the Bolsheviks, the reactionary group, with the active support of the Allied nations, staged a government overthrow by arresting two members of the Directory. Admiral Kolchak was proclaimed the "supreme ruler." This new man at the helm, with no strong views of his own, unstable emotionally and even subject to hysteria, soon became the puppet of the reactionaries who surrounded him. The country was militarized by application of the so-called rule by court-martial; even under autocracy, this method of government had been practiced for a short time only and had been abolished in early 1907. The military units behind the lines were charged with purely police functions. Punitive detachments operated everywhere, engaging, as often as not, in plundering and dealing arbitrarily with those of opposing views. Kolchak's government, instead of fortifying the front against the Bolsheviks, opened up a second, inner front and began persecuting those who had earlier fought the Bolsheviks. The struggle against the Bolsheviks, instead of a fight for freedom, became an occupation of foreign territory. It is difficult to understand how the government proposed to continue this struggle while distrusting the masses of its own people. By pursuing a policy of persecution and annihilation of the socialist intelligentsia, Kolchak's government stripped itself of the very slogans and ideals in the name of which it could have continued the struggle against bolshevism. It ignored the fact that on both sides of the front the overwhelming majority of the armies was composed of workers and peasants who did not want a return of the old order.

All this arbitrariness and the drastic measures taken in dealing with the populace brought forth a reaction that became the partisan movement. There were, perhaps, some rare exceptions; but on the whole, this should be viewed not as a movement organized by the Bolsheviks, but as one that arose out of the need for self-preservation, for protection against unlawful infringement on the personal rights and economic well-being of the people.

The Siberian liberation movement, begun with great success, failed under the onslaught of two reactionary forces. Conducting a war against the Red force, the leaders of the democratic movement were unable to deal with the steadily growing Black force, and it was by this force that they were overcome. The underlying reason for this was, of course, the international situation, which made it possible for representatives of foreign powers to take advantage of these reactionary groups and use them to promote their own interests.

The tragedy of Russian democracy was that by urging the fight against the Bolsheviks it alienated American and European liberal circles, who considered it reactionary; the bourgeois merchant class considered it pro-Bolshevik. The idea of a democratic form of government in Russia held no appeal for either group.

From the moment of the Siberian uprising, the question of the struggle against reactionary dictatorship—a dictatorship hiding behind workers' slogans—ceased to be a question affecting the Russian people only. This reactionary power, having spread its influence far beyond the boundaries of Russia, is a threat to the peaceful existence of many peoples. An ominous force, it is represented in Europe and America as the progressive movement of a freedom-loving nation.

The Siberian liberation movement differed in essence from analogous attempts that took place on the other borders of Russia in that the banner of war was raised in the name of establishing a democratic order. In May 1918, when the uprising began, the call was for a Constituent Assembly and autonomy for Siberia. One and a half years later, units of the Siberian Army in Tomsk, Krasnoyarsk, Novonikolaevsk, and Irkutsk staged an uprising against Kolchak's government, again calling for a Constituent Assembly and autonomy for Siberia.

Difficult as it was to organize the uprising, it was, as became only too apparent, still more difficult to create a working apparatus for a democratic government power. What was lacking was practical experience and a certain amount of decisiveness. What was needed were more men with clear heads, stout hearts, and firm wills—men who could stand up to responsibility.

But this movement has not yet lost either its historic significance or the practical conclusions that arose from it. The Soviet regime has deprived the Russian people of all civil liberties and downgraded them to the position of trained animals in a circus. To end this slavery and to achieve the rights of man, the Russian people must depend solely on themselves.

The sacrifices that have gone into the struggle are not lost. The fight for the rights of man—the liberation of the individual and the securing of his right to take part in government—goes on.

> Ere the last wave can crash ashore,
> The fateful ninth, as reckoned,
> Lesser waves have to crest before—
> The first wave—and the second . . .
>
> Revolutsyonnaya Rossiya, 1905

Appendix A
Chronology of Events

1917

February 23–26. Revolution. Tsar Nicholas II, emperor of all the Russias, abdicates his power to the Provisional Government.

March 20–30. I. M. Sverdlov organizes the first cell of the Leninist Bolshevik splinter group in Krasnoyarsk, Siberia.

April 30. The Krasnoyarsk Bolsheviks break with the Social-Democrats and create their own Leninist Bolshevik Party.

May. The proponents of Siberian autonomy, *oblastniki*, organize a bureau in preparation for an all-Siberian congress of their activists. In Petrograd, the Bolsheviks attempt to seize power.

August. General Kornilov marches on Petrograd with the aim of creating a more conservative government.

September. The Central Committee of the Bolshevik Party sends several groups of party activists, together with five hundred sailors from the Baltic fleet, to Siberia as reinforcements for the local party organizations.

October 23. The Bolsheviks seize power in Petrograd.

November. An uprising by military cadets occurs in Omsk.

December 4–15. The All-Siberian Congress of Oblastniki in Tomsk draws up a program founding the Siberian Oblast Duma (Parliament).

December 8–15. The Siberian Bolsheviks decide to disarm all military units in Irkutsk that do not recognize their authority.

1918

January 7. The Constituent Assembly in Petrograd is dispersed.

January 17. The Cossack uprising in Krasnoyarsk serves as a pretext for mass arrests of opponents of the Soviet regime. The Bolsheviks declare the abolition of city and rural councils.

February 6. The Siberian Oblast Duma is dispersed and several of its members are arrested. The duma then proclaims the need to combat the Soviet regime.

February 28. The Second All-Siberian Congress of Soviets passes a resolution condemning the Treaty of Brest-Litovsk concluded with imperial Germany.

March. An agreement between the Czech Legion (formerly serving on the Ukrainian front) and Commissar Stalin is concluded, permitting the Czechs to proceed to the Far East with part of their military equipment. In Irkutsk, the Provincial Congress of Peasants' Deputies is dispersed by the Soviets by force.

April 5. Japanese troops land in Vladivostok.

May 14. A skirmish occurs in Chelyabinsk between the Czech detachment and Hungarian elements of the Soviet Red Guard.

May 21. S. I. Aralov, chief of operations of the Military Commissariat, sends a telegram proposing to the Czechs that they form a special unit within the Red Army.

May 23. Aralov cables the Soviets: "Take all necessary action forthwith to detain, disarm, and disband all units of the Czech corps."

May 25. Commissar Leon Trotsky cables: "Under penalty of death, it is the duty of all Soviet forces on the railroad to disarm the Czechs."

May 25. The Soviets set up a military headquarters in Omsk, Siberia.

May 25. The Omsk soviet attempts to disarm the Czech detachment at the Kulamzino Station.

May 26. The Czech Legion receives the order to seize control of all railroad movement in West Siberia.

May 26. The West Siberian Commissariat of the Siberian government gives the order to begin the uprising against the Soviets.

May 26. The Czech detachment, along with units of the Siberian government, overthrows the Soviets in Novonikolaevsk.

May 26. The Czechs occupy Mariinsk.

May 28. Units of the Siberian government carry out an unsuccessful assault on Tomsk.

May 29. The Bolsheviks attempt to disarm the Czech detachment at the Kansk railroad station, and Kansk is captured by the Czechs.

May 29. The Tomsk soviet evacuates the city, accompanied by the international brigades.

May 30. Units of the Siberian government occupy Tomsk.

May 30. Units of the Siberian government, along with the Czech detachment, occupy Taiga Station and the town of Petropavlovsk.

May 31. The French Mission cables the Czechs: "Your actions have forced the French Mission to wash its hands of your affairs."

June 1. The West Siberian government declares it has seized power. At the Mariinsk station, the Omsk soviet and the Czechs agree upon a four-day cease-fire.

June 2. The French military attaché telegraphs the Czechs: "Do not permit yourselves to become embroiled in their internal political conflicts."

June 2. The U.S. representative to the Inter-Allied Railway Commission requests that the U.S. consul instruct Gaida and the other Czech commanders to cease fighting and meddling in politics.

June 2. A detachment of Czechs occupies Kurgan.

June 4. With foreign government representatives participating, a ten-day cease-fire on the Mariinsk front is negotiated between the Czechs and the Soviet forces.

June 6. At the conclusion of the cease-fire, the Czechs begin an assault at the Marianovko Station, where they rout a Soviet army of twenty-five hundred men.

June 7. The commander of the Soviet forces of Yeniseisk province makes a speech.

June 7. Using 27 ships, the local soviet and the international brigades evacuate the city of Omsk.

June 7. Units of the Siberian government assume control of Omsk.

June 9. A Czech detachment arrives in Omsk.

June 10. Semipalatinsk is captured by troops of the Siberian government.

June 14. An unsuccessful uprising is led by units of the Siberian government against the Soviets in Irkutsk.

June 16. With the aim of ending the cease-fire, the Czechs, reinforced by units of the Siberian government, launch an attack on Mariinsk, where they destroy a Soviet army of three thousand.

June 18. The town of Achinsk is taken by a combined force of Czechs and troops of the Siberian government.

June 18. In Krasnoyarsk, the Siberian government mounts a successful uprising against the Soviets, who, with the international brigades, evacuate the city in five ships. Military units of the Siberian government storm the local prison and free the head of the Siberian Oblast Duma, members of the Siberian government, and a number of Czechs.

June 20. Gaida's and Pepelyaev's forces arrive in Krasnoyarsk.

June 20. Biisk is captured by Siberian government forces.

June 20. An unsuccessful revolt is attempted against the Soviets in Ekaterinburg.

June 28. The West Siberian Commissariat rescinds the nationalization of industry in all territories under its control.

June 29. The Czech Legion overthrows Soviet forces in Vladivostok.

June 30. The West Siberian Commissariat cedes its power to the Siberian government.

July 4. The Provisional Government declares Siberia an autonomous state.

July 10. Irkutsk is taken by the Czechs with forces of the Siberian government.

July 13. A coalition of politicians in Omsk declares opposition to the convening of the Siberian Oblast Duma.

July 15. The Siberian Provisional Government passes and publishes a law regarding the procedures of declaring territories to be put under martial law.

July 15. The first conference on the structure of a government for all territories freed from the Bolsheviks is convened in Chelyabinsk.

July 18. In Omsk, the Trade-Industry Conference passes a resolution for the abolition of the Siberian Oblast Duma and the establishment of a strong, unified government.

July 25. Gaida declares the existence of a state of siege from Krasnoyarsk to the Far East and sets up a system of military field tribunals. Ekaterinburg is occupied by Siberian troops.

July 27. Grishin-Almazov telegraphs Gaida demanding an explanation for his having violated the Siberian government's edict on law and order by declaring a state of siege.

July 31. The Siberian government orders a mobilization of various draft-age groups.

August 3. British and Japanese troops land at Vladivostok.

August 5. The U.S. government sends a diplomatic note regarding the Allied intervention.

August 6. Japan declares intervention.

August 15. The Siberian Oblast Duma is convened in Tomsk.

August 16. American troops arrive in Vladivostok.

August 20. By request of the Siberian Provisional Government, the provincial duma closes its session.

August 20. Soviet power falls in Verkhneudinsk.

August 23. The second Chelyabinsk conference is convened.

August 24. The Siberian government founds its administrative council (soviet).

August 25. Soviet power falls in Iakutsk.

August 26. Soviet power falls in Chita.

August 28. At the Uralga station of the Baikal Railway Line, the Conference of Soviets decides to cease hostilities and dissolves all military units. The soldiers scatter across the taiga.

September 3. Combined forces take Stretensk, Troitskosavsk, and Kiakhta.

September 5. Grishin-Almazov is dismissed from his post as minister of defense and replaced by Ivanov-Rinov.

September 6. Ivanov-Rinov orders the reintroduction of epaulets.

September 6. Khabarovsk is captured by the Cossacks.

September 1–8. Peasants revolt against the Siberian government in the Slavgorodsk district of Altai province.

September 8–25. Various local governments hold a conference in Ufa.

September 18. The Ufa Conference resolves to convene the Constituent Assembly (formerly the Constituent Commission) on January 1, 1919.

September 18. Soviet power falls in Blagoveshchensk.

September 21. The renegade paramilitary organizations of Volkov and Krasilnikov arrest members of the Siberian government, as well as the president of the Siberian Oblast Duma.

September 21. Officers of Krasilnikov's group murder Novoselov, a member of the Siberian government.

September 24. The five-member Directory is formed.

October 9. The Directory arrives in Omsk.

October 14. Admiral Kolchak arrives in Omsk.

October 14. An all-Siberian railway strike is declared.

October 22. A banquet is held in Krasnoyarsk for officers of the British Expeditionary Forces commanded by Colonel Ward.

October 22. V. M. Chernov puts forth a charter.

October 24. Five members of the Communist Party are forcibly removed from the Krasnoyarsk prison by Czechs and shot.

October 26. B. N. Moiseenko, member of the Constituent Assembly, is murdered in Omsk by officers of Krasilnikov's organization.

October 30. Peasants revolt in seven sectors of the Mariinsk district of Tomsk province.

November 1. Army recruits revolt in Tomsk.

November 2. All provincial governing bodies are dissolved.

November 5. An all-Russian government is established.

November 5. The Siberian Oblast Duma dissolves itself.

November 9. Peasants revolt in the Minusinsk district of Yeniseisk province.

November 18. A change of power is forced in Omsk. Two members of the Directory are arrested.

November 18. Admiral Kolchak is appointed head of state.

November 19. Members of the Constituent Assembly refuse to recognize Kolchak's mandate.

November 19. Members of the Socialist-Revolutionary Party are arrested in Ekaterinburg.

November 21. Volkov, Katanaev, and Krasilnikov, engineers of the coup, are tried and exonerated.

November 21. The arrested members of the Directory are deported.

November 22. The Czechs protest Kolchak's usurpation of power.

November 23. General Boldyrev, a member of the Directory, is forced to leave the country.

November 30. Kolchak orders the arrest of all Socialist-Revolutionary Party members in the Constituent Assembly.

December 21–22. An unsuccessful uprising is led by the Bolsheviks in Omsk; Ivanov-Rinov uses it as a pretext to deal with all political opponents, including those who had no part in the revolt.

December 23. The city of Perm, far from the boundaries of Siberia, is taken by troops of the Siberian government commanded by Gen. A. Pepelyaev.

December 30. The Volsky group, a self-appointed faction of the Socialist-Revolutionary Party made up of a few members of the Constituent Assembly, enters into negotiations with the Soviets.

1919

January 23. The Entente Cordiale proposes to all protagonists in the civil war that they send representatives to confer in the Prinkipo Islands.

February 8. Admiral Kolchak departs for the front. The Socialist-Revolutionary Party conference condemns the Volsky group for irresponsibility in entering into negotiations with the Soviet government.

March 12. I. Sukin, Kolchak's foreign affairs adviser, cables all ambassadors that the Volsky group is concluding an agreement with the Soviet regime without authorization by the Socialist-Revolutionary Party.

March 13. Siberian troops advance on all fronts.

March 14. Admiral Kolchak declares all railroad lines under martial law.

April 7–18. Siberian troops advance.

April 20. The Western Army is defeated on the central front.

May 23. The Southern Army withdraws. The Red Army goes on the offensive in the Perm region.

May 26. General Gaida telegraphs Vologodsky demanding that General Lebedev be relieved of his command.

June 3. The five Great Powers appeal to Kolchak.

June 4. Kolchak replies.

June 8. The Western Army evacuates Ufa.

June 19. The State Economic Conference opens.

June 20. General Gaida is dismissed.

June 20. A delegation of the Central Committee of the Socialist-Revolutionary Party sends a declaration to the Allies stating that in the struggle with the Bolsheviks, democracy alone will prevail.

June 24. The Allies promise to aid Kolchak.

July 8. Siberian troops evacuate Perm.

July 16. Siberian troops evacuate Ekaterinburg.

July 26. Siberian troops evacuate Chelyabinsk.

August 9. Siberian troops evacuate Tiumen.

August 16. Siberian troops evacuate Kurgan.

September 17. Kolchak puts forth a zemstvo charter. U.S. military and diplomatic representatives confer in Vladivostok. Partisans capture Tomsk.

September 21. The French Mission leaves Omsk.

October 15–20. Final battles are fought with the Red Army in the Tobol and Ishim River region.

October 25. Tobolsk is evacuated.

October 30. Petropavlovsk is evacuated.

November 8. In Omsk, the Council of Ministers has a final conference with Kolchak presiding.

November 10. The government evacuates Omsk.

November 12. Kolchak leaves Omsk.

November 14. Omsk is abandoned without a struggle.

November 17–20. In Vladivostok, General Gaida and the president of the Siberian Oblast Duma lead an uprising against the government.

November 19. The government declares its willingness to work with the citizens.

November 23. The chairman of the Council of Ministers, P. Vologodsky, resigns; V. Pepelyaev is appointed in his place.

December 6. The commander of a group of Siberian troops leads an uprising against Kolchak and occupies Novonikolaevsk. He demands a convocation of the Siberian Constituent Assembly. By order of General Voitsekhovsky, the commander and 32 other officers are shot.

December 7. Gen. A. Pepelyaev demands Kolchak's dismissal and the immediate convocation of the Siberian Constituent Assembly.

December 9. Gen. A. Pepelyaev and the chairman of the Council of Ministers, V. Pepelyaev, arrest General Sakharov, army commander-in-chief, for chaotic and disgraceful withdrawals in general and for dereliction of duties at Omsk in particular. They demand Kolchak's dismissal and his departure from Siberia.

December 11. Semipalatinsk is taken by the Red Army.

December 11. General Kappel is appointed army commander-in-chief.

December 12. Partisans take the town of Minusinsk, Yeniseisk province.

December 14. Novonikolaevsk is overrun by the Red Army.

December 16. At a conference in London, the Entente Cordiale resolves to discontinue aid to the anti-communist forces.

December 19. The commander of the First Division of the Siberian Army demands Kolchak's dismissal and transfers civil powers in Yeniseisk province to rural and city institutions.

December 20. Tomsk is occupied by partisans.

December 21. An uprising in Cherenkhov is led by the Political Center.

December 23. Kolchak designates Ataman G. Semenov as supreme commander, Far Eastern region.

December 24. An uprising in Irkutsk is led by the Political Center.

December 24. The Red Army reaches Taiga Station.

December 25. The Red Army enters Mariinsk.

1920

January 2. A truce is concluded between the local government and the Irkutsk garrison, loyal to Kolchak.

January 4. Admiral Kolchak transfers power to General Denikin.

January 5. The Irkutsk local government assumes the reins of power from the weak remnants of Kolchak's government.

January 7. The Red Army arrives in Krasnoyarsk.

January 14. The diplomatic corps departs Irkutsk.

January 15. Kolchak is handed over to the local government.

January 16. The Allies sign a trade agreement with Soviet Russia abolishing all trade restrictions.

January 21. The Political Center transfers power to the Revolutionary Committee.

January 25. General Kappel dies.

January 31. General Rozanov, commander of the Primorskii (maritime) province, leaves Vladivostok; power is passed to the Zemskaia Uprava (zemstvo administration).

February 3. General Voitsekhovsky demands of the Revolutionary Committee that Admiral Kolchak and some gold reserves be handed over to him.

February 7. Admiral Kolchak and V. Pepelyaev, chairman of the Council of Ministers, are executed in Irkutsk in accordance with a decree of the Revolutionary Council.

Appendix B

Chernov Memorandum

The Socialist-Revolutionary [S-R] Party. "In struggle you will win your right." To all party organizations.

In the struggle under way between Soviet Russia and Russia of the Constituent Assembly, between ochlocracy and democracy, the latter is threatened by counterrevolutionary elements who are joining with the aim of enslaving it.

Therefore, the S-R Party, at the center of the struggle for the Constituent Assembly, must first and foremost guarantee that it does not become engulfed by the wave of counterrevolution, much as a year ago it was engulfed by the wave of bolshevik anarchy.

One of the surest guarantees against such a danger is the formation, on Russian territory liberated from bolshevism, of a central governmental authority to carry high the banner of popular sovereignty untarnished by dealings with open or secret enemies, to energetically consolidate the organization of laboring democracy, and to equally energetically defeat all efforts to organize counterrevolutionary plots and forces.

Moreover, the existence of such an authority would serve as a pledge of the popularity of the cause of the Constituent Assembly among the toiling masses in soviet Russia, and therefore, as a pledge of its [the Constituent Assembly's] ultimate triumph.

But a satisfactory resolution of the tasks of organizing an authority was not achieved at the state conference at Ufa.

The circumstances complicating the correct resolution of the task included: the press of an exceedingly difficult international situation, com-

---

SOURCE: V. M. Chernov collection, Hoover Institution Archives, Stanford.

pounded by the absence of a single central authority; the determined resistance of a reactionary imperialist group entrenched in the Siberian government and aided by the ruling circles of the Cossacks; and the threat of conspiracies fraught with civil war in an atmosphere of military losses on the front of the Constituent Assembly, weakened by secret and open defeatists.

On the other hand, the outcome of the conference was shaped by the general weakness of the position of the S-R faction, which suffers from insufficient unity and discipline and is terrorized by military losses and the threatened actions of rightist elements; consequently, the faction is unable to guarantee the S-R Party the place in the government that is commensurate with its moral and political authority among the masses.

The major triumph of the party at the Ufa Conference—the recognition by the conference of the party as the legal majority of the Constituent Assembly as elected—threatens to become a purely nominal one because, in their latest pronouncements, Cossack leaders and Kadet supporters of the Siberian orientation seem to be ignoring altogether the general political promises they took upon themselves at Ufa. As far as the points on which the party was forced to yield, such as the questions of the makeup and lack of authority of the Directory and the fixing of a date for the convocation of the Constituent Assembly, these points' significance is now becoming clear in the series of political misdeeds unmasked by the Provisional Government.

These misdeeds include: the selection of an official residence; the territorial separation of deputies of the Constituent Assembly from the congress; the transfer of all general governmental functions to the corresponding ministries of the Siberian government; the confirmation of the temporary dispersal of the Siberian Oblast Duma; the ongoing failure to punish the inspirers and leaders of the Omsk counterrevolutionary conspiracy; the reinstatement of epaulets and discipline of the old army; the attempt to abolish agitational, cultural, and enlightenment work in the army; and a whole series of personnel appointments giving the army over into the hands of reactionary generals and atamans.

Despite these misdeeds and the signs of weakness and indecision, the S-R Party, in accordance with the promises made at Ufa, continues to support fully the central government in its struggle with the "commissarocracy" and is prepared to render it full support in its struggle with reactionary adventurist groups, into whose hands has fallen local power in places and who are trying to render purely nominal the authority of the all-Russian provisional government.

The S-R Party is further prepared to render full support to the Provisional Government in the defense of democratic freedoms and the independence of Russia and in the establishment of normal relations with allies, on condition that the occupation of territory by foreign troops will not encroach on the sovereignty of the nation. At the same time the party presumes that the nation has the right to be adequately informed about the appropriate measures of the Provisional Government, whose formal lack of legal authority in no way should be license for a return to all the defects of the former secret diplomacy.

Irrespective of the strength and readiness of the Provisional Government, in its current makeup, to act vigorously in all the noted directions, the S-R Party must make its central tactic the gathering of its own democratic forces and those sympathetic to it around the Constituent Assembly and its precursor, the Congress of Deputies of the Constituent Assembly.

The work of the congress must be propaganda for laboring democracy in favor of a future government responsible to the Constituent Assembly, in accordance with the social and political lines of its majority, and homogeneous enough in its makeup to implement its policies, not only on paper but in fact, with the determination and energy dictated by the urgency of the present moment.

In accordance with this, the Congress of Deputies of the Constituent Assembly should begin immediately the working out and widespread publicizing of legislative bills for the Constituent Assembly and prepare a plan for the organization of a state in accordance with the federal structure of Russia. The activity of the congress should be directed toward affirming among the masses the idea of popular sovereignty and toward the mobilization of society's democratic forces in the name of the defense of the Constituent Assembly, such that, in the event of an encroachment on its rights, the congress could become the organizing center for a revolutionary all-Russian authority in defense of the assembly.

The party, for its part, must close and tighten its ranks, cure itself of its lack of confidence, vacillation, unhealthy fear of responsibility, and tendency to capitulate readily before external pressure. Such ailments have worked their way into the ranks and threaten to isolate the leadership from the lower layers of the party who are oversensitive to their own vacillations as well and serve to prepare the ground for defeat.

If this condition is satisfied, the sobering of the masses from the mirages of bolshevism and Left S-Rism and the political bankruptcy of those fanatics and adventurers who are leading them will naturally return to the party's sphere of influence those mass elements who were torn away from it by the shameless demagogy and revolutionary intoxication of the recent stormy period.

In expectation of the possibility of political crises that might be provoked by counterrevolutionary conspiracies, all party forces must be mobilized now, trained for military action, and armed so that they are ready at any moment to withstand the blows of the counterrevolutionary organizers of civil war in the rear of the anti-bolshevik front.

The gathering, rallying, comprehensive political instruction, and purely military mobilization of the party's forces must be the major focus of activity of the Central Committee and should provide the Central Committee with reliable points of support for its ongoing influence in the civilian sphere.

Party activity in Soviet Russia should be a natural supplement to the work of the Central Committee by attracting to the banners of the party all those mass elements who have come to be sobered up from the bolshevik intoxication. [The Party] must demonstrate to them that only the workings of the Constituent Assembly and the leading faction of S-Rs in that body is capable of guaranteeing the people that dominance by Bolsheviks will not be replaced by that of the counterrevolution.

The party must be radically purged of all alien elements who are responsible for its demoralization, for eroding the steadfastness of its socialist positions and the unity of its tactics and, thereby, undermining its discipline and energy.

Only through such a rectification of its political behavior can the activity of the S-R Party stand equal to the current tragic period of Russian and world history. With each new step it can take in new layers of the masses who were once seduced and then taught by life's bitter experience and become more and more a genuine party of the people. And in this once and for all indestructible tie with the people, the party can draw on its strength to resolve those political issues which, for the Russian people, are now questions of life and death.

The Central Committee of the Socialist-Revolutionary Party
Ufa, October 22, 1918.

Notes

Introduction

1. There were two types of exile. Administrative exile was by order of the secretary of the interior, could be from one to five years, and did not strip a person of civil rights. Furthermore, the government gave monthly financial assistance for living expenses, the amount depending on the locale and the climatic conditions. The second type of exile denied the accused civil rights and was the result of a court order after a trial. Such sentences were for life, without any government assistance.

2. In July 1917 R. Eideman, together with other Left Socialist-Revolutionaries, left the party and worked with the Bolsheviks. In 1937, when he was head of the Military Academy of the Red Army, he was shot, together with Tukhachevsky. (Boris Levytsky, *The Stalinist Terror in the Thirties* [Stanford: Hoover Institution Press, 1974], pp. 61–62.)

Chapter 1

1. S. G. Svatikov, "Rossiia i Sibir'," *Vol'naia Sibir'*, no. 4 (1928): 86.

2. Ibid., p. 91.

3. Ibid., p. 90.

4. G. N. Potanin (1845–1920) was a Siberian Cossack officer who, for his participation in the movement for an autonomous Siberia, served time at hard labor and in exile from 1865 to 1874. He was an outstanding scholar and writer in geography, ethnography, and folklore. His more important works deal with the culture, customs, and folk art of the many Turkoman and Mongolian tribes in Siberia and Central Asia as well as the Mongols of northern China.

5. N. A. Lapin, *Revoliutsionnoe demokraticheskoe dvizhenie 60-godov XIX veka v zapadnoi Sibiri* (Sverdlovsk: Sredne-Ural'skoe Knizhnoe Izd-vo, 1967), pp. 112–13.

6. Svatikov, "Rossiia i Sibir'," p. 118.

7. M. M. Stishov, *Bol'shevitskoe podpol'e i partizanskoe dvizhenie* (Moscow: Moskovskii Universite, 1962), p. 12.

8. N. V. Blinov, "Sotsial-demokraticheskaia organizatsiia v Sibiri," *Sibirskie ogni* 8 (1929).

9. Stishov, *Bol'shevitskoe podpol'e*, p. 15.

Chapter 2

1. R. Eideman, "Ulichnye boi," *Sibirskie ogni* 6 (1927).

2. V. I. Lenin, "O politicheskom poloshenii," July 23, 1917, in *Works*, 5th ed. (Moscow: Izd-vo Politicheskaia Literatura, 1974), 34:1–5.

3. V. Safronov, *Oktiabr v Sibiri* (Krasnoyarsk: Krasnoiarskoe Knizhnoe Izd-vo, 1962), p. 319.

4. Ibid., p. 320.

5. Lenin, "Odin is Korennukh Voprosov Revoliutsii," in *Works*, 34:204.

6. Safronov, *Oktiabr*, p. 346.

7. M. Frumkin, "Fevral-Oktiabr v Krasnoiarske, 1917," *Proletarskaia revoliutsiia* 21 (1923): 146.

8. Ibid., p. 145.

9. Safronov, *Oktiabr*, p. 145.

10. Ibid., pp. 473–85.

11. M. A. Gudoshnikov, *Ocherki po istorii grazhdanskoi voini v Sibiri* (Irkutsk: Irkutskoe Knizhnoe Izd-vo, 1959), p. 7.

12. Ibid., p. 15.

13. Safronov, *Oktiabr*, p. 355.

14. Ibid., p. 355.

15. Ibid., p. 503.

16. Frumkin, "Fevral-Oktiabr," p. 149.

17. Ibid., pp. 150–51.

18. Safronov, *Oktiabr*, p. 484.

19. See Safronov's conclusions about this period: "The lessons that the revolutionary events in Siberia have taught have been instrumental in laying bare the propaganda of the bourgeoisie and its lackeys to the effect that the Communists in Russia wrested power from a democracy by way of force. To show the inconsistency of these assertions, it is enough to be reminded that in Siberia and the Far East, where the population is almost ten million and where there were not more than ten thousand Bolsheviks, the Socialist Revolution triumphed by peaceful means." (Ibid., p. 606.)

20. V. D. Vegman, "Sibirskaia krasnaia gvardiia," *Prosveshchenie Sibiri* 88 (1931): 39.

21. Safronov, *Oktiabr*, p. 600.

22. Vegman, "Sibirskaia krasnaia gvardiia," p. 38.

23. Safronov, *Oktiabr*, p. 506.

24. B. Shumiatskii, *Tovarisch* (Irkutsk), April 7, 1918.

25. Frumkin, "Fevral-Oktiabr," p. 152.

26. Safronov, *Oktiabr*, p. 607.

27. Frumkin, "Fevral-Oktiabr," p. 151.

28. Vegman, "Sibirskaia krasnaia gvardiia," p. 38. Other Soviet accounts repeat this picture of bolshevik failure. "There was no unity and no support on the part of the villages for the workers" (V. Maksakov and A. Turunov, *Khronika grazhdanskoi voini v Sibiri* [Moscow: Gos. Izd-vo, 1926], p. 3). "Soon the villages began to show rather a lack of unanimity toward Soviet power— interest in the new regime waned since there are no large landowners in Siberia and there is nothing to divide" (P. S. Parfenov, *Uroki proshlogo* [Harbin, 1921], p. 18). "The soviets in Siberia were created as a direct reaction to the revolutionary struggle in the center. The Bolsheviks played a decisive role in their formation. However, here, as in the entire country, the Socialist-Revolutionaries and the Mensheviks seized the leadership. The impact of the petty-bourgeois element in Siberia, where there was a lack of any significant industrial proletariat, was especially strong." (Stishov, *Bol'shevitskoe podpol'e*, p. 24.) "It was thus in Siberia's agrarian structure itself—in the character and special quality of the social groups among the Siberian peasantry— that lay the foundation that determined the difficulty and peculiarity of the process of forming a union between the working class and the peasantry" (ibid., p. 43).

29. Maksakov and Turunov, *Khronika*, pp. 149–51.

30. *Delo Narodh*, December 2, 1917.

31. P. Mikhailov was a member of the West Siberian Commissariat; Colonel Grishin-Almazov was deputy minister of war.

32. Parfenov, *Uroki proshlogo*, p. 29.

Chapter 3

1. F. Shteidler, "Vystuplenie chekhoslovakov v Rossii 1918 goda," *Vol' naia Sibir'*, no. 4 (1928): 15.

2. Ibid., p. 23.

3. Ibid., p. 24.

4. M. Frumkin, "K istorii sverzheniia sovetskoi blasti v Sibiri," *Proletarskaia revolutsiia*, 4 (1922): 17.

5. Ibid., pp. 19–21.

6. E. Harris, Archive, File on Omsk political situation, Box 2, Hoover Institution Archives.

7. Ibid.

8. Ibid.

9. *Dokumenty geroicheskoi bor'by: Arkhiv krasnoiarskogo kraia* (Krasnoyarsk: Krasnoiarskoe Knizhnoe Izd-vo, 1959), pp. 42–45.

10. Ibid., p. 50.

11. Arkipova, "Evakuatsiia krasnoiarskogo soveta," *Proletarskaia revoliutsiia* 5 (1922): 312.

12. Ibid., p. 315.

13. A. N. Reznichenko, *Bor'ba bol'shevikov protiv "demokraticheskoi" kontrrevoliutsii v Sibiri* (Novosibirsk: Zap.-S.b. Knizhnoe Izd-vo, 1962), states (p. 75) that "the Red Guardsmen of Dubrovinsky's detachment were arrested the very next day." This is sheer fiction on the part of this "historian," who has distorted the truth. It was in my name that the railroad workers on the train conducted negotiations with Dubrovinsky. On December 13, 1918, I relinquished my authority in governing the district. Up to that time not one Red Guardsman had been arrested.

14. I. N. Smirnov, *Bor'ba za Ural i Sibir'* (Moscow: Gos. Izd-vo, 1926), p. 187.

15. *Arkhiv krasnoiarskogo kraia*, p. 44.

16. Ibid., p. 42.

Chapter 4

1. P. Vologodskii, Dnevnik, p. 15, Hoover Institution Archives.

2. Ibid., p. 19.

3. Ibid., p. 26.

4. *Zaria* 28 (July 18, 1918).

5. *Sibirskaia Rech'* 38 (1918).

6. A. V. Stepanov-Ivanov, Letter, January 27, 1950, Hoover Institution Archives.

7. Vologodskii, Dnevnik, p. 40.

8. Ibid., p. 68.

9. I. I. Serebrennikov, *Moi vospominaniia* (Tientsin, 1937–1940), p. 113.

10. Vologodskii, Dnevnik, p. 56.

11. Harris, Archive.

12. Arkhipova, "Evakuatsiia krasnoiarskogo soveta," pp. 314–15.

13. Vologodskii, Dnevnik, p. 44.

14. G. K. Guins, *Sibir', soiuzniki i Kolchak* (Peking: Izd-vo Russian Mission, 1921), 1:199–201.

15. Ibid., 2:96.

16. Parfenov, *Uroki proshlogo*, p. 74.

17. Approximately from the mid-fifteenth century, at the time of the emergence of the Cossack military communities, the Cossacks had elected by universal and free vote an ataman from among their ranks, whose duties were purely administrative. The responsible decisions were made by the military government. In times of war, a campaign ataman was elected. Beginning with the eighteenth century, the ataman was expected to coordinate his operations with other military groups, and he was subordinate to the all-Russian commander-in-chief. Atamanshchina is an ugly parody of the Cossack form of government. This term is used to describe what happened when military opportunists would proclaim themselves atamans and organize detachments, ignoring the laws, acting arbitrarily, and, as a rule, refusing to subordinate themselves to the central power.

18. *Vol'naya Sibir'*, no. 4 (1928): 80.

19. *Zemskoe delo* (Krasnoyarsk), no. 4 (1918): 20–21.

20. Guins, *Sibir', soiuzniki*, 1:178.

21. *Vol'naya Sibir'*, no. 4 (1928): 81.

22. Vologodskii, Dnevnik, pp. 98–99.

23. A. Gan (Gutman), *Rossiia i bol'shevizm* (Shanghai, 1922), p. 239.

24. Guins, *Sibir', soiuzniki*, 1:239, 241.

25. Stepanov-Ivanov, Letter, p. 3.

26. Guins, *Sibir', soiuzniki*, 2:242.

27. S. P. Mel'gunov, *Tragediia Admirala Kolchaka* (Belgrade: Russkaia Tipografa, 1931), 2:11.

28. Harris, Archive, File on Omsk political situation, May–November 1918, p. 12.

29. Vologodskii, Dnevnik, p. 127.

30. Ibid., pp. 98–99.

31. Ibid., p. 110.

32. Maksakov and Turunov, *Khronika*, p. 240.

33. Vologodskii, Dnevnik, p. 110.

Chapter 5

1. *Byloe* 20 (1923): 15.

2. K. V. Sakharov, *Belaia Sibir'* (Munich, 1923), p. 15.

3. V. G. Boldyrev, *Direktoriia, Kolchak i interventi* (Novonikolaevsk: Sibkraiizdat, 1925), p. 84.

4. Sakharov, *Belaia Sibir'*, p. 28.

5. J. D. Ward, *Soiuznaia interventsiia v Sibiri* (Moscow: Gos. Izd-vo, 1923), p. 71.

6. Ibid., p. 71.

7. Ibid., p. 74.

8. Literally, an association for freeing. Members included socialists and liberals who had no official status in their parties. The goal of the organization was the overthrow of Soviet power and the establishment of a bourgeois republic.

9. Boldyrev, *Direktoriia*, p. 96.

10. Vologodskii, Dnevnik, p. 211.

11. Parfenov, *Uroki proshlogo*, p. 82.

12. Stepanov-Ivanov, Letter, p. 3.

13. V. D. Nabokov, *Ispytaniia diplomata* (London: Duckworth, 1921), p. 245.

14. Ward, *Soiuznaia interventsiia*, p. 82.

15. Sakharov, *Belaia Sibir'*, p. 19.

16. Ibid., p. 19.

17. Serebrennikov, *Moi vospominaniia*, p. 218.

18. Vologodskii, Dnevnik, p. 223.

19. Guins, *Sibir', souizniki*, 1:308–9.

20. Ibid., 1:315.

21. Boldyrev, *Direktoriia*, p. 61.

22. Vologodskii, Dnevnik, p. 319.

23. Guins, *Sibir', soiuzniki*, 1:264.

24. Ibid., 2:21.

25. Ibid., 1:264.

26. Harris, Archive.

27. A. P. Budberg, "Zapiski belogvardeitsa," p. 95, Hoover Institution Archives.

28. Guins, *Sibir', soiuzniki*, 2:42.

29. Ibid., 2:368.

Chapter 6

1. Guins, *Sibir', soiuzniki*, 1:312.

2. In November 1918 at Lenin's suggestion, the Soviet of People's Commissars decided to establish an Extraordinary Commission to Combat Counterrevolution and Sabotage (Cheka). This commission was entrusted with unlimited powers to arrest, conduct investigations, try cases, pass sentences (including death), and see that punishments were carried out. In many cases, the reason for the arrest was not for a crime against the Soviets, but because of a person's education, profession, or upper-class origins.

3. Guins, *Sibir, soiuzniki*, 2:96.

4. Vologodskii, Dnevnik, p. 273.

5. I. Subbotovskii, *Soiuzniki i russkie reaktsionery* (Leningrad: Vestnik Leningradskogo Soveta, 1926), p. 295.

6. Ibid., p. 300.

7. M. Girs, File of telegrams, Hoover Institution Archives.

8. *Byloe* 21 (1923).

9. Ward, *Soiuznaia interventsiia*, p. 99.

10. Guins, *Sibir', soiuzniki*, 2:99.

11. Kolosov, "Kak eto bylo," *Byloe* 21 (1923).

12. Guins, *Sibir', soiuzniki*, 2:398.

13. Vologodskii, Dnevnik, p. 255.

14. Guins, *Sibir', soiuzniki*, 1:312.

15. Sakharov, *Belaia Sibir'*, p. 47.

16. Mel'gunov, *Tragediia Kolchaka*, p. 120.

17. V. I. Vyrypaev, manuscript, Box 1, pp. 70, 71, Hoover Institution Archives.

18. Harris, Archive, File on U.S. Legation, Peking, January 1919, telegram no. 24.

19. Ibid., telegram no. 69.

20. Vyrypaev, p. 74.

21. Ibid., pp. 17, 61.

22. Sakharov, *Belaia Sibir'*, pp. 55, 57.

23. Ward, *Soiuznaia interventsiia*, p. 109.

24. Vologodskii, Dnevnik, p. 233.

25. A. Turunov, *Partizanskoe dvizhenie v Sibiri* (Moscow, 1925), p. 174.

26. Ibid., p. 115.

27. B. Solodovnikov, *Sibirskie avantury i General Gaida* (Prague: Tip. Politika, 192–?), pp. 86–87.

28. Mel'gunov, *Tragediia Kolchaka*, p. 224.

29. E. Varnek and H. H. Fisher, *The Testimony of Kolchak* (Stanford: Stanford University Press, 1935), p. 213.

30. Mel'gunov, *Tragediia Kolchaka*, p. 214.

31. Turunov, *Partizanskoe dvizhenie*, pp. 147–48.

32. P. S. Troitskii, *Krasnyi arkhiv*, no. 6 (1937): 119–20.

33. K. Seleznev, *Partizanskoe dvizhenie v zapadnoi Sibiri, 1918–1919* (Novosibirsk: Zapadno-Sibirskoe Izd-vo, 1936), p. 144.

34. Vologodskii, Dnevnik, pp. 98–99.

35. Turunov, *Partizanskoe dvizhenie*, p. 20: letter from author to minister of interior.

36. Ibid., p. 22: report of author.

37. Ibid.: report of General Shil'nikov, head of the detachment.

Chapter 7

1. Budberg, "Zapiski belogvardeitsa," p. 167.
2. Guins, *Sibir', soiuzniki*, 1:168.
3. Vologodskii, Dnevnik, p. 302.
4. Ibid.
5. Vyrypaev, p. 91.
6. P. P. Petrov, *Ot Volgi do Tikhogo Okeana* (Riga: M. Didkovsky, 1930), pp. 75–76, 80.
7. Ibid., p. 92.
8. Vyrypaev, p. 98.
9. Petrov, *Ot Volgi*, pp. 241, 242.
10. Vologodskii, Dnevnik, pp. 359–60: telegram from Gaida to Vologodskii, May 26, 1919.
11. A. A. Kirilov, "Sibirskie armie v bor'be za osvobozhdenie," *Vol'naia Sibir'*, no. 4 (1928): 66.
12. Serebrennikov, *Moi vospominaniia*, p. 270.
13. Ibid., p. 243.
14. Vologodskii, Dnevnik, p. 411.
15. Budberg, "Zapiski belogvardeitsa," p. 174.
16. Quoted in V. S. Dragomiretskii, *Chekhoslovakii v Rossii* (Paris: Praga, 1928), p. 144.
17. Sakharov, *Belaia Sibir'*, p. 152.
18. V. N. Pepeliaev, "Razval Kolchakovshchiny," *Krasnyi archiv*, no. 31 (1928): 76.
19. Budberg, "Zapiski belogvardeitsa," p. 125.
20. Ibid., p. 176.
21. Ibid., p. 130.
22. Ibid., p. 138.
23. Ibid., p. 113.
24. Vologodskii, Dnevnik, pp. 436–37.
25. Pepeliaev, "Razval Kolchakovshchiny," p. 76.
26. Vologodskii, Dnevnik, p. 422.
27. Guins, *Sibir', soiuzniki*, 2:251, 253.
28. Ibid., p. 253.
29. Ibid., pp. 245, 246, 249.
30. A. Denikin, *Ocherki russkoi smuty* (Berlin: Izd-vo Slovo, 1923), p. 3:259.
31. Sakharov, *Belaia Sibir'*, p. 177.
32. N. Kalashnikov, *Sibirski arkhiv* 2 (1929): 81.

33. Ibid., p. 84.

34. General Puchkov, "Ledianoi pokhod," *Vestnik O'va Russkikh veteranov*, no. 46/47 (1947): 33.

35. V. Konstantino, *Poslednii dni Kolchakovshchiny* (Moscow: Gos. Izd-vo, 1926), p. 146.

36. Vyrypaev, p. 117.

37. Ibid., pp. 109, 110.

38. A. P. Budberg, Dnevnik, Hoover Institution Archives.

Chapter 8

1. E. Sychev, "Zapiski," Hoover Institution Archives.

2. E. Dzhemson, *Peregovori o sdache vlasti Omskim pravitelstvom Politicheskomu Tsentru* (Harbin, 1921), p. 23.

3. Anatolii Markov, "Encyclopedia of the White Movement," Hoover Institution Archives, 2:265a.

4. Sakharov, *Belaia Sibir'*, p. 190.

5. Ibid., p. 320.

6. Dzhemson, *Peregovori*, pp. 6–7.

7. General Zankevich, "Obstoiatel'stva soprovozhdavshie vydachu Adm. Kolchaka," *Beloe delo* 2 (1956): 152.

8. Ibid., p. 154.

Chapter 9

1. W. Graves, *America's Siberian Adventure, 1918–1920* (New York: J. Cape & H. Smith, 1931), p. 9.

2. Ibid., p. 4.

3. Harris, Archive, File on U.S. Legation, Peking, March 1919, no. 194.

4. Graves, *America's Siberian Adventure*, pp. 341–42.

5. Harris, Archive, File, "Kolchak, Adm.-government."

6. M. A. Inostrantsev, "Pervoe poruchenie Kolchaka," *Beloe delo* 1 (1956): 107.

7. Ibid., p. 108.

8. Socialist-Revolutionary Party Archive, file no. 467, International Institute of Social History, Amsterdam.

Chapter 10

1. Guins, *Sibir', soiuzniki*, 2:397.

2. Ibid., 2:438.

3. Girs, Archive, Box 50–1, pp. 143–44: telegram from Sukin to Ambassador Sazonov in Paris.

4. Ibid.

5. L. M. Spirin, *Klassy i partii v grazhdanskoi voine v Rossii* (Moscow: Mysl', 1968).

6. *Delo Naroda*, no. 1 (March 20, 1919): 3.

7. V. Vol'skii, *K prekrascheniu voiny vnutri demokratii* (Moscow, 1919), p. 103.

8. *Sibirskie ogni* 2 (1922): 131.

9. Vera Vladimirova, "Rabota Eserov v 1918 g.," *Krasnyi archiv*, no. 20 (1927).

10. An exception to this may have been witnessed at the open trials of Communists, who praised their party and its leader; but this must be looked upon as a very special achievement of the Soviet regime.

11. *Revoliutsionnaia Rossiia*, no. 21/22 (1922): 22.

Bibliography

Agabekov, G. S. *Zapiski chekista* [Notes of a Chekist]. Berlin: Izd-vo Strela, 1930.

Agalakov, V. M. *Iz istorii stroitel'stva sovetskoi vlasti v vostochnoi Sibiri* [A history of the establishment of Soviet power in East Siberia]. Irkutsk: Irkutskoe Knizhnoe Izd-vo, 1958.

Akulinin, I. G. *Orenburskoe kazach'e voisko v bor'be s bol'shevikami* [The Orenburg Cossacks' struggle against the Bolsheviks]. Shanghai: Slovo, 1937.

Alekseev, S. A. *Grazhdanskaia voina v Sibiri i severnoi oblasti* [The civil war in Siberia and the northern provinces]. Moscow: Gos. Izd-vo, 1927.

Argunov, A. A. *Mezhdu dvumia bol'shevizmami* [Between two bolshevisms]. Paris: Izd-vo Union, 1919.

Aripov, R., and Mil'shtein, N. *Iz istorii organov gos bezopasnosti Uzbekistana* [A history of the organs of state security in Uzbekistan]. Tashkent: Uzbekistan, 1967.

Arkhipova. "Evakuatsiia krasnoiarskogo soveta" [The evacuation of the Krasnoyarsk Soviet]. *Proletarskaia revoliutsiia* 5 (1922).

Baz, I. *Pochemu my pobedili v grazhdanskoi voine* [Why we won the civil war]. Moscow: Gos. Izd-vo, 1930.

Berk, Stephen M. "The Coup d'Etat of Admiral Kolchak." Manuscript. Hoover Institution Archives, Stanford.

Blinov, N. V. "Sotsial-demokraticheskaia organizatsiia v Sibiri" [Social-democratic organizations in Siberia]. *Sibirskie ogni* 8 (1929).

Boldyrev, V. G. *Direktoriia Kolchak i interventi* [The Directory, Kolchak, and the Allied interventionists]. Novonikolaevsk: Sibkraiizdat, 1925.

Borisov, V. *Dal'nii vostok vesna 1921 g.* [The Far East in spring 1921]. Vienna: Izd-vo Novaia Rossiia, 1921.

Bozhenko, L. I. *Sibirskaia derevnia v period 1921–1928* [The Siberian country-side, 1921–1928]. Tomsk: Izd-vo Tomskogo Universiteta, 1978.

Budberg, Gen. A. P. Dnevnik [Diary]. Hoover Institution Archives, Stanford.

————. "Zapiski belogvardeitsa" [Notes on the White Guards]. Hoover Institution Archives, Stanford.

Bullard, Arthur. *The Russian Pendulum*. New York: Macmillan, 1919.

Bunyan, James. *The Origin of Forced Labor in the Soviet State*. Baltimore: Johns Hopkins University Press, 1967.

Burevoi, K. S. *Kolchakovshchina* [The Kolchak regime]. Moscow: Gos. Izd-vo, 1919.

Chernov, V. M. *Pered burei* [Before the storm]. New York: Izd-vo Chekhov, 1953.

————. *Zapiski sotsialista-revoliutsionera* [Notes of a Socialist-Revolutionary]. Berlin: Izd-vo Grzhebin, 1922.

Denikin, A. I. *Ocherki russkoi smuty* [Essays on the Russian uprisings]. Berlin: Izd-vo Slovo, 1923.

Dokumenty geroicheskoi bor'by: Arkhiv krasnoiarskogo kraia [Documents of a heroic struggle: Archives of the Krasnoyarsk district]. Krasnoyarsk: Krasnoiarskoe Knizhnoe Izd-vo, 1959.

Dragomiretskii, V. S. *Chekhoslovakii v Rossii* [The Czechoslovaks in Russia]. Paris: Praga, 1928.

Dubina, I. D. *Partizanskoe dvizhenie v vostochnoi Sibiri, 1918–1920* [The partisan movement in East Siberia, 1918–1920]. Irkutsk: Vostochno-Sibirskoe Knizhnoe Izd-vo, 1967.

Dvorianov, N. V. *V tylu u Kolchaka* [Behind Kolchak's lines]. Moscow: Izd-vo Sovetskoi Lit-ry, 1963.

Dzhemson, E., ed. *Peregovori o sdache vlasti Omskim pravitelstvom Politiche-skomu Tsentru* [Negotiations regarding the Omsk government's relinquishing of power to the Political Center]. Stenographic notes. Harbin, 1921.

Eideman, R. "Ulichnye boi" [Battles in the streets]. *Sibirskie ogni* 6 (1927).

Eihe, G. I. *Oprokinutyi tyl'* [The rear overrun]. Moscow: Gos. Izd-vo, 1966.

Footman, David. *The Last Days of Kolchak*. Oxford: Oxford University Press, 1953.

————. *Siberian Partisans in the Civil War*. Oxford: Oxford University Press, 1954.

Frumkin, M. "Fevral-Oktiabr v Krasnoiarske 1917" [Krasnoyarsk, February–October 1917]. *Proletarskaia revoliutsiia* 21 (1923).

————. "K istorii sverzheniia sovetskoi blasti v Sibirii" [A history of the overthrow of Soviet power in Siberia]. *Proletarskaia revoliutsiia* 4 (1922).

Gan, A. (Gutman). *Rossiia i bol'shevizm* [Russia and Bolshevism]. Shanghai, 1922.

Girs, M. Archive. Hoover Institution Archives, Stanford.

Graves, W. *America's Siberian Adventure, 1918–1920*. New York: J. Cape & H. Smith, 1931.

Gudoshnikov, M. A. *Ocherki po istorii grazhdanskoi voini v Sibiri* [Essays on the history of the civil war in Siberia]. Irkutsk: Irkutskoe Knizhnoe Izd-vo, 1959.

Guins, G. K. *Sibir', soiuzniki i Kolchak* [Siberia, the Allies, and Kolchak]. 2 vols. Peking: Izd-vo Russian Mission, 1921.

Harris, E. Archive. Hoover Institution Archives, Stanford.

Iakovlev, N. *Bol'sheviskoe podpol'e v tylu Kolchaka* [The bolshevik underground behind Kochak's lines]. Krasnoyarsk: Krasnoiarskoe Knizhnoe Izd-vo, 1941.

Inostrantsev, M. A. "Pervoe poruchenie Kolchaka" [Kolchak's first mission]. *Beloe delo* (Berlin), 1 (1956).

Ivanov, G. M. *Taseevskaia Respublika* [The Taseev Republic]. Krasnoyarsk: Krasnoiarskoe Knizhnoe Izd-vo, 1969.

Janin, P. T. *Ma mission en Sibérie* [My mission in Siberia]. Paris: Payot, 1933.

Kavraiskii, V. *Klassovoe rassloenie sibirskoi derevni* [The class stratification of the Siberian village]. Novosibirsk: Sibkraiizdat, 1927.

Kiriliov, A. A. "Sibirskaia armiia v bor'be za osvobozhdenie" [The Siberian Army in the struggle for freedom]. *Vol'naia Sibir'* (Prague), no. 4 (1928).

Kolosov, E. E. "Kak eto bylo" [The way it was]. *Byloe* (Petrograd), 21 (1923).

Konstantinov, K. *Poslednii dni Kolchakovshchiny* [The last days of the Kolchak regime]. Moscow: Gos. Izd-vo, 1926.

Kravchenko, A. *Kamarchaginskii front za vlast Sovetov* [The Kamarchaginsky front for Soviet power]. Novosibirsk, 1947.

Krol, L. *Za tri goda* [For three years]. Vladivostok: Izd-vo Svobodnaia Rossiia, 1921.

Krusser, G. *Sibirskie oblastniki* [Siberian autonomists]. Novosibirsk, 1931.

Lapin, N. A. *Revoliutsionnoe demokraticheskoe dvizhenie 60-godov XIX veka v zapadnoi Sibiri* [The revolutionary democratic movement in West Siberia of the 1860s]. Sverdlovsk: Sredne-Ural'skoe Knizhnoe Izd-vo, 1967.

Lavrov, I. A. *Na rubezhe* [Abroad]. Harbin: Izd-vo N. V. Zaitsev, 1937.

Lebedev, V. I. *The Russian Democracy in Its Struggle Against the Bolshevik Tyranny*. New York: Izd-vo Narodo-pravstvo, 1919.

Lenin, V. I. *Works*. 5th ed., vol. 34. Moscow: Izd-vo Politicheskaia Literatura, 1974.

Levytsky, Boris. *The Stalinist Terror in the Thirties*. Stanford: Hoover Institution Press, 1974.

Lockhart, R. *Buria nad Rossiei* [A storm over Russia]. Riga: Zhizn' i Kultura, 1933.

Maddox, Robert James. *The Unknown War with Russia*. San Rafael, Calif.: Presidio Press, 1977.

Maiskii, I. M. *Demokraticheskaia kontrrevoliutsiia* [The Democratic counter-revolution]. Moscow: Gos. Izd-vo, 1923.

Maksakov, V., and Turunov, A. *Khronika grazhdanskoi voini v Sibiri* [A chronicle of the civil war in Siberia]. Moscow: Gos. Izd-vo, 1926.

Manning, C. A. *The Siberian Fiasco*. New York: Library Publishers, 1952.

Margulies, M. S. *God interventsii* [The year of the intervention]. Berlin: Izd-vo Grzhebin, 1923.

Markov, Anatolii. "Encyclopedia of the White Movement" [in Russian]. 4 vols. Hoover Institution Archives, Stanford.

Maslov, S. S. *Rossiya posle chetyrekh let revoliutsii* [Russia after four years of revolution]. Paris: Russkaia Pechat', 1922.

Mel'gunov, S. P. *Tragediia Admirala Kolchaka* [The tragedy of Admiral Kolchak]. 2 vols. Belgrade: Russkaia Tipografiia, 1930–1931.

Miakotin, V. "Na chuzhoi storone" [On the other side]. *Editor Mel'gunov* (Berlin), no. 1 (1923).

Molchanov, N. *Nezabyvaemoe* [The unforgettable]. Krasnoyarsk, 1957.

Momet, L. *Ocherki natsional'nogo osvoboditel'nogo dvizheniia i grazhdanskoi voiny na gornom Altaie* [Essays on the national liberation movement and the civil war in the Altai mountain range]. Moscow, 1930.

Morozov, K. I. "Organizatsiia opozitsii protiv Bol'shevikov" [The organization of opposition to the Bolsheviks]. Mel'gunov collection, Box 13, Hoover Institution Archives, Stanford.

Nabokov, V. D. *Ispytaniia diplomata* [The trials of a diplomat]. London: Duckworth, 1921.

Ogorodnikov, R. E. *Udar po Kolchaku vesnoi 1919 g.* [The thrust against Kolchak in spring 1919]. Moscow: Voennoe Gos. Izd-vo, 1938.

Olitskaia, E. *Moi vospominaniia* [My reminiscences]. Frankfurt/Main: Izd-vo Posev, 1971.

Papin, L. M. *Krakh Kolchakovshchiny* [The collapse of the Kolchak regime]. Moscow: Izd-vo Moskovskogo Universiteta, 1957.

Parfenov, P. S. *Grazhdanskaia voina v Sibiri, 1918–1920* [The civil war in Siberia, 1918–1920]. Moscow: Gos. Izd-vo, n.d.

——. *Uroki proshlogo* [The lessons of the past]. Harbin, 1921.

Pavlovskii, P. I. *Annenkovshchina* [Annenkov's rule]. Moscow: Gos. Izd-vo, 1928.

Pepeliaev, V. N. "Razval Kolchakovshchiny" [The disintegration of the Kolchak regime]. *Krasnyi arkhiv*, no. 31 (1928).

Petrov, P. P. *Ot Volgi do Tikhogo Okeana* [From the Volga to the Pacific]. Riga: M. Didkovsky, 1930.

Plotnikov, I. F. *Geroicheskaia podpol'e* [The heroic underground]. Moscow: Izd-vo Mysl', 1968.

Popov, G. K. *The Tcheka*. London: A. Philpot, 1925.

Puchkov, General. "Ledianoi pokhod" [The icy march]. *Vestnik O'va Russkikh veteranov* (San Francisco), no. 46/47 (1947).

Reznichenko, A. N. *Bor'ba bol'shevikov protov "demokraticheskoi" kontrrevoliutsii v Sibiri* [The bolshevik struggle against the "democratic" counterrevolution in Siberia]. Novosibirsk: Zap.-Sib. Knizhnoe Izd-vo, 1972.

Rogozin, T. *Partizany stepnogo Badzhaia* [The partisans of the Badzhai steppes]. Moscow: Izd-vo Novaia Moskva, 1926.

Safronov, V. *Oktiabr v Sibiri* [October in Siberia]. Krasnoyarsk: Krasnoiarskoe Knizhnoe Izd-vo, 1962.

Sakharov, Gen. K. V. *Belaia Sibir'* [White Siberia]. Munich, 1923.

Seleznev, K. *Partizanskoe dvizhenie v zapadnoi Sibiri, 1918–1919* [Partisan movements in West Siberia, 1918–1919]. Novosibirsk: Zapadno-Sibirskoe Izd-vo, 1936.

Semenov, I. M. *Siberia: Its Conquest and Development*. Baltimore: Helicon, 1963.

Serebrennikov, I. I. *Moi vospominaniia* [My reminiscences]. Tientsin, 1937– 1940.

Shornikov, M. M. *17 god* [1917]. Novosibirsk: Zap.-Sib. Knizhnoe Izd-vo, 1967.

Shteidler, F. "Vystuplenie chekhoslovakov v Rossii 1918 goda" [The activities of the Czechoslovaks in the Russia of 1918]. *Vol'naia Sibir'* (Prague), no. 4 (1928).

Smirnov, I. N. *Bor'ba za Ural i Sibir'* [The battle for Siberia and the Urals]. Moscow: Gos. Izd-vo, 1926.

Snow, R. *The Bolsheviks in Siberia, 1917–1918*. Madison, N.J.: Fairleigh Dickinson University Press, 1975.

Solodovnikov, B. *Sibirskie avantury i General Gaida* [Siberian adventures and General Gaida]. Prague: Tip. Politika, 192–(?).

Spirin, L. M. *Klassy i partii v grazhdanskoi voine v Rossii* [Classes and parties in the civil war in Russia]. Moscow: Mysl', 1968.

Stepanov-Ivanov, A. V. Letter, January 27, 1950. Hoover Institution Archives, Stanford.

Stishov, M. M. *Bol'shevitskoe podpol'e i partizanskoe dvizhenie* [Underground and partisan bolshevik movements]. Moscow: Moscovskii Universite, 1962.

Subbotovskii, I. *Soiuzniki i russkie reaktsionery* [The Allies and the Russian reactionaries]. Leningrad: Vestnik Leningradskogo Soveta, 1926.

Svatikov, S. G. "Rossiia i Sibir'" [Russia and Siberia]. *Vol'naia Sibir'* (Prague), no. 4 (1928).

————. *Rossiia i Sibir'* [Russia and Siberia]. Prague: Izd-vo Obshchestva Sibiriakov, 1929.

Troitskii, P. S. "Raport" [Report (to the minister of interior)]. *Krasnyi arkhiv,* no. 6 (1937).

Turunov, A. *Partizanskoe dvizhenie v Sibiri* [The partisan movement in Siberia]. Moscow, 1925.

Unterberger, B. *American Siberian Expedition.* Durham, N.C.: Duke University Press, 1956.

Varneck, Elena. Papers. Hoover Institution Archives, Stanford.

Varneck, Elena, and Fisher, H. H. *The Testimony of Kolchak.* Stanford: Stanford University Press, 1935.

Vegman, V. D. "Kak i pochemu pala v 1918 g. sovetskaia vlast v Tomske" [How and why Soviet power fell in Tomsk in 1918]. *Sibriskie ogni* 1/2 (1923).

————. *Povstancheskoe dvizhenia na Altae* [Uprisings in the Altai]. Novosibirsk: Zapadno-Sibirskoe Kraevoe Izd-vo, 1935.

————. "Sibirskaia krasnaia gvardiia" [The Siberian Red Guard]. *Prosveshchenie Sibiri* 88 (1931).

Vladimirova, Vera. "Rabota Eserov v 1918 g." [The work of the Socialist-Revolutionaries in 1918]. *Krasnyi arkhiv,* no. 20 (1927).

Vol'skii, Nikolai V. (N. Valentinov). *The New Economic Policy and the Party Crisis After the Death of Lenin.* Edited by J. Bunyan and V. Butenko. Stanford: Hoover Institution Press, 1971.

Vol'skii, V. *K prekrashcheniu voiny vnutri demokratii* [The termination of the war inside the democracy]. Moscow, 1919.

Vologodskii, P. Dnevnik [Diary]. Hoover Institution Archives, Stanford.

Vyrypaev, V. I. Manuscript. Hoover Institution Archives, Stanford.

Vyshniak, M. "Grazhdanskaia voina" [The civil war]. *Sovremennye zapiski* (Paris), no. 45 (1931).

Ward, J. D. *Soiuznaia interventsiia v Sibiri* [The Allied intervention in Siberia]. Moscow: Gos. Izd-vo, 1923.

White, John A. *Siberian Intervention.* Stanford: Stanford University Press, 1947.

Zankevich, General. "Obstoiatel'stva soprovozhdavshie vydachu Adm. Kolchaka" [The circumstances accompanying the handing over of Admiral Kolchak]. *Beloe delo* (Berlin), 2 (1956).

Zemskoe delo (Krasnoyarsk), no. 4 (1918).

Zhurov, U. V. *Yeniseiskoe krest'ianstvo v gody grazhdanskoi voiny* [The peasantry of Yeniseisk province during the civil war]. Krasnoyarsk, 1972.

Index

SIBERIA

100 0 100 200 300 400 KM.

BARENTS

SEA

KARA SEA

EUROPEAN
USSR

OB. R.

YENISEI R.

TURUKHANSK

Ekaterinburg

Tiumen

Chelyabinsk

Kurgan

OB. R.

Petropavlovsk

YENISEI

ANGA

Omsk

Tomsk

Achinsk

Kansk

Taiga

Mariinsk

Ta

Novonikolaevsk

Krasnoyarsk

Nizhneudinsk

Barnaul

Minusinsk

Biisk

Semipalatinsk

- ·—·—· RAILROADS
- ········ FRONTIERS
- ▲ TERRITORY LIBERATED
  FROM SOVIET POWER
  MAY 26 - JULY 10, 1918

- ■ ADDITIONAL TERRITORY
  LIBERATED FROM
  SOVIET POWER
  JULY 10 - SEPTEMBER 8,
  1918